MUGHAL ARCADIA·

MUGHAL ARCADIA

∿ *Persian Literature* ∿
in an Indian Court

Sunil Sharma

Harvard University Press

Cambridge, Massachusetts   London, England

2017

Library of Congress Cataloging-in-Publication Data
Names: Sharma, Sunil, 1964– author.
Title: Mughal Arcadia : Persian literature in an Indian court /
Sunil Sharma.
Description: Cambridge, Massachusetts : Harvard University Press,
2017. | Includes bibliographical references and index.
Identifiers: LCCN 2017006230 | ISBN 9780674975859 (alk. paper)
Subjects: LCSH: Indo-Iranian literature—History and criticism. |
Mogul Empire—Court and courtiers—History. | Mogul Empire—
Civilization. | Mogul Empire—Intellectual life.
Classification: LCC PK80 .S53 2017 | DDC 891 /.5509954—dc23
LC record available at https://lccn.loc.gov/2017006230

For Ebba Koch

Contents

Illustrations

MUGHAL ARCADIA

The Persianate World

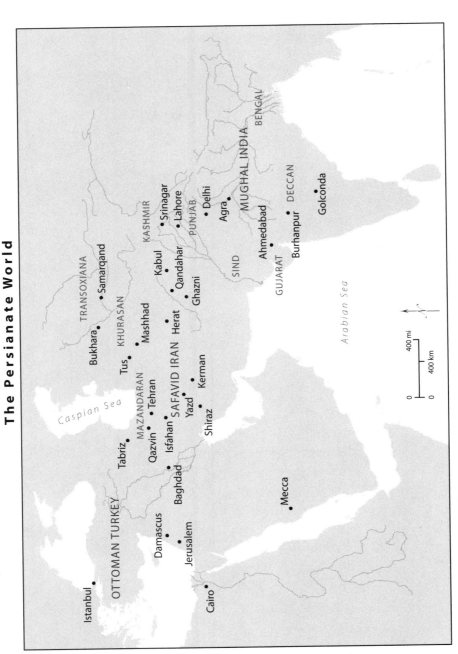

Map of the Persianate world

Introduction
Lingua Persica

⌣ *India capta victorem cepit* ⌢
Conquered India captured its conqueror

When the renowned Persian and Urdu poet Sir Muhammad Iqbal
visited the valley of Kashmir in the early twentieth century, he wrote
about the land of his ancestors with a profound sense of attachment
and nostalgia, comparing the golden past of the land to the grim
present. In these Persian verses he declared, "My body is a flower
from the avenues of paradisiacal Kashmir. / My heart is from the holy
shrine in the Hijaz and my song from Shiraz" (*tanam guli zi khiyaban-i
jannat-i Kashmir / dil az harim-i Hijaz u nava zi Shiraz ast*).[1] For him and
other poets, Kashmir was the memory of a pristine and happy place
favored by nature, the Hijaz was the symbol of the most revered Muslim
religious space situated in the Arabian peninsula, and Shiraz in Iran
was the imagined original home of classical Persian poetry. These
diverse places had come to be linked together in poetic geography as
central to Muslim civilization in the Indian subcontinent. The representation of Kashmir as a paradise on earth, an image that was a
staple of twentieth-century Bollywood films and that persists to this
day despite the ironical fact of the valley being more akin to a lost
paradise, has been imagined this way for more than a millennium.
Iqbal's evocation of the happier days of Kashmir, which continues to

move people in the same manner to this day, was really of the period when the valley was ruled and beautified by people connected to the Mughal Empire in the seventeenth century.

The Persian language, although one of many in use in premodern India along with Sanskrit and others, was closely tied to the Mughals who ruled various parts of the Indian subcontinent from the sixteenth to the nineteenth centuries. Vestiges of their cultural legacy are present everywhere in contemporary South Asia in many facets of daily life, from artifacts of high culture such as magnificent palaces in Agra, Delhi, and Lahore to the gardens of Kashmir, but also from paintings, culinary cultures, and sartorial fashions to popular films and love songs in the *ghazal* form in languages such as Urdu that have been deeply influenced by Persian. In fact, the most lasting contribution of the Mughals is the prized quality of cosmopolitanism, and the culture of *adab,* understood as both good manners and belles-lettres, which lingers on in myriad forms from Lahore to Lucknow. In order to understand the Mughal cultural and literary legacy to which Iqbal was heir, and how Kashmir came to be an important locus amoenus in the poetic imagination, it is necessary to first consider the place of the Persian language and literature in early modern India.

Increasingly referred to as Farsi in English, Persian enjoyed the status of being a literary language in several premodern societies, while serving as the lingua franca of a large part of the non-Arab Islamic world. Its history in the second millennium was to a large extent linked to the spread of Islam although it was not the language of religion, but rather of literature, administration, and diplomacy. Persian had been in use by Muslim elites for over five centuries in many parts of the Indian subcontinent by the early modern period, and particularly by the time of the Mughals when it attained a prestigious status, sometimes at the expense of other languages. Despite its wide currency it was neither the mother tongue of a large community of speakers in India, nor was it a "dead" or scriptural classical language such as Arabic or Sanskrit. In this regard the role of Persian in India was somewhat analogous to the use of classical Chinese in the medieval courts of Japan and Korea, Greek in the Hellenistic world, or even similar to the way both the vernacular French and the classical Latin languages were used in medieval Europe.[2]

European travelers in several parts of Asia in the early modern period found that their Persian, and less often Turkish, language skills served them well in communicating with people from different backgrounds and social classes. In 1623 the Italian traveler Pietro della Valle noted that Persian was more used in Ahmedabad, capital of the province of Gujarat, than the local language: "Nor let it seem strange that in India, in the countries of the Moghol, the Persian tongue is us'd more perhaps than the Indian itself, since the Mogholian Princes being originally Tartars, and of Samarkand, where the Persian is the natural tongue of the country, have therefore been willing to retain their natural speech in India; in brief, the Persian is the language of the Moghol's court, most spoken and us'd in all publick writings."[3] Della Valle explains to his reader that Persian is the language of the Mughal ruling house—his transcription of their name as Moghol, the Persianized form of Mongol, was more historically correct. Of course, there was no single "Indian" language, and Persian served the Mughals well to connect them to the wider world in the Middle East and Central Asia.

In the sixteenth and seventeenth centuries Persian poetry had a flowering in the Mughal Empire, and many members of the imperial family were generous patrons of men of letters at the courts in Agra, Delhi, and Lahore, as well as provincial governors and other officials in Kabul, Kashmir, Gujarat, Khandesh, and Bengal. Even before Mughal rule began in north India in 1526, scores of men of letters, as well as artists, scholars, and other professionals, from the eastern Islamic world—mainly the Iranian plateau and Persophone Central Asia or Transoxiana—had begun to come to India in order to seek employment at the courts of the rulers of the Muslim kingdoms in Central and South India, the so-called Deccan sultanates, and then under the first six Mughal rulers from Babur to Aurangzeb. Most often all that was needed for a person to succeed was a sound knowledge of Persian and a spirit of adventure during their residence in different parts of the subcontinent, much like native English speakers who go abroad to teach the language around the world today. It was through the cultural commodity of language and poetry that negotiations over shifting cultural, political, and even religious authority were conducted by various participants in a multilingual literary culture dominated by Persian. Persian poets who chose not to leave their homes to start a new life in India were entertained by dazzling tales of the liberal patronage of Indian rulers and the strange customs and cultures of India. In the sixteenth and seventeenth centuries, hopes of employment in the courts of the Mughal emperor, or princes and nobles, was not the only reason to migrate to a country that was perceived as exotic. At different moments in time, there were other economic, political, and religious considerations that motivated Persophone individuals to leave their homelands, whether temporarily or permanently.

Although Persian had been in use in parts of the Indian subcontinent for several centuries, the arrival of the Mughals marked a new phase in history. With a gradual increase in its currency among new communities and engagement with local cultures, it maintained its place as a courtly language of empire, but at the same time it became a vehicle for almost every form of written expression, from the classical literary genres used in the Perso-Islamic textual traditions to translations and new works originating in India. The analogy in the Latin epigraph to this chapter may not hold true in every detail, but its essential point is certainly applicable in this case. India was conquered by a Persophone Muslim conqueror of Turkish background, but over time he and his descendants were captivated by the literary, religious, artistic, and intellectual traditions of the land. The Persian language played a central role in the articulation of this process and in the recasting of knowledge about India into new forms through the medium of texts on a range of topics for audiences in the wider Persophone world. The role of poetry was also central in redefining the image of India, which had largely been imagined as a place of wonders and riches for centuries.

Several overlapping views regarding the Mughal Empire contributed to it being viewed in a favorable way. The literary term "Arcadia" denotes an idealized space that was peaceful and close to nature, which is apt for a phenomenon that culminated in the celebration of the imperial landscape, especially in the gardenlike province of Kashmir. The Mughal domains initially came to be celebrated as *dar al-aman,* land of security, as India became a refuge for literati, scholars, and mystics and Sufis in the late sixteenth and first half of the seventeenth century, most of whom had their origins in Safavid Iran. Given the ubiquity of the garden metaphor in classical Persian literature and the actual place of gardens in courtly life, the empire was also often described by historians and poets as a garden with the ruler as its gardener. The concept of a garden in turn was linked to that of paradise, going back to the ancient Persian *pairidaeza,* which became *firdaus* in later Persian and Arabic, signifying a park or enclosed garden in several cultural and religious contexts. In Islam as well, paradise or heaven is *janna,* the eternal garden that holds the promise of peace and delights. Thus, Mughal India, and various places and spaces within it, came to be described as a veritable paradise, the *firdaus* or *jannat* of both the cultural and religious imagination of Persophone communities. With Emperor Akbar's policy of universal civility (*sulh-i kull*), the pax mughalica, or more correctly pax mongolica, made it seem like a utopian society in which multiple cultures flourished, people were free to practice their different faiths, and poets and poetry were held in high regard. This was the subject of a great deal of praise in prose and poetic texts.

Fortunately for us, there is an enormous archive of texts and visual objects from this time in the form of poems, histories, paintings, and buildings that helps us to understand what these ideas signified in terms of the quotidian lives of actual people. Special spaces, such as the river-front mansions of Agra or the gardens of Kashmir, allowed the staging of convivial gatherings where poetry was recited and wine was drunk. Such scenes would be replayed over and over again all over the empire in Ahmedabad, Burhanpur, and Lahore. The Mughals evinced a fondness for not just urban imperial centers, where many of the imperial architectural moments were located, but also the unspoiled countryside. By the time Shah Jahan began his reign in 1628, certain places such as the Kashmir valley, with its salubrious climate and a topography that was thought to actually approximate the experience of paradise, became enshrined as the microcosm for

Mughal Arcadia. Kashmir was a favorite retreat for the court and émigré poets from Iran. Underlying the valorization of Kashmir was a desire to recreate Iran, the land of roses and nightingales and the supposed true homeland of Persian poetry, in India. This was true of other places in the Mughal Empire as well, but Kashmir was particularly suited to become "Little Iran" as it came to be called. The project to resituate the Persian classical tradition through the imitation of earlier poems, buildings, and paintings in a distinctly Indo-Persian context, inevitably drew on local cultural practices and Indic traditions. This phenomenon of intertwining cultural strands manifested itself time and again in Mughal Persian literary texts, through the use of a number of old and new tropes and themes by poets. This was the Kashmir that Iqbal invoked in his verses.

This book is about the process by which the metaphor of Mughal Arcadia came to be articulated in the literature of Shah Jahan's reign, especially in the Persian topographical narrative poem, mostly written in the rhymed couplet or *masnavi* form. The gardens and landscape of the pristine valley of Kashmir was the chief topic for such poems, although other places such as the capital cities and the province of Bengal were also described in verse. This was a rather unique phenomenon in the context of Persian literary history, in which Persophone poets of different backgrounds made contributions to and shaped Mughal Persian literary culture. But the beginning of the story that culminated in the flowering of this literary genre is the arrival of the Mughal conqueror Babur in 1526 in a place that was viewed as a land of wonders. It ends about a century and a half later in the early reign of the emperor Aurangzeb, when India lost much of its attraction for Persophone migrants. Ultimately, like other Arcadias, such as al-Andalus in Muslim Spain or Renaissance England, the idealized world of the early Mughals too receded into cultural memory and became a fixed image for what posterity viewed as the embodiment of the finest cultural achievements: artistic and literary refinement, an engagement with the larger world with equal attention to the local, and lavish patronage of scholars and literati from different cultural, religious, and linguistic backgrounds. How, then, did the reception of the classical Persian literary tradition at the Mughal court promote the conditions for constructing this Arcadia? Why did the century-long encounter of émigrés from Persophone lands with India begin with enthusiasm and end in disaffection? Providing answers to these questions requires a new approach to the literary history of Mughal Persian in the seventeenth century. In this study, I introduce individuals whose lives were marked by a great degree of mobility and their writings about places they lived in, loved, loathed, visited, or left behind. This remarkable body of literature has not been studied seriously and is certainly worthy to claim our attention.

Characterized by a cosmopolitan outlook and cherished values of refined conduct (*adab*) and ethics (*akhlaq*), Mughal literature was written in a number of languages, from Persian, Turkish, Hindi, and Urdu, even Arabic and Sanskrit, by a wide range of authors, from kings and Sufis to princesses, physicians, and professional poets, who came from different social and ethnic backgrounds. The corpus of literary texts produced during the Mughal period easily equals the impressive production of artistic objects—paintings, bindings, calligraphy, carpets, jewelry, gardens, and buildings—from the same period, though the latter are better known today. Few good translations of Mughal literary texts in any language are available today, especially poetic works that were among the chief achievements of this literary culture.

Poetry was prized over prose and, in fact, there were few prose texts without verses. Poetic works were created and enjoyed in a variety of ways: panegyric odes were declaimed on formal occasions at court, lyric poems were sung to music in private and public settings for entertainment or to induce a mystical state, autobiographies and histories were written to be read by courtiers or studied by princes to learn from the lives of great rulers. There were far-reaching networks for the circulation of texts, whether in an oral or written form, so that a Persian poem produced in Agra in the sixteenth or seventeenth century would a few weeks later be read in Istanbul or sung in Bukhara. Persian poetry as a social activity was particularly widespread in the fifteenth and sixteenth centuries among people of all social levels, from princes to artisans.[4] The situation in India was not quite the same as in Iran or Central Asia. Knowledge of Persian and its classical tradition was increasingly widespread in multilingual India, but, because it was a learned language and not the native speech of the large majority of the population, it was limited to classes and groups of people who participated professionally or culturally in the machinery of administration. This group of Persian learners grew over time, especially in seventeenth- and eighteenth-century Mughal society, well into the colonial period, before English entirely replaced Persian in the nineteenth and twentieth centuries.[5]

Mughal literary culture was never exclusively tied to the Persian language, nor was it solely a court-centered activity. However, there is no denying the hegemony of Persian literature and the elite position of speakers of the language at this time, which was a major historical and social phenomenon in South Asia. An example of how a single individual could influence history in the seventeenth century is the empress Nur Jahan, who along with her extended family commissioned the grandest Mughal gardens and became patrons to the most talented Persian poets during the reigns of Jahangir and Shah Jahan. To put in another way, the period of Mughal rule in South Asia, from 1526 to 1858, is the story of how a small Turko-Persian Central Asian princely family, along with a large and diverse group of courtiers, administrators, and men of letters, headed a vast empire that by the end of its time was steeped in local traditions.

In terms of Persian literary culture, the Mughal period can broadly be divided into two ages, that of the first six Mughals, a century and a half from the short four-year rule of Babur to the early years of Aurangzeb's long reign in the latter half of the seventeenth century; and the age of the later Mughals, from the time when Aurangzeb left his capital in 1681 for the Deccan, never to return, to 1858, when the British banished the last emperor, Bahadur Shah "Zafar," into exile in Burma. In the first period, Persian was the chief literary language and émigré poets from Iran and Central Asia dominated the scene at court. Persian continued to be important in the second age, but early forms of Urdu and Hindi were increasingly if not equally favored as languages of literary expression at this time, and poets of Indian origin—Muslims and non-Muslims—played a major role in producing literature and directing literary tastes. From around the end of the seventeenth century poetry was no longer only a courtly and elite activity but produced in all segments of Mughal society.[6] Over time non-Muslims were fully integrated into this culture, especially in the homosocial world of Persian poetry. Women, though not totally absent, were largely invisible as authors. The vernacular sphere is where women found their own voices.

For over a century or so Mughal Persian poetry was fashionable in literary circles in the entire Persophone world, which included societies from the Balkans to Bengal. Studying the textual corpus of this period presents several daunting challenges. How does one write about a literary culture whose output of written texts is huge by any standard, running into hundreds of thousands of verses and scores of volumes in prose? Scholarly studies have usually provided surveys of the whole range of textual production, or focused on one genre—that is, the *ghazal* or love lyric that enjoyed great popularity then as it does now and was the chief matrix of literary taste.[7] Overwhelmed by the sheer volume of texts, several such studies fashion themselves on traditional anthologies of Persian poetry (*tazkira*s) that are partly biographical and also useful as sources of literary history. *Tazkira*s contain a great deal of anecdotal information and can be useful to gauge the prevailing aesthetic tastes at a given moment in history, as well as being highly entertaining for their gossip. There were also other kinds of texts that are worthy of interest from this period, some that we would call literary criticism in the form of treatises or introductions to collections of a poet's own or another's verses, in which poets discuss their own position in relation to the poetic canons of the past and literary circles of the present. But most valuable are the *divan*s of poets, a complete or partial collection of their poetic works.

While the older standard histories of Persian literature describe the early modern period, both in the connected worlds of Safavid Iran and Mughal India and separately, as an age when there was an "extraordinary dearth of notable poets" or literature being in steep decline, the attitude of literary scholars and historians has taken a more favorable turn in recent decades.[8] Paul Losensky, a textual scholar who engages with early modern literary works at a micro level in their social, cultural, and political contexts, admits that "our critical understanding of the period remains hampered by an inadequate conceptual framework."[9] In this work, I use Persian largely as a linguistic category rather than a cultural one, to avoid conflating nationality with language. Iranian is, of course, used not in the presentist sense but as a civilizational category with an awareness that there is a great deal of gray area. But confusion often arises because Persian can signify "Iranian" with respect to culture, but it is also as a linguistic term denoting the semantic world of "Farsi." Thus, the medieval Persian poet Amir Khusrau was not Iranian but wrote in Persian. He is part of the history of Persian literature—that is, literature in Persian but not exclusively of Iran. Although it is not necessary to reinvent the wheel at every instance, it is worthwhile to recall Marshall Hodgson's statement that Persian "was to form the chief model for the rise of still other languages to the literary level. . . . Most of the more local languages of high culture that were later used by Muslims likewise depended upon Persian wholly or in part for their literary inspiration. We may call all these cultural traditions, carried in Persian or reflecting Persian inspiration, 'Persianate' by extension."[10] Persianate and Indo-Persian are both useful terms that are used when "Persian" as a cultural category is not quite the correct designation. In the context of this book, Persianate literature describes works in Ottoman and Chaghatai Turkish, Dakhni and Urdu, or even Brajbhasha Hindi in certain instances, when the influence of established Persian-language poetic forms or imagery is discernable. Similarly, Indo-Persian is not used here as a linguistic register but for the body of Persian literature that was produced in and consciously crafted as belonging to the subcontinent, whether the author was of Indian or Iranian origin.[11]

The history of early modern Persian literature is often dominated by the study of the *ghazal* because it was at this time that at the hands of master poets it transformed from a simple love lyric to a complex Baroque poem in the "fresh style" (*taza-gu'i, sabk-i Hindi*). Later, at least in Iran, there was a return to the earlier style in its neoclassical phase.[12] The *ghazal* was unquestionably a vibrant and dynamic literary form in the early modern period, and because of its quotability and particular aesthetics of ambiguity, it enjoyed a great deal of popularity outside court circles. To this day, *ghazal*s continue to flourish in a range of South Asian languages, although in Iran the form is mostly linked to the classical tradition. The premodern *ghazal* has received a great deal of scholarly attention because the subject of stylistics has played a large role in the fragmentation of the Persianate world and formation of literary canons based on nationalist criteria. But a purely stylistic approach can overlook some pivotal social and cultural aspects of Indo-Persian literary culture. In addition, other kinds of poetic writings, particularly poems about praise of patrons and places composed in the formal *qasida* and narrative *masnavi* forms, were as much in vogue in courtly circles across early modern Persianate societies. Innovative literary developments tied to several historical factors occurred in literary circles not just with respect to the *ghazal,* but also in other poetic forms and genres. The study of these various texts needs to be integrated much more in current scholarship.

The rhetoric of "newness" that seemed to be the mark of the age was found not only in Persian but also in other literary traditions of this period.[13] Audrey Truschke's observation in her study of the Sanskrit phenomenon at the Mughal court helps in further understanding the Persian situation here. Although poets and scholars in both traditions had "a yearning for fresh, transformative ideas," it seems that "newness was generally unmarked as such, and authors tended to stress continuity rather than rupture with the prior practice."[14] It is noteworthy that the flowering of Mughal Persian poetry about place coincided with the court's engagement with Sanskrit, with both phenomena ending in the early Aurangzeb years. Truschke's conclusion that two discernable shifts, linguistic and political, led to its end is also applicable to some degree to Persian. The recent scholarship of Allison Busch on the Hindi poetry of this period and Rajeev Kinra on the integration of Hindus into the world of Indo-Persian further elucidates the making of Mughal literary culture in its first century.[15] This book brings previously unstudied Persian poetry and the influential community of Persian émigré poets, mainly Iranians, more squarely into the picture.

I have chiefly been inspired by the New Historicist approach, which maintains "the primacy and distinctiveness of the literary document, which communicates knowledge not simply about the ideology of the cultural moment that produced that text but most specifically about how this particular literary text responded to the conditions of its own production."[16] I have especially been drawn to the way Stephen Greenblatt and others practicing the New Historicism have incorporated the study of a broad range of textual and material practices in their analysis of literary cultures. Mughal Persian literary culture in its early phase is particularly suited to this approach because of the vast and varied archive of texts, images, and buildings. There is no disputing the fact that poetry, along with historical chronicles and other texts, is central in this project, and its study is indispensable on the larger canvas of Indo-Muslim and Mughal studies, because, as noted by Paul Losensky, poetry becomes an "important element in a network of semiotic and economic practices, both shaping and being shaped by its social nature and context."[17] Another point worth noting is that early modern Persian literature was not solely caught up in a particular historical moment but was also responding to a longer classical tradition.[18] Thus, the role that mono- and multilingual poets played in this period's literary culture is fundamental to the study of the Mughals across the disciplines.

A few centuries before the Mughals arrived in India, the Muslim rulers of Andalusia in southern Spain had achieved a high degree of civilization, with Arab as the literary language and Muslims, Jews, and Christians participating to different degrees in the creation of its literatures. These achievements were celebrated in Arabic poetry in the praise of courtly gardens and palaces such as the Alhambra in Granada, and also in Cordoba and Valencia. The concept of *convivencia* in the context of Andalusian civilization, signifying the coming together of different religious communities in a multilingual environment and contributing to a golden age of cultural production, is an attractive approach. But although there are some intriguing parallels with the Mughal case, there are salient differences as well, the chief being the longer history of Islam in India before and after the Mughals. A question often asked about Andalusian literature is whether this literature was different from the Arabic literature produced in the central lands in the Middle East? As Salma Khadra Jayyusi, a scholar of classical Arabic literature, explains, "there is no accurate gauge by which to measure the stimuli evidently exerted on

Arabic poetry in al-Andalus (and in the East) by the fantastic bringing together of races and cultures under the unifying banner of Islam, but whatever their precise nature, they became assimilated into the poetry, were fused with its spirit and naturally expressed in its particular idiom."[19] This situation is analogous to the one regarding Mughal Persian literature, which is connected to the larger history of Persian literature in Iran and other Persophone lands, especially since in the early period it was a culture dominated and shaped by Iranian émigrés. At the same time, this literature is also very much part of multilingual India. But both literary traditions have had, and to a great extent continue to have, difficulty integrating it into their own national narratives, in much the same way that in some large museums around the world the art of Mughal India has an awkward representation in both their Islamic and South Asia collections.

A comparison with the two great Islamic empires, Ottoman and Safavid, which overlapped with the Mughals in time and place, is in some ways a more viable approach, although here too one must be sensitive to both the differences and similarities.[20] The three polities had much in common other than sharing the Persian language as the chief literary medium. The splendor of the courts, the heterogenous composition of the populations, not to speak of the administrative and military setups, and most of all, an awareness of political and cultural developments and changes in each other's territories make this both a challenging but compelling comparison. The newfound awareness of translocal literature manifested itself differently in the Iranian heartland in the writings of Safavid poets than in the works of Mughal authors, and interestingly the visual archive with respect to painted representations of cities and landscapes is rich in the Mughal, and Ottoman, case but negligible in the Safavid tradition. Although part of a connected literary and artistic tradition through Perso-Islamicate cultural practices, the differences in the way that places were praised and represented in their poetic and historical texts can then provide a useful matrix for a comparative study of the cultural history of the two polities.

Safavid and Mughal literary cultures are sometimes viewed as entirely separate, whereas there was a great deal of mobility of court poets between the two domains. The overlapping literary spheres can be compared to the situation with British and American literatures in English where the two have an overlapping canon but also cater to distinct local markets and reading tastes. The circulation of texts and people played a significant role in the dynamics of how the various Persianate literary cultures transformed over time. The story about the people who were actors in the staging of Mughal Arcadia overlaps to some extent with the broader subject of the history of travel and migration of Iranians to different parts of Asia in the early modern period. A variety of textual sources from travelogues to poetry have been useful in studying the mobility of Persophone people in the premodern period.[21] Given the great degree of self-fashioning in the literature of this period, some caution must be used in taking a writer's statements about feelings on experiences such as emigration, displacement, and exile at face value, especially when studying poetic texts in which empirical information is often insubstantial or even absent and the context must be teased out through a careful study of metaphors and allusions. Many people attached to the Mughal court experienced a tremendous zeal for travel, both on a transregional level and within the subcontinent. At the same time, the texts they produced also traveled great distances in oral and written forms.

With the study of Mughal literature in its range of languages it is necessary to comprehend the complex social networks of poets and patrons, the multilingual nature of overlapping literary spheres, and the shift over time in the way the literature was produced and enjoyed. Since it is impossible to write a literary history of the period that would take into account all these aspects in detail, it is far more productive to focus on a set of related themes in representative texts of a period. The complex literary and cultural phenomenon of the sixteenth and seventeenth centuries that I study in this book is encompassed under the umbrella term "Mughal Arcadia." The reality and imagery of travel and topography were central in the literary works of this period and shifted over the course of a century and half of Mughal rule in response to the changing composition of the poetic community. These motifs emerge in writings about newly constructed and "discovered" places becoming part of the empire, and how places such as Kashmir and Bengal with their manmade and natural landscapes came to exemplify some of the highest ideals of the Mughal Empire. Of equal significance was the continuity of an Indo-Persian project that was the legacy of an earlier cultural high-point in Delhi that can be traced back to the polymath classical poet Amir Khusrau, who was active in the thirteenth and fourteenth centuries, when the city had welcomed refugees fleeing the onslaught of the Mongols in Central Asia. Amir Khusrau's presence is pervasive throughout the entire Mughal period. Aside from him, there was also the larger burden of the classical Persian literary past. By the time that Mughal literature began to take shape, the project of preserving the vast corpus of texts and forging an identity based on its reception weighed heavily on litterateurs.

ONE

Mughal Persian Literary Culture

∿ Poeta fit, non nascitur ∿
A poet is made, not born

COMMUNITIES OF POETS

An understanding of the complex nature of early modern Indo-Persian literary culture is necessary in order to understand how the notion of Mughal Arcadia came to be realized. The starting point may well have been the movement of Persophone people to the Indian subcontinent. The story of émigré Persians and the formation of an expatriate Persophone community in Mughal India is part of a larger narrative about the migration of people in early modern Asia. This emigration of Iranians from their homeland is comparable to their exodus to the West after the Islamic Revolution in 1979. Earlier waves of large-scale movements of Iranians had also taken place when Zoroastrians left in great numbers to settle on the west coast of India after the Arab conquest of the seventh century. With the Mughals in power the boundaries between Persianate societies became even more porous than they had been and people came to different parts of the subcontinent because their Persian skills allowed them to settle there with relative ease. Individuals from an astonishing variety of social and professional backgrounds, due to their linguistic proficiency in speaking and writing Persian, made successful careers at various courts in the Mughal north and Deccan, some of them continuing a peripatetic lifestyle in the subcontinent. Not all of them were poets, of course, but almost all of them composed the occasional verse to facilitate their upward social mobility.[1] Apart from the small group of full-time poets, many did double duty as librarians, physicians, calligraphers, courtiers, even soldiers.[2] Many of these men intermarried with local women and their offspring inherited a composite Persianate culture. But there was an older history of India playing host to Persophone people who had then made it their home.

The city of Delhi had been the seat of Islamic rulers for several centuries by the time the Mughals arrived. Especially under the various sultans of the thirteenth and fourteenth centuries, when it became a refuge for learned men and Sufis who were forced to flee the Mongol invasions of large parts of Asia and the Middle East, there had been a long tradition of literary production in Persian in the region around the capital. This was true in the case of the poet Amir Khusrau's father's family that had come to India from Central Asia in the early thirteenth century. In a long narrative poem on a historical theme composed in 1289, *Qiran al-Sa'dain* (Conjunction of Two Auspicious Planets), and dedicated to the short-reigned Sultan Kay Qubad to commemorate his reconciliation with his father Bughra Khan,[3] Amir Khusrau lavishly praises Delhi's architectural monuments and includes a lyrical paean in the *ghazal* form to the Hindu youths of the city. In these lines he celebrates the city (*Hazrat-i Dihli*):

Delhi, refuge of religion,
Refuge and paradise of justice.
Long may it endure.
Since it is a heavenly paradise
In every essential quality,
May God keep it from calamity. . . .
It has become the shelter of Islam in the world
And its dependencies the cupola of the seven heavens.
Its inhabitants are all notables of the land.

In every corner are pillars of the state.

It is the seat of mighty rulers.

It enjoys the good fortune of kings.

The corner of every home here is a wondrous paradise;

All manner of gold was spent in its design.

In every street there is a row of great people.

In the niches of every house are hidden costly articles.

People of one house with a hundred joys;

Home of one people with a hundred human qualities![4]

This view of India as a refuge for oppressed people in the Muslim world would persist in one form or another and be reused by the Mughals in the context of their historical situation.

Amir Khusrau's other innovative work in verse, *Nuh sipihr* (Nine Spheres), was written toward the end of his life and went further in his praise for the paradisiacal land of India. The work is a poetic encyclopedia of Indian knowledge and practices written to celebrate the land of his birth that in the author's mind deserved its rightful place on the map of Islam as much as the Middle East. In one section of the *Nuh sipihr* Amir Khusrau described all the quintessentially Indian cultural aspects from yogis to mangoes, extolling its superiority in terms of climate and the openness of the culture. Amir Khusrau continuously had a profound influence on not only the Persian literature that was produced in subsequent centuries wherever Persian was in use, but also on Persianate cultural practices in India such as devotional music and folk songs. Indian poets and scholars drew on his writings for their ethnographic descriptions of India up to the nineteenth century. In the area of Persian belles lettres, many common images and topoi originated from his poems, such as the likening of the Hindu woman, the *sati* or suttee, to a moth extinguishing itself in a flame. The *sati* later became an iconic symbol of India, as we will see later on. Amir Khusrau made a boastful claim about India being akin to paradise in grandiose terms, the chief reason being that it was the place where the first man Adam first came to Earth.[5] Almost three centuries later, the Mughal historian Abu'l-Fazl, in a rather unusual section on outsiders who came to India, also begins with

Adam and continues the memory of an Indo-Persian tradition.[6] The legacy of Amir Khusrau was present in multiple ways in the works of Mughal men of letters.

By the early fifteenth century, several poets writing in Persian, mainly Sufis, lived in the region of Delhi that already had a long history as a city of saints. The Lodi rulers just before the Mughals did not cultivate a glamorous style in their patronage of the arts as some earlier rulers had done and the Mughals would revive, and the court had less of a focus on Persian literature.[7] It was with the coming of a small and intimate Persophone literary community that accompanied Babur from Kabul to Delhi in 1526 that Mughal Persian literary culture began to take shape. By the time of Shah Jahan, the literati formed a hierarchical and extremely professionalized cadre of poets, historians, and secretaries just over a century later.

People from different parts of the Iranian plateau—Iraqis, Khurasanis, Gilanis, and so on—formed factions and subcommunities in diaspora and their relationship with each other was constantly changing in response to the politics of the day. Those who were from Transoxiana, mainly Uzbeks and Chaghatais, were more conscious of their Central Asian shared culture with the Mughals and were often at odds with the Iranians.[8] Although the category "Iranians" obscures a great deal of diversity among the inhabitants of and migrants from the plateau, the sense here is basically "people from the Safavid territory." Many Iranians were bilingual or multilingual, speaking Turkish and other languages, but the subcontinental view is indeed to view them as one group.[9] In any case, Iranians were relative latecomers at the Mughal court since Babur, the first Mughal ruler, and the people who accompanied him, were mainly from Central Asia (i.e., the regions of Uzbekistan and Afghanistan today). The composition of the poets also changed over time: from almost exclusively Central Asians in the beginning to an Iranian majority, and finally Persophone Indians being in a sizeable majority only toward the end of Shah Jahan's rule. The reign of Babur's son and successor Humayun—ten years from 1530 to 1540 and then eleven months in 1555–1556—was interrupted by a prolonged exile that included a year-long sojourn outside India and a short visit to the Safavid court in Tabriz. Reclaiming his kingdom with the help of the Safavid ruler Shah Tahmasp I's forces, he brought two master artists, 'Abdus-Samad and Mir Sayyid 'Ali, and several poets with him to Delhi, such as Qasim Kahi of Kabul. This interlude proved to be culturally significant and marked the beginning of an intimate Iranian encounter with India for just over a century that would leave its mark on both societies in several ways.

As purveyors of cultural prestige, the historian Juan Cole writes, "The Iranis came to be the wealthiest faction, with the highest salaries, below only the Chaghatai ruling family of Timurids itself." In fact, they were very conscious of "the way Shah Tahmasp had provided Humayun, the second Mughal ruler, with the arms and material to make a second assault on India, thus in effect bearing responsibility for the establishment of the Mughal Empire as an ongoing concern as opposed to Babur's mere adventure. Given this debt, Mughal India would always be in some sense subsidiary to Iran."[10] Nevertheless, the literary culture at the early Mughal court to a great degree came to be characterized by a tension between Iranian émigré poets and Persophone Indians even as they served in the common endeavor of producing literary works that best represented and served the political and cultural ambitions of the ruling house.[11]

What was the reason for the huge brain drain from Safavid Iran to India in the early modern period? Scholars agree that there was no single reason for this social phenomenon. The explanation that the Safavid Shah Tahmasp's so-called second sincere repentance in 1556, which brought in a form of *shari'a* with strict standards regarding public morality and piety—the first was in 1532—was the chief cause for a decline in the arts, spurring a large-scale emigration from Iran, does not account for the prolonged mobility of people from the plateau.[12]

Nonetheless, when it comes to poets, one of the plausible causes for the early phase of the migration could have been the negative attitude of the Safavid kings toward court poetry and non-Shia literature in general. The Safavid chronicler Iskandar Beg Munshi, writing several decades after the fact, described Shah Tahmasp's attitude to poetry: "During the latter part of his life, however, when the Shah took more seriously the Koranic prescription to 'do what is right and eschew evil,' he no longer counted poets pious and upright men because of the known addiction many of them had to the bottle. He ceased to regard them with favor and refused to allow them to present him with occasional pieces and eulogistic odes."[13] This can be contrasted with the words of Abu'l-Fazl, the Mughal emperor Akbar's chronicler, who also records an ambivalent attitude toward professional poets: "Poets strike out a road to the inaccessible realm of thought, and divine grace beams forth in their genius. But many of them do not recognize the high value of their talent, and barter it away from a wish to possess inferior store: they pass their time in praising the mean-minded, or soil their language with invectives against the wise. . . . For this reason his Majesty does not care for poets; he attaches no weight to a handful of imagination. Fools think that he does not care for poetry, and that for this reason he turns his heart away from the poets."[14] Akbar's attitude was not so different from that of Shah Tahmasp, who wanted his court poets to devote themselves to composing religious poems, but as is clear in Akbar's case the negative view of some aspects of verbal skills in no way indicated a lack of interest or patronage in all poetry. At the Safavid court poets began to compose vast numbers of poems in praise of the venerated Shia figures such as 'Ali and the later imams, while Mughal poets wrote a great deal of praise poetry about powerful men who ruled the empire, especially since there was stiff competition to gain the favor of a generous patron.

Combined with the less than positive attitude of Shah Tahmasp toward nonreligious poetry, whatever its long-term repercussions, was the fact that employment opportunities for poets were brighter in the subcontinent. As Kausari, a Safavid poet at the court of Shah Tahmasp declared in despair:

darin kishvar kharidar-i sukhan nist / kasi sargarm-i bazar-i sukhan nist
sukhan ra qadr u miqdari namanda / ma'ani ra kharidar namanda
ki dar Iran kasi nayad padidar / ki bashad jins-i ma'ni ra kharidar . . .
dar Iran talkh gashta kam-i janam / bi-bayad shud su-yi Hindustan
hama tuti-mazaqan-i shikarkha / bi-mulk-i Hind azan kardand mava[15]

> There is no buyer of poetry in this land;
> no one is active in the market of poetry which has no value or
>   appreciation.
> There is no purchaser of meaningful verse . . .
> My life has become intolerable in Iran; I should go to India.
> All the poets like sweet parrots have made India their home.

It should not be surprising that poetry is mentioned as a product in
a consumer market. This was the world of professional poets, not that
of Sufis who composed mystical literature for no ostensible material
gain. The Mughals also recruited heavily among the Persian speakers
of Iran and Central Asia because as the newcomers among gunpowder empires they needed to fill their court with the best available talent. On Akbar's orders the physician Hakim Humam Gilani
went to Iran to recruit men of letters among his compatriots to come
and seek employment at the Mughal court. An imperial *farman*
penned by Abu'l-Fazl proclaimed, "Love of the people of Iran has
been deeply ingrained in his [Akbar's] heart from the very beginning; it is his desire that this exalted community should come close
to him spiritually as well as materially, . . . and the high and low (that
is, all classes) of that community should partake of imperial favor."[16]
The two brothers in imperial service Faizi and Abu'l-Fazl also served
as headhunters on a trip to the Deccan, seeking out Persophone
scholars and poets who had settled there. In response to favorable reports about certain individuals, Akbar would send personal invita-
tions to them, even offering to take care of their traveling expenses.[17]
    The brain drain from Iran had huge implications within Iranian
society over time. Historian Colin Mitchell argues that the crisis
brought on by the emigration of men of letters to the Mughal court
in the late sixteenth century, when the eastward movement was at
its peak, resulted in the imperial chancery (*dar al-insha*) to be "under
conservative and inexperienced stewardship."[18] Certainly a cause for
great concern in Safavid courtly circles, the general depopulation of
the country was noticed decades later by the French traveler Jean
Chardin, who arrived in Iran in 1666; one of the reasons he gave for
the situation was that, "within this last Century, a great many Per-

sians, and even entire Families, have gone and settl'd in the Indies.
As they are a handsomer, wiser, and more polite People, beyond all
Comparison, than the Mahometan Indians, who are descended from
the Tartars, in the Country of Tamerlane; they all advance themselves
in the Indies. The Courts of the Indian Mahometan Kings are all full
of them, particularly that of Golconda and Vijapour. As soon as any
of them are well establish'd, they send for their Families and Friends,
who go willingly where Fortune invites them, especially into a
Country, which is one of the most plentiful of the World."[19] But by
the time Chardin was writing these words, emigration from Iran to
India had already peaked and was on the decline. But at its peak, the
market for Persian poets in Safavid Iran was saturated, and "the as-
piring professional might find little demand for his wares and easily
be lured away by the new, rich markets of India."[20]

The textual archive of this period includes thousands of lines of
poetry by men debating the pros and cons of moving to India. In
fact, this subject had become a common poetic trope. Individual lines
of poetry regarding a poet's attitude toward India, his nostalgia for
home and family, and the vagaries of fate, range widely in tone, from
elation to despair, and should not necessarily be taken at face value.
A poet might have been writing for a Mughal patron in which case
his verses would be celebratory about India, but if he were ad-
dressing a more private group of friends or family he would have
been more honest and damning about "liver-eating India" (*Hind-i
jigarkhvar*). This popular metaphor involved a play on the word Hind,
which means both "India" and also refers to the aunt of the prophet
Muhammad who ate the liver of one of the early converts and de-
fenders of Islam before she converted to the new faith. But despite
all the pressure to succeed in India, poets from Iran did achieve the
highest position at court: the first Mughal poet laureate (*malik al-
shu'ara*) was an Iranian, Ghazali of Mashhad, and in fitting with the
policies of Akbar, who always sought a balance of the different factions, his replacement was the Indian poet Faizi, who also wrote
under the pen name Fayyazi. The next, and in fact the last, two
were both Iranians—Talib of Amul under Jahangir and Kalim of
Hamadan under Shah Jahan.[21] Not surprisingly, Iranian émigrés

overwhelmingly comprised the most elite coterie of poets at the courts of these three rulers.

The openness of the Mughals to people of various religious and sectarian backgrounds was another reason for the choice some people made to relocate from Safavid lands to Mughal territory. Sufis were persecuted in Iran by the Safavid ruling house, who ironically had Sufi connections themselves, to make room for the establishment of a Shia state.[22] Akbar's court, and India once again in the post-Mongol period, came to be regarded as the *dar al-aman,* the abode of peace, and this image persisted all the way down to the age of Shah Jahan in the mid-seventeenth century.[23] The Mughal code of universal civility (*sulh-i kull*) assured, in Rajeev Kinra's words, an "atmosphere of cultural hospitality, of bureaucratic and administrative meritocracy, of value for scholarly inquiry and the arts, and of respect not only for the diversity of the subcontinent itself but also for the intellectual and commercial capital brought by travelers from around the world."[24] A poet named Ghuyuri of Badakhshan in a humorous vein compared Akbar's court to paradise in these verses:

> *bar dar-i shah-i Akbar-i ghazi / ki bihisht ast pur zi asayish*
> *man agar rish-i khud tarashidam / na zi pay-i zinat ast u arayish*
> *chun gunah az siyah-ru'i, nist / rish ra dar bihisht gunjayish*[25]

> At the threshold of the *ghazi* king Akbar, which is reposeful paradise,
> If I shave my beard it would not be to appear well groomed.
> What is the sin in being clean-shaven? A beard has no place in
>   paradise.

The poet refers to the plentiful youths (*ghilman*) of paradise who are supposed to be beardless. Years later when these lines were repeated before the next emperor, Jahangir, he was pleased and wondered why his father had not shared them with him when he was alive.

In 1579, Emperor Akbar took the bold step of getting the highest religious authorities of his realm to issue a document, known as the *mahzar,* that proclaimed him as a just king who "outranked the qualified interpreters of Islamic law (the *mojtahed*s) and could, therefore, choose between conflicting opinions of the legal scholars that version which best served the nation and good order."[26] When he became emperor his son Jahangir described the open atmosphere of his father Akbar's realm in these words:

> Followers of various religions had a place in the broad scope of his peerless empire—unlike other countries of the world, like Iran, where there is room for only Shiites, and Rum [Ottoman territory], Turan [Central Asia], and Hindustan, where there is room for only Sunnis. Just as all groups and the practitioners of all religions have a place within the spacious circle of God's mercy, in accordance with the dictum that a shadow must follow its source, in my father's realm, which ended at the salty sea, there was room for practitioners of various sects and beliefs, both true and imperfect, and strife and altercation were not allowed. Sunni and Shiite worshiped in one mosque, and Frank and Jew in one congregation. Utter peaceableness was his established way. He conversed with the good of every sect and gave his attentions to each in accordance with their station and ability to understand.[27]

To whatever degree this may have held true on the ground level, effective propaganda promulgated the view that Akbar's India was the ideal place for people of all faiths to live in. In a letter to Philip II of Spain, Akbar had written, "everyone continues, without investigating the arguments and reasons, to follow the religion in which he was born and educated, thus excluding himself from the possibility of ascertaining the truth, which is the noblest aim of the human intellect. Therefore, we associate at convenient seasons with learned men of all religions, and thus derive profit from their exquisite and exalted aspirations."[28] His interest in comparative faiths led him to eventually found a short-lived divine cult of his own, the *Din-i ilahi,* which was considered heretical by the orthodox faction at his court. Mughal India would have appeared as an attractive and fabled place to many Safavid subjects, even if they had no desire to uproot themselves.

A large number of Muslims who were Sunnis, Sufis, or belonged to marginal communities with no place in the twelver-Shia Safavid state, did make their way to India to enjoy religious freedom.[29] Unusual examples of individuals from minority religious groups were the Zoroastrian priest Azar Kaivan, who headed an esoteric religious sect that was a cross between illumationist philosophy and Sufism, and his disciple Mubad Shah, who authored a remarkable encyclopedia of comparative religion, *Dabistan-i mazahib* (School of religions).[30] The Azar Kaivanis had a utopian vision of "a mighty king named Bahram, who would gather together the armies of India and China and liberate the Persian homeland from the tyranny of the black-clad Muslims."[31] Perhaps the Mughal emperor was going to be this savior. A few decades later, an antinomian poet by the name of Sarmad, a Jewish convert to Islam, besotted by a Hindu lad, wandered naked around India while pushing the boundaries of propriety in composing blasphemous Sufi poetry. He met his end by being beheaded at the order of Emperor Aurangzeb in 1666 in front of the Jama Masjid, the main mosque of Delhi, where his tomb is a venerated shrine today. Sarmad's devotion to his beloved and his martyrdom made a deep impact on people and his memory is still very much alive.

Another poignant narrative about being struck by the desire to travel in the late sixteenth century is of an émigré by the name of 'Arif Igi who told his life story to a compatriot, 'Abdun-Nabi Fakhruz-Zamani from Qazvin, whom he met up with in later years in India. 'Arif narrated that after his brother inherited the post of mayor (*kalantar*) from their father in their hometown, he, the brother, began to behave in an ungenerous manner toward him. 'Arif revealed that "for a long time I had the desire to travel and often it became an obsession. My brother's hostility was the cause of my traveling and at the age of twenty-eight I left my hometown. First I travelled around Kirman and Yazd near my home, after a while I set out by the Kark desert in Sistan for India. When I reached my destination, I saw a country that was well populated and built up; I saw cities that were extremely pleasing for repose and comfort. I decided that I would spend my whole life there. In short, I found occupation in India and in every city that I went to I spent a few days with the nobles and poets there."[32] After being part of the young prince Salim's entourage he was again struck with wanderlust and left for Iran, then returned to

India despite being fearful that Salim, now Emperor Jahangir, would not have forgiven him for leaving. He was welcomed back and spent his retirement in comfort in Bihar. There were even some individuals who ostensibly traveled for reasons that today we would call sexual freedom. The two poets Qadri and Qaidi from the city of Shiraz in Iran were lovers who moved to India to be together. After traveling around for some time, they died in their adopted land, though not in the cause of love.[33] Later we will encounter the stories of other individuals whose travels led them to the ultimate destination of their age, the Shangri-La and Eldorado both rolled into one that was the realm of the Mughals in the early modern age.

The migration of Iranians continued at a robust rate in the first half of the seventeenth century, especially spurred by the welcoming atmosphere fostered by Emperor Jahangir's chief wife, Mihrunnisa, who took the title Nur Jahan (Light of the world). The Mughal empress was sympathetic to her compatriots since she was born in Qandahar while her family was itself on the road to India. Her extensive network of family members in high imperial posts provided many lucrative opportunities for accomplished Iranian men of letters. The seventeenth century also witnessed a greater degree of people going back and forth from Iran, with some individuals choosing to reside temporarily in India and then returning home, and then sometimes coming back again because life at home was not the same once they had gotten a taste of the world outside Iran. By Shah Jahan's reign, about a dozen court poets at the highest level were almost all of Iranian extraction and recent émigrés, although chroniclers and historians were increasingly Indians.[34] The second level of poets and secretaries, who were from diverse social and ethnic backgrounds and also included Indians, served the various princes, nobles, and other administrators in the capital and the provinces.

An analogous situation existed at the Ottoman court, home of another variety of Persianate court culture, where Iranians were welcomed for the same reasons: they were native speakers of Persian and well versed in the classical literary tradition. This led to a tension between different groups: "early-modern Ottoman elites saw their primary cultural influences as coming directly from Persia and the historical culture of the Arabs and that many of them complained bitterly about the favored treatment that any literarily inclined visitor or refugee from Persia received from Ottoman patrons of culture."[35] In terms of an even wider comparison historically, Gülru Necipoglu explains the cultural context: "The cosmopolitan ethos of the new capital and the sultan's court provoked resentment, much as Alexander the Great's 'policy of fusion' had been criticized by the Macedonians. As a Turkish poet named Çatladı put it, 'If you wish to stand in high honor on the sultan's threshold / You must be a Jew or a Persian or a Firengi [Frank].'"[36] We will see that some Indian poets felt a similar sense of resentment about the partiality toward native Persian speakers at court. Although there have been no comparative studies in terms of numbers, it appears that for certain communities of Iranians, especially those who had seen friends and relatives bringing or sending remittances back home, India remained a more lucrative and attractive destination than the Ottoman court. In the sixteenth and seventeenth centuries Persian was also much more in use among the Mughals who did not incorporate vernacular languages in the domain of high court culture as easily. Urdu became the primary language of the later Mughals, virtually replacing Persian, but as a literary language of the court it had a much later start than Turkish at the Ottoman court. In this regard, the Muslim rulers of the 'Adilshahi and Qutbshahi sultanates in the southern part of the Indian subcontinent were more similar to the Ottomans in not privileging Persian over other local languages, and for this reason the vernacular Dakhni flourished much earlier in their courts than did Urdu among the Mughals as a literary language.

Already by the seventeenth century Mughal India was "too 'full,' not only of Iranians but of other groups who are all vying for the same position and privileges."[37] Jumping ahead to the eighteenth century, things by this time reached a point of no return with the history of Iranian presence in India having entered a new phase, when Mughal Arcadia was merely a forgotten dream. A young Iranian in India, Valih Daghistani, describes the embarrassment caused by the behavior of his older compatriot Hazin of Lahijan, who was also displaced in the aftermath of the fall of the Safavids in 1722:

Hazin has satirized the people of this country from among kings and nobles in an obscene manner that is not worthy of a *shaikh*. As much as I have tried to prevent him from this indecent behavior, it was no use and he continues to do what he does. Since I am beholden by the kindness of the king and rights of companionship of the nobles and other acquaintances who are blameless, I have been forced to give up my friendship and interactions with this great man and to overlook many things. Bravo to the generosity and munificence of these nobles who despite their power have not resorted to revenge, but rather do not spare themselves with regard to his situation. This matter is of great embarrassment for the Iranian scholars who live in exile in this country.[38]

The attitude of cultural superiority on the part of Iranians in India, which to some degree or other must have existed right from the beginning of their presence at the Mughal court, no longer worked in their favor since by this time there were sufficient Indians selling their talents in the market of Persian. But it is worth bearing in mind that the story of one individual does not reflect an entire cultural phenomenon in all its complexities. Rather there were different phases of interface between the various ethnic, religious, and social groups in the Mughal Empire.

The works of several major Mughal poets circulated beyond local audiences to the larger world of Persian, but within the subcontinent the spread of Persian learning had a great impact on professional men of letters of Indian origin, both Muslim and Hindus, at different social levels. Over time Persianate Indians flocked to provincial capitals or Delhi and Agra in larger numbers in search of employment and traveled extensively within the Mughal domain in the entourage of their patrons, seeing for themselves the glory of the vast empire. In comparison to Iranians and Central Asians coming to India, Indian Persian poets rarely traveled to Iran or Transoxiana to sell their Persian skills, a fact that was noted by Safavid men of letters. Of course, it would have been a case of taking coals to Newcastle. Places such as Shiraz and Bukhara were a major part of the cultural geography of Persophone people but not many Indian poets visited those places.[39] It is only the exceptional poet, such as Mazhari of Kashmir from Akbar's court, who visited Iran. An embassy from Jahangir's court to the Safavids during the years from 1613 to 1619 included at least one artist, Bishandas, but no poet.

Among the non-Muslim Persian poets of Indian origin, there were few noticed by court chroniclers until the hegemony of Iranians was ceded to indigenous Muslim poets by the middle to late seventeenth century. But even early on, a desire to learn Persian and advance themselves in bureaucratic careers had inspired many Hindus, especially in the province of Punjab. In a letter to his son written in the middle of the seventeenth century, the Mughal courtier Chandarbhan offers advice on the importance of studying the Persian classics: "Although the field of Persian is vast, almost beyond human grasp, to open the gates of the language one should read the classics. When you have advanced a bit, you should read the key texts on ethics as well as works of history. The benefits of these will be to render your language elegant, and also to provide you knowledge of the world and its inhabitants. These will be of use when you are in assemblies of learned men. When you have some leisure, read the master poets; they will give you both pleasure and relief, increase your abilities, and improve your language."[40] These words reveal a remarkably humanistic outlook on education in Mughal society. Chandarbhan "Brahman" of Lahore was one of the Hindu secretaries-poets (*munshi*) in the imperial chancery of Shah Jahan. His son Tejbhan also later served in a similar capacity. Not only was Chandarbhan an accomplished stylist in Persian, he also displayed an impressive knowledge of the canons of classical and contemporary Persian literature. By his time, Mughal cultural practices and the Persian language were no longer mere skills that one picked up in order to advance one's career. In fact, an entire way of life to which a serious knowledge of Persian poetry was central was being developed and embraced by several non-Muslim communities in early modern India.[41]

Where were women in this multiethnic and diverse community of poets? Although historical sources provide evidence of womenfolk accompanying men in this migration, whether permanently or temporarily, there are very few female literary voices from this period, at least if we go by the sources available to us.[42] A few princesses of the imperial family, such as Babur's daughter and Humayun's sister Gulbadan Begum, Shah Jahan's daughter Jahanara, and Aurangzeb's daughter Zebunnisa, are remembered for their writings as well as for their patronage of poets. This was in keeping with the tradition of their Timurid ancestors. A few verses are also attributed to the empress Nur Jahan, and many other educated women in the harems would have participated in secluded poetry recitations (*musha'iras*) or written verses for private circulation. Non-elite women are also occasionally mentioned in the sources, sometimes as poets, but Indo-Persian was really an overwhelmingly male-centered literary culture. Women came into their own in the use of Urdu and Hindi with the end of Persian hegemony when space was opened up for other groups to participate in the literary life of the period.

THE LIVES OF MUGHAL POETS

Several salient characteristics of Mughal literary culture emerge when comparing the career trajectories of two poets of Akbar's court, one of Iranian origin and the other of Indian background. Jamaluddin Muhammad 'Urfi, a native of Shiraz, arrived in India in 1584 as a young man in his twenties.[43] Attached to Akbar's court, 'Urfi was a skilled panegyrist who found a worthy patron in the young prince Salim. In these lines from a longer poem, 'Urfi offers career advice couched in metaphorical language to a young man about life in the age of Akbar, speaking from personal experience:

> *shi'ar-i millat-i islamiyan bugzar agar khahi*
> *ki dar dair-i mughan a'i u asrar-i nihan bini*
> *tu az mulk-i 'Iraqi vazhgun kun 'adat-i pishin*
> *agar khahi ki husn-i raunaq-i Hindustan bini*
> *zi mulk-i nur az anru takhti dar kishvar-i zulmat*
> *ki husn-i chiniyan ra dar libas-i zangiyan bini*[44]

Abandon the customs of the Muslim people if you want
To enter the temple of the Magis, where hidden secrets will be
    revealed to you.
You are from the land of Iran, change your old ways,

If you want to see the beauteous splendor of India.
You have sailed from the realm of light to the land of darkness
To see the beauty of the Chinese in the garb of the blacks.

The call to find freedom in India was the new slogan for many émigré poets of the age and it was rhetoric their Mughal patrons were pleased to hear from their poets. 'Urfī's image of India as the land of darkness (*kishvar-i zulmat*) is an image that developed out of an older trope of the dark-skinned Hindu whose lowly status is akin to the suffering lover in Sufi poetry, in opposition to the fair-skinned Turk who is the cruel beloved.[45] Darkness was also associated with the more positive image of the elusive water of life (*ab-i hayat, ab-i zulmat*), most famously figuring in the Persian Alexander narratives where the Macedonian hero is unsuccessful in reaching it. These stock images were now being put to a new use by 'Urfi and others. The one about India as the land of darkness would be exploited in every possible way, both in a positive and negative sense, by poets in the next two centuries to metaphorize a whole spectrum of emotions toward the land of India.

In the years after Akbar's court had moved operations to Lahore, 'Urfī's brief but brilliant career was cut short by his early death in 1591 at the age of thirty-six from dysentery, which was the fate of many visitors to the subcontinent from time immemorial. Even at a young age 'Urfi had become a literary sensation, being highly regarded as far away as the Ottoman court and to this day considered a major practitioner of an abstract or baroque style of the *ghazal*. Despite his fine poetic skills, at least one chronicler of Akbar's reign, 'Abdul-Qadir Badauni, narrated that 'Urfi was a young man of lofty disposition and understanding who was versatile in his composition, but he was also very haughty and pompous, which caused him to lose favor with people. He was said to be ugly to boot because of a pockmarked face, one reason that was actually offered for his offensive behavior. Later biographers narrated that 'Urfi had a bit of a crush on Prince Salim, his chief patron for a time.[46] Given the competitive atmosphere and the tension between native and nonnative speakers of Persian at court, it is likely that 'Urfi offended people by flaunting his superior credentials as an Iranian—and that too as a native of

Shiraz, the city of the great classical poets, Sa'di and Hafiz. Badauni records that initially 'Urfi and the emperor's favorite Faizi were on cordial terms, but then the relationship soured and 'Urfi found a more congenial atmosphere among his compatriots. There is a telling anecdote that describes 'Urfi shortly after his arrival in Agra. He made a courtesy call at the home of the Indian poet laureate Faizi. Finding Faizi playing with his dog, 'Urfi asked what its name was. In a display of quick wit, Faizi responded laconically making a pun on his visitor's pen name. "It is known" (i.e., 'urfi).[47] This anecdote illustrates the competitive, though cordial for the most part, relationship between Iranian and Indian poets of the time.

Faizi's father, Shaikh Mubarak, was a respected scholar of Islamic law and philosophy during the age of Akbar. He ran a madrasa in Agra and was frequently at loggerheads with the more conservative ulema of the time. Shaikh Mubarak had connections with the heretical Mahdavi movement and was a major supporter of Akbar in his efforts to curtail the power of the religious establishment. Faizi entered imperial service at the age of twenty in 1567, serving as tutor to the emperor's sons Salim, Murad, and Daniyal. His younger brother Abu'l-Fazl became one of the court historians and among the emperor's favorite courtiers. At age forty-two Faizi became the poet laureate (*malik al-shu'ara*), succeeding the Iranian poet Ghazali in this position. He died six years later in 1595.[48] Faizi's career as Akbar's premier poet and role as key player in the project of creating a distinct body of Mughal Persian literature was sufficient to leave a permanent legacy in the Indo-Persian tradition. Faizi was a committed poet with a strong sense of his own worth, but he also disapproved of the hyperprofessionalism around poetry that drew hacks and charlatans whose only claim was to be native speakers of Persian. In these particularly vitriolic lines he lashes out against such poets:

> Now there are innumerable poets, but they have chosen the fray of
>   dogkeepers over an angelic disposition.
> With the hunger of dogs sunk into running around with greed,
>   having poured onto the ground a hundred honors from lack of
>   bread.

> With dazzled eyes blackening rejected designs, with confused souls
> polishing the mud of the pit of blathering.
> In the marketplace of blame, with the dust of the ages on it, prisoners
> to buying and selling regal commodities.
> Sometimes they spit coarse expressions from their lips, where their
> words look like caftans on the body of meaning.
> Sometimes they import cool images into hot idioms like cold water
> into a bathhouse in winter.
> Shaven unbaked potsherds on which they have placed the value of
> Badakhshani turquoise.
> So coarse that never will their speech stick to the heart even if you
> attach it with glue.
> Like blowing sand it comes out dry even if you dunk their poetry into
> the seven seas.
> A hundred volumes of poetry made by plundering the masters, that
> the pillaged goods are beyond number.

The metaphor of commerce and materiality is foregrounded in these
lines to highlight the fact that poetry is an easily available product
for sale in an open bazaar. Faizi also brings in the familiar image of
blackness, used as a literary trope rather than laden with racist overtones. He continues to speak about how special he is among the sellers
of poetry:

> Since there was no one else left in the world, today I am he who has
> renewed poetry with a fresh collection of poems.
> Stranger from the realm of meaning I am in this caravanserai, from
> the caravan of poetry with lots of goods.
> Now heaven has entrusted the key to poetry to me. From the heart
> opening and from me key-shaking.
> My inner meanings turn the denizens of paradise of the subtle abode
> of thought into houris and ghilman.[49]

Faizi's scathing assessment of the raw ambition and desperation
exhibited by poets—and many of these would have been émigrés—
attests both to the sheer number of candidates in the field and

the fierce competition among them. Only he has the superior poetic skills that transfer the pleasures of paradise to the realm of
reality. Faizi was rightfully proud of his talent as a poet, but he
was also buoyed by the favor shown him and his family by the
emperor.

Despite his display of self-confidence, Faizi's sense of isolation
among the Iranian elites at court comes through occasionally in his
poetic oeuvre. Although he was close to Emperor Akbar and had
achieved the highest honor that a court poet could aspire to, he was
anxious about his stature being dwarfed by those with stronger
claims on the language. But he did become famous, and, in reality,
he was the only Indian-born Mughal poet who was celebrated beyond the Indian Persianate domain until the time of the literary giant
Bedil, who flourished in the late seventeenth and early eighteenth
centuries.[50] The two major chroniclers of Akbar's reign, his brother,
Abu'l-Fazl, and Badauni, both wrote the longest biographical accounts of him in their works, comprising twenty pages in print as
compared to the half page or less allotted to other individuals. This
was despite the antipathy that Badauni felt toward the entire clan of
Abu'l-Fazl, thus attesting to his genuinely fine skills as a professional
poet.

Faizi expresses his emotions about being an Indian poet among
Iranians more candidly in a prose introduction to his collection of
poems (*divan*). First he boasts about his prowess as a poet of Persian:
"My elegant verses nourish the intellect of friends. They are fine and
meaty all over, and black-skinned of Hindustan. In these times they
have come forth from the great land of Hindustan to the inhabited
world and chosen exile (*ghurbat*) over homeland (*vatan*)." He then
goes on in a self-deprecatory vein: "What is my rank as an Indian
(*Hindustani*) with this twisted language (*kaj-maj zabani*) and champi-
onship in mastering Persian (*pahlavani u Pahlavi-dani*)! I can be like
the magicians of Hind with their charms and spells—they make
imaginary forms and spirits appear, which do not exist outside."[51]
Faizi realized that he was in a somewhat unique position at court
where not many men who had acquired Persian as a learned language had gained the high position and prestige that he did. The

situation would not change for some decades until a critical mass of poets of Indian origin arose who also wrote in Persian and made up a community of their own.

Under the emperors Jahangir and Shah Jahan there were no Persian poets of Indian origin who would match Faizi's stature, even as the highest literary circles at court opened up to men of diverse backgrounds. A painting from around the 1630s depicts one of the lively poetic assemblies (*majlis*) of the Mughal governor of Kashmir, Zafar Khan, about whom we will hear more later (see Figure 1). Zafar Khan is shown with poets, musicians, and even the artist Bishandas in advanced years. Among the group of old and venerable poets seated in a row in the presence of this enlightened patron who was a poet himself is an individual with a dark complexion. His appearance indicates his Indian origin among the other poets, two of whom are the Iranian senior poets Qudsi and Kalim. The Indian poet is seated at the edge of the group. His marginality is characteristic of the situation at this time, but it also reflects a distinct, and now fixed, presence in the elite assembly. Given the particular historical context of this painting, it is possible that this person is the young Indo-Persian poet from Lahore named Munir.

Active a couple of decades after Faizi's death, Abu'l-Barakat "Munir" of Lahore was in the service of several of Shah Jahan's administrators as a *munshi*. He was already a precocious poet in his youth. According to one source he got into a literary debate with Talib of Amul, Emperor Jahangir's poet laureate.[52] A somewhat shadowy figure in Mughal literary history, Munir did not attain the same fame beyond India that his more illustrious predecessor Faizi did, but he was remarkable in the way he wrote poetry about different places in the Mughal Empire, as we will see later. Munir expressed frustrations similar to Faizi's about the elitist attitude in Mughal society that favored native speakers of Persian. A sense of kindred spirit with Faizi is discernable in Munir's writing, especially in the way that he calls himself a person of Indian stock who speaks the twisted language (*Hindi-nizhad-i kajmaj-zaban*). In a treatise on poetics where he lauds the classical poets over the fashionable "fresh" style of the day, Munir offers a tantalizing glimpse into the stressful aspects of being a professional poet in his time:

> In the past if you were a young master poet, you would be considered old by virtue of your intelligence and wisdom. If you were poor, you would be reckoned a rich man by virtue of the wealth of your poetic skills. If you were retiring, you would be considered famous by virtue of your renowned verses. And if you were not Iranian, you would be considered noble by virtue of your good temperament. Today if you don't possess those four qualifications, you are considered to be nothing and your poetry useless. With respect to the quality of being noble, especially, in this age unless a poet's birthplace is in that country, i.e., Iran, his poetry will not be ranked high. My father was from Lahore and I have mastered the art of poetry, but I am forced to lie that I am from Khurasan so that my poetry and verses find buyers.[53]

In order to bolster his pedigree as an Indo-Persian poet, Munir goes on to name five renowned classical poets who emerged from the land of India: Mas'ud Sa'd Salman and Abu'l-Faraj Runi of Lahore, Amir Khusrau and Hasan of Delhi, and the more recent Faizi of Nagor, thus providing an alternate literary canon to one that centered on poets of the Iranian heartland. Like 'Urfi, he died young, at the age of thirty-four in 1644.

There were scores of other poets with more unusual life stories than those of 'Urfi, Faizi, and Munir who did not belong to the highest cadre of court poets and were not remembered by posterity. One such person was Rasmi Qalandar of Yazd, who as his name indicates was a dervish from Iran, but at some point in his life served as a mercenary soldier in Kashmir and then reinvented himself as a poet in Lahore. In a formal poem in the *qasida* form, which served as a petition in verse, he sought the patronage of the Mughal Maecenas, the general 'Abdur-Rahim Khankhanan, a poet himself who rivaled the munificence of the emperor. In his poem Rasmi dazzles the reader with a catalogue of contemporary and classical poets in order to flatter 'Abdur-Rahim:

FIGURE 1 Zafar Khan's *majlis* (above and opposite)

zi yumn-i madh-i tu an naghma-sanj-i Shirazi / rasid sit-i kalamash bi-Rum
  az khavar

bi-tarz-i taza zi madh-i tu ashna gardid / chu ru-yi khub ki bayad zi mashatta
  zivar

zi faiz-i nam-i tu Faizi girift chun Khusrau / bi-tigh-i Hindi, iqlim-i sab'a ra
  yaksar

zi rizachini-i khvanat Naziri-i sha'ir / rasida ast bi-ja'i ki sha'iran-i digar

kunand bahr-i madihash qasidaha insha / ki khun zi rashk fitad dar dil-i
  sukhanparvar

savad-i shi'r-i Shakibi chu kuhl-i Isfahan / bi-tuhfa su-yi Khurasan barand
  ahl-i basar

zi madhat-i tu Hayati hayat-i digar yaft / bali murabbi-i tab' 'arz buvad jauhar

hadis-i Nau'i u Kufri chisan bayan sazam / chu zinda'and bi-madh-i tu ta
  dam-i mahshar

zi ni'mat-i tu bi Nau'i rasid an maya / ki yaft Mir Mu'izzi zi ni'mat-i Sanjar

zulal-i madh-i tu ta rahnuma-yi Rasmi gasht / sarab az qadamash shud chu
  chashma-yi kausar[54]

Due to the auspicious praise of you, the fame of that accomplished
  poet from Shiraz (*'Urfi*) went from East to West. He became
  familiar with a new style, like a beautiful face that is made over by
  a bride's waiting woman.

By the grace of your name, *Faizi* like [Amir] *Khusrau* conquered the
  seven climes all at once with his Indian sword.

With crumbs from your table, the poet *Naziri* has reached a position
  that other poets compose *qasida*s in *his* praise and the hearts of
  poets bleed with jealousy. . . .

Connoisseurs take as gifts the works of *Shakibi* to Khurasan, like the
  kohl of Isfahan.

By praising you *Hayati* found a new life; indeed, talent is patronized
  by a generous temperament.

How can I describe the case of *Nau'i* and *Kufri*, they will live until the
  day of resurrection for praising you. From your generosity *Nau'i*
  received the wealth that *Mir Muizzi* did from Sanjar. . . .

Until the limpid water of your praise became the guide for *Rasmi*,
  there was a mirage of his footsteps, like the spring of paradise.

The names in italics are all names of poets, the last one being the one who penned this poem. Apart from Mir Muizzi and Khusrau who represent the past, and Faizi who is Indian, the rest are all contemporary poets from Iran who enjoyed the patronage of 'Abdur-Rahim Khankhanan. This galaxy of poets cleverly worked into a single poem is a compliment to a patron who is responsible for collecting a distinguished entourage. The significant point in these verses is that the direction that Persian poetry traveled has reversed in this age—it now goes from India to Iran, rather than the other way around. The names of the classical poets also add the authority of tradition here. There is a more than a tacit acknowledgment in these lines that Iran is no longer the home of Persian poetry.

Historians from Akbar's court describe the Mughal Persian literary community in various ways. Three versions of a grouping of poets who were from Akbar's time illustrate this point. In volume one of the encyclopedic work *A'in-i Akbari*, Abu'l-Fazl lists fifty-nine best poets of the age who were presented to the emperor, beginning with his brother Faizi who gets the longest notice. While his list of scholars, Sufis, and musicians shows these people were overwhelmingly of Indian background, the vast majority of poets are émigrés from Iran and Central Asia; only two men originated from Punjab and two from Kashmir. One of the latter is Mazhari Kashmiri who is described by Abu'l-Fazl as having been in Iran where "from living together with good people, acquired excellent habits."[55] There was much more to Mazhari, as we shall see.

In contrast to Abu'l-Fazl's list, that of the historian Badauni begins with Ghazali Mashhadi, Akbar's first poet laureate, while not surprisingly given the enmity between the Badauni and Abu'l-Fazl, Faizi stands at number 107 and is reviled in the harshest terms for his sycophancy and heretic beliefs. A useful feature of Badauni's list is the fact that he includes the widest representation of Persian poets active in India in terms of place of origin, social class, religious community, and sex. Here is found the only mention in this period of a Hindu poet of Persian, a young man named Manohar whose *takhallus* was "Tausani." Tausani was the son of Lon Karan, Raja of Sambhar, and according to the author, "although he was not acceptable to the emperor (*marzi-yi tab'-i padshahi nabud*) he has poetic genius (*tab'-i nazmi*)." Badauni adds that "since a Hindu had so much poetic genius (*tab'-i shi'r*) and ecstatic feeling (*halat-i gharib*) he thought fit to record these verses.[56] The only mention in this period of a female poet is one Nihani of Agra who is compared to the classical poet Mahsati of Herat (*za'ifa'i bud dar Agra qarina-yi Mahsati Haravi*). Nihani's son, apparently, was in imperial service.[57] Another unusual inclusion in Badauni's list is Tifli, son of Mulla Darvish of Fatehpur, in the service of Prince Salim. Tifli is said to have "a most generous nature (*tab'i bi-ghayat fayyaz darad*) and an admirable taste in poetry (*saliqa-yi u bi-shi'r basi munasib*)." Badauni goes on to say, "It is marvelous that a lad of Tifli's years should understand and speak Persian; much more so that he should be able to compose poetry in the language (*farsi fahmidan u guftan dar in sinn 'ajab buvad chi ja-yi shi'r guftan*)."[58] Mazhari Kashmiri is included at number 144, but only described as being in imperial service in Kashmir without any mention of his sojourn in Iran.[59] Putting all these biographical accounts together, along with references from court chronicles, allows for a fuller picture of the composition of the Mughal Persian literary community to emerge.

The third chronicle of Akbar's reign that offers a different listing of eighty-one poets is by Nizamuddin Ahmad,[60] a man who was in imperial service in the province of Gujarat in the 1580s, overlapping with the governorship of the aforementioned patron-poet 'Abdur-Rahim Khankhanan. Therefore, the poets in his chronicles, who come after the "account of amirs of high rank, shaikhs of Hindustan, physicians," do not reflect an Agra-Delhi-centered who's who of notables. The list begins with the most distinguished names among the professional poets, two of whom were poet laureates: Ghazali, Qasim Kahi, Husain Marvi, and Faizi. The account of Faizi is short in comparison to the other Mughal chroniclers, but more flattering than the one by Badauni. Regarding Mazhari Kashmiri, Nizamuddin merely states that "he is one of the servants of the threshold." The value of Nizamuddin Ahmad's work is that it mentions local poets of Persian such as Malik Mahmud Pyare Gujarati and provides a glimpse into the Persianate community in Gujarat. It should be noted that none of these works describes the multilingual nature of the literary circles, whether in Agra or Ahmedabad, that in the early Mughal period would also have been composed of Chaghatai and Hindi poets. Poets who we know to have been multilingual are only mentioned as writing in Persian. Someone like 'Ishqi Khan, who composed poems in old Urdu (*rekhta*), is only mentioned here as a Persian poet. Another person named 'Itabi is said to have composed poetry in Persian and Arabic, but that is as far as it goes. No examples of non-Persian verses are ever offered in these works.

Comparing how the lives of court poets were being recorded at the Safavid court, the "poets" section of the chronicle of Shah 'Abbas I's reign, Iskandar Beg Munshi's *'Alamara-yi 'Abbasi*, has a list that is similar but nowhere as long as in the Mughal histories.[61] Only eighteen poets are described as writing by the time of the passing of Shah Tahmasp I in 1576 and an additional five men who were not professional poets. In the ranking of the court poets, major figures such as Maulana Zamiri Isfahani who appears first as the "peerless poet of the age," followed by Maulana Muhtasham, Maulana Vali, Maulana Vahshi Yazdi, are those who did not migrate to India. Iskandar Beg only mentions three court poets who left Iran for India, Mir Haidar "Mu'amma-yi Kashan" (identified as Rafi'i in Mughal texts), and Maulana Malik Qummi, who spent his entire career at the Adilshahi court in the Deccan, the third is a bazaari poet by the name of Sultan-i Fuqara, who was a moneychanger turned dervish whose career as a poet flourished upon his return to Iran. Surprisingly, we encounter Mazhari Kashmiri again here, who is said to have visited Iran "with the object of meeting Persian poets" and whose good looks created a sensation there and verses "created an equal sensation among contemporary poets."[62] These last intriguing details are not found in the Mughal texts; perhaps the Indian chroniclers had no idea what Mazhari had gotten up to in Iran. By including a small but diverse group of poets, the Safavids acknowledge an awareness of the expanding and connected Persianate world, with a movement of men of letters in *both* directions, although this list does not portray realistically the large scale of migration to India. The Mughals, of course, did not show much interest in the activities of Persian poets of Iran who had chosen to stay home, although their poems would have been known to some degree.

Having become a magnet for Persian poets of diverse backgrounds from all over the Persophone world, India and its Persianate center, the Mughal court, continued to promote the idea of a welcoming land inhabited by peoples of all nations and social classes who possessed valuable skills that they contributed to the cultural life of the times. Although the Mughal court was remarkably tolerant of diversity compared to their contemporaries in Europe and Asia, in her study of the patronage of Sanskrit by the Mughals, Audrey Truschke cautions that, "the Mughal brand of multiculturalism was not an open stage where all traditions were equally esteemed, nor was it a utopia of religious toleration."[63] But the propagation of a positive view of India was integral to the success of the imperial vision of a ruling polity that was committed to establishing its distinct identity in the Islamic world. In the early seventeenth century, the poet Kalim declared that India "could be called a second paradise in the sense that anyone who left this garden regretted it" (*tavan bihisht-i duvvum guftan bi-in ma'ni / ki harki raft azin bustan pashiman shud).*[64] The association of India with the metaphor of paradise in Persian literature already had a long history, although what that signified changed over time. For people like Kalim, it meant a place for Persian poets to practice their craft and be handsomely rewarded for it. Such was the state of Persian poetry at the Mughal court, but how did things actually work in a society that was more like the tower of Babel and what relationship did Persian have to the many other languages encountered by the Mughals?

MULTILINGUALISM

Early Mughal literary culture was multilingual, with both Chaghatai Turkish, or Turki as the family language of the early Mughals was known, and Persian being used for writing and spoken communication. Then there were various registers of a north Indian vernacular that can be grouped under the term Hindi or Hindavi, Braj-bhasha and Avadhi. These formed a continuum with Dakhni in the southern region. Like many people of the cultural milieu he originated from, the first Mughal ruler Babur was at least bilingual, as is evident in his poetry and prose. On the threshold of the Indian subcontinent, as Babur prepared to enter a new world, he made a note in his autobiography of the number of languages spoken just in the province of Kabul: Arabic, Persian, Turkish, Mongolian, Hindi, Afghani, Pashai, Parachi, Gabari, Baraki, and Lamghani.[65] This was even before he entered the plains of India! Babur and his descendants would encounter the many languages of India as they settled there and initiated a process of mutual linguistic exchange. Yet Persian stood out among the languages used by them. The influx of native speakers of the language from Khorasan, the region in Eastern Iran and present-day Afghanistan, in the early modern period, was certainly "a factor enhancing the role of the Persian language in its formation."[66] Persian would be the most indispensable tool to keep the machinery of empire running smoothly and for people from disparate backgrounds to achieve social mobility.

In a letter authored by the Mughal emperor Aurangzeb to his son Muhammad Sultan in 1654, the learned father emphasizes the merits of writing and reading of Persian, specifying a suitable time for the activity, such as after lunch: "But if the meal alone suffices to refresh you, spend the interval in improving your handwriting, composing letters, or reading Persian prose and poetry." The well-meaning father goes on to give more specific direction to this son: "Read the *Akbarnamah* [History of Akbar] at leisure, so that the style of your conversation and writing may become pure and elegant. Before you have thoroughly mastered the meanings of words and the proper connection in which they may be used, do not employ them in your speeches or letters. Ponder carefully on what you speak or write."[67] This snippet of domestic life shows that Persian was the language privileged by the imperial family over family languages such as Turki or Hindi. Apparently, lessons in Turkish would have been continued out of respect for their heritage but were not enjoyable for the princes by this time, as was true even earlier in the case of Shah Jahan when he was prince Khurram.

Persian continued to be cultivated by the court until the very end of Mughal rule in 1858, but in the later period most people had a somewhat bookish knowledge of it since the nineteenth-century was the age of Urdu. Chiefly cultivated as a classical language and mark of prestige, Persian was symbolically so important for the last Mughal court poet Ghalib that he is said to have invented an Iranian tutor for himself to bolster his claims to being a master of it.[68] Over the course of time, Persian was increasingly considered to be of no real use in modern South Asia. Today, most scholars and nonspecialists are familiar with the history of the Mughal period through translations or vernacular languages, and not through the original texts in Persian or even those in Hindi, because Braj-bhasha is quite different from the modern standard language. This is analogous to the situation in modern Turkey where most people cannot access Ottoman Turkish texts, let alone Ottoman Persian ones, in the original. Urdu literature produced in Mughal society in the eighteenth and nineteenth centuries is far more accessible to South Asians.[69]

In her study of premodern Hindi literature, Allison Busch discusses the problem of neglecting the rich body of vernacular poetry from the Mughal court for a number of reasons, one being a discomfort with courtly literature that is viewed as elitist.[70] Serious attention to Persian court poetry also suffers from the same problem. The point is that the enjoyment of Braj-bhasha Hindi poetry was also essential to the appreciation of the arts, especially poetry and music, for all courtiers.[71] While the basic challenge of acknowledging the multilingualism of Mughal literary culture has been overcome by several young scholars recently, there is a need for more comparative work on how Persian and Hindi poets interacted with each other and the shared features of the works they composed under imperial patronage.

Hindi was firmly rooted in subimperial and Rajput Hindu courts all over north India, and although Hindi poets had a secure place at the Mughal court, Persian received more attention due to a sense of "superiority attached to the Persianate episteme."[72] Scores of praise poems and historical texts were composed in Hindi for Mughal rulers and nobles, and the vogue of Persian's "fresh style" (*taza-gu'i*) of poetry coincided with what in retrospect is called the *riti* style of Hindi, both being complex and rhetorical with similarities to the metaphysical poets of English literature. History was also an important subject for poetry in both literary traditions: the anomalous history of the battles of Humayun and Akbar in Sanskrit, *Jagadagurukavya,* written by the Jain Padmasagara in 1589,[73] and other texts in various Indian languages were clearly in direct or indirect conversation with Persian texts. Appreciating the multilinguality of the early modern period enriches our understanding of Mughal cultural life in all its manifestations.[74] Nevertheless, the fact that the sheer number of Persian texts from this period far outnumber those in other languages is indisputable, many of which are also part of the Safavid Iranian archive because of the links between the two societies. But it must be kept in mind that the ultimate purpose of Mughal court literature, irrespective of language, was to espouse an imperial ideology, as the art historian Ebba Koch has shown with respect to architecture and painting: "The written texts and the arts were equally seen as necessary means to represent the ruler and his state for a wider public and of providing a lasting memorial to his fame."[75] Persian was the language that reached the larger Perso-Islamic world, while Hindi, and later Urdu, connected the Mughal court to other parts of the Indian subcontinent.

When it came to being polylingual no one could match the larger-than-life 'Abdur-Rahim Khankhanan. The son of Bairam Khan, a Turkmen from Khurasan who had accompanied Babur to India and was for a time regent to the child ruler Akbar, 'Abdur-Rahim personified the cultural synthesis that the early Mughals were striving to achieve. His biographer 'Abdul-Baqi Nihavandi, who was the recipient of generous hospitality when he arrived from Iran in 1614, lavishly praised his knowledge and enjoyment of literature in various languages:

India has many languages such that in every region there are urban (*shahri*) and regional (*vilayati*) languages. This general speaks them all well. He has full command of Turki; since it is the language of his ancestors and knowing it is not surprising. Since Turki is not used in India and there are others of Turkish stock, such as the sons of Chaghtai amirs, Qizilbash nobles, and Uzbek notables, but due to the fact that they are born in India and raised among the people here, they do not know it. Only this linguist who knows the secrets of the unseen and heavenly world speaks Turki of this tribe, i.e., Uzbeki, Qizilbashi, and Rumi, with perfect fluency.

He was even said to have picked up a smattering of Portuguese, no doubt from his dealings with traders and Jesuits. For Nihavandi, only one other person could match this amazing linguistic ability, Shah 'Abbas I of Iran "who also knows and speaks with perfect fluency with many of the groups in their own language. Especially the languages of the people of Iran that are Gilani, Mazandarani, Shirvani, Georgian, Qalmaq, Circassian, Turkoman, and others. Most areas of Iran have their own languages and they repose in the shadow of his kindness."

'Abdur-Rahim's repertoire of languages connected him to a larger Persianate community of people, both Indians and Iranians. More than a hundred people—poets, artists, scholars, and so on—were said to have benefited from his patronage:

> If I were to include in my summary the names of panegyrists and poets who have praised him in Hindi and were to pay attention to the biographies of that group, it would be interminable and words would fail me. The rewards and favours that were given to them cannot be described in brief. A great number of chroniclers among them were and are always attached to him as beneficiaries in his felicitous service. It would not be surprising if I write about the rewards and gifts that were more than those awarded to poets of Persian. This general has also composed sound poetry and charming verses in Hindi.[76]

Certainly there were others like the general among the Mughals, especially some of the princes of the ruling house, who knew a number of languages and spent time in different parts of the empire, but 'Abdur-Rahim, known as Rahim in the context of Hindi poetry, remains a legend in modern India.

According to an anecdote illustrating 'Abdur-Rahim's generosity, the Hindi poet Gang uttered this verse before him on a certain occasion as a tribute to his generosity:

sikhe kahan navab-ju aisi deni dain
jyon jyon kar uncho kare tyon tyon niche nain

Where did my lord learn such generosity?
The more your hands are raised [to give],
the lower your eyes are.

Rahim responded with an appropriate verse displaying his mastery in repartee:

denhar kou aur hai bhejat so din rain
log bharam mo pe dharai yate niche nain[77]

The giver is someone else—He bestows continuously.
But people think it's me, hence my downcast eyes.

Unlike other great patrons of poetry, 'Abdur-Rahim was also a poet who forged intimate relations with people around him and supported people in Iran.[78]

It is unfortunate though not surprising that although Nihavandi refers to the patronage received by Hindi poets at 'Abdur-Rahim's court, their lives and verses are actually not recorded in his biography, for works like his were meant for a Persian audience. Much of 'Abdur-Rahim's own Hindi poetry, the most popular being Rahim's *dohas*, aphorisms in rhymed couplets, has a murky manuscript tradition, probably due to its transmission in a largely oral context, with some verses also attributed to other Hindi poets such as Tulsidas, Surdas, and Biharilal, among others.[79] Despite being a discerning connoisseur of Persian poetry, surprisingly 'Abdur-Rahim was not really a poet in that language and only a couple of *ghazals* by him seem to have survived. In a study of his workshop, where many ambitious manuscript projects were completed, John Seyller concludes that he "continued his exceptional cultivation of *Indian* literature even as he pursued a more *traditional* interest in Persian classics."[80] It would seem that 'Abdur-Rahim's talents lay in the field of Hindi poetry, rather than Persian, though he was a patron to poets in all languages that were used around him.

Almost all of the Mughal rulers composed occasional verses in Hindi while being expert at judging the merits of good literature. Much of the court poetry written at this time was for entertainment or in praise of the emperor, princes, and other men, and occasionally women, in positions of power. This held true for both the Persian and Hindi poetic traditions. Panegyric poetry whether in the Persian *qasida* form or the Hindi *prashasti* have been neglected by readers and scholars as being too ornate and not lyrical, but there is much that is innovative and exciting in them. For instance, the Hindi poet Keshavdas praises Jahangir in his rhetorical work *Jahangirjas-chandrika* (Moonlight of Jahangir' renown), combining images from Hindu culture with the stock images of panegyric:

> See how the emperor Jahangir is as astonishing as the god Indra.
> In his court are poets and generals,
> skilled artists and discerning scholars,
> warriors, officers, stable masters, sheikhs, masterminds,
> a range of entertainers and their companions.
> There are beautiful songs, haunting to the soul.
> Keshavdas says, Jahangir is a capable ruler in every respect—
> he is kind to the deserving and
> harsh toward those who break the law.[81]

Another Hindi poet Kavindra lauds Shah Jahan's "multicultural competency" in these lines from his work *Kavindrakalpalata* (Wish-fulfilling vine of Kavindra):

> He knows the Qur'an and the Puranas,
> he knows the secrets of the Vedas.
> Say, where else can one find so much connoisseurship,
> so much understanding.[82]

The allusions to both Muslim and Hindu scriptural texts in these verses allowed diverse audiences to derive aesthetic pleasure from listening to or reading them. Sung Hindi poetry was equally enjoyed as Persian in musical assemblies by all courtiers, while books with illustrations in a more general Rajput style took their place next to those from Persian classics. In both praise and love poetry, the two most important topics, the poetics of the two traditions come close together and some degree of cross-fertilization would have been in play.

In his autobiography, Emperor Jahangir mentions that in the year 1608 he was enraptured by the "subtle conceits" in the verses recited to him by a Hindi bard (*charan*) in the entourage of the Rajput prince Raja Suraj Singh.[83] Alas, he did not record the original verses, but rather a Persian version of them done by one of the court poets. In other situations, poetry could also provide entertainment or elicit astonishment. It is narrated in one the chronicles of his reign that in 1629 someone brought two Hindus from Bihar before Shah Jahan claiming that they "were able to commit to memory, on only one hearing, ten related Hindi verses which had only recently been composed by ten different poets; and moreover, they could then reconstruct the sequence in which the verses had been composed, and also compose additional verses extemporaneously on the same subject and in same meter." When the emperor witnessed this marvelous feat, he rewarded them handsomely.[84] In addition to an appreciation of the quality of poetry, this anecdote speaks of an interest in unusual skills in memorizing and extemporizing verses.

The second half of the seventeenth century witnessed a flowering of both Hindi and Persian literature by Hindu and Muslim authors; many Persophone Indians were chiefly from the *kayasth* and *khatri* communities seeking employment in the imperial bureaucracy.[85] The increasing popularity of Urdu poetry in the eighteenth and nineteenth centuries, which rendered Persian more of a classical language, resulted in literary texts becoming more accessible to nonelite groups. Mughal literature of this period was no longer limited to courtly circles but was produced and enjoyed in a larger social arena. The political upheavals of the eighteenth century, from weakening of Mughal power, incursions by Nadir Shah of Iran, Ahmad Shah Durrani of Afghanistan, and the Marathas, as well as finally British rule in many parts of India, all influenced the kind of literature that was produced and the way it became part of people's lives. Major Urdu poets of the seventeenth century, such as Mir Taqi Mir, Mir Hasan, and Sauda, were bilingual or multilingual. They composed poetry chiefly in Urdu, occasionally in Persian, sometimes Hindi and even Punjabi. Historians often focus on the cultural decline of the later Mughal period and cite the genre of *shahrashob* in Urdu as a poetic expression of this downward cultural turn. But there was a flourishing literary scene in many provincial cities of the erstwhile Mughal Empire that were successor Muslim kingdoms, such as Awadh, Bengal, Hyderabad, and Rampur.[86]

READING, RECITING, AND WRITING OF POETRY

In its sumptuousness Mughal literary culture was a continuation of the brilliant Timurid courtly tradition of the fifteenth and early six-teenth century, which had its center in Herat, in present-day Afghan-istan. In Timurid culture poetry was part of a daily life of gatherings in gardens where wine and opium were freely consumed. In fact, as heirs of this courtly culture, the Mughals who referred to themselves as Timurids were proud of this rich legacy and it was continued in many forms, all the while absorbing local practices as well. Timurid literary culture was multilingual, with men of letters using Persian and Chaghatai Turkish as the two main languages. In keeping with this tradition, the first Mughal ruler Babur's circle of courtiers was smaller and more intimate than what the Mughal court would be-come under Akbar and his descendants. As a result, the community of prince, courtiers, and poets was less hierarchical and more like a large clan. In addition to converting to Shiism as a condition of mili-tary help from the Safavids in order to win back his kingdom, Hu-mayun brought several poets and artists from Iran and transformed the character of Mughal court life.[87] Thus, Mughal literature had both a diachronic and synchronic relationship to the larger Persianate world: first, as conscious heirs to a powerful Timurid heritage, and second, by its connection to other Persian and Persianate literary cultures. The cultural links between Mughal and Safavid literary worlds, and to some extent Ottoman, existed both in terms of the mobility of people and readership since texts moved freely across im-perial boundaries. There are useful comparisons to be made between Persian literary cultures in these three great early modern empires, especially between the Mughal and Ottoman who were Persianate in that they derived inspiration from Persian and Iranian artistic forms but also integrated elements from the local non-Persian cul-tures into their arts.

Ghazali, Akbar's first poet laureate, described the cherished values associated with *adab* that were central to all Muslim and Persianate societies in these verses:

birun zi tariq-i kufr u din ast adab / dar khatim-i mardumi nigin ast adab
dar majlis-i 'ishq agar darun miayi / az khvish birun a ki hamin ast adab[88]

Adab is beyond the way of infidelity and faith.
Adab is the seal in the ring of humanity.
If you enter the assembly of love,
leave yourself behind for that is *adab*.

What was this elusive concept of *adab*? The basic ideas of *adab* were common to all Perso-Islamicate societies, but there were also more localized aspects tailored to different cultural situations. Related to the word for literature, *adabiyat* and its plural *adab*, which bears the meaning of "customs," meant possessing refinement and good manners, the skill to use the apt turn of phrase, as well as a good measure of chivalry. As a code of comportment, it was central to all forms of social intercourse in Mughal society, and one could best be educated in it through reading, composing, and listening to good poetry.

Poetry was a vibrant part of an oral culture, as much as it was in the copying and reading of books. Staged and extemporaneous recitations of poems (*musha'ira*) or reading of prose tales were part of the daily life of courtiers. Professional poets sometimes composed and declaimed their own verses, and individuals for this activity were especially chosen for their mellifluous voice, physical beauty, place of origin, or connection to powerful people. Formal panegyric odes were composed and recited on festive occasions such as the Perso-Islamic festivals *'id al-fitr* and *nauruz,* or to mark a military victory or accession. Poets also composed poems to mark other special events such as births, deaths, completion of buildings, and book projects, which at the same time were commemorated by court artists.

In this way, the visual and verbal arts come together to provide snapshots of episodes in the lives of the Mughals. Commemorative poems that included the year of an event in a chronogram (*tarikh,*

meaning history) were often recorded by chroniclers, and their authors were rewarded by their patrons in proportion to a poem's merit
and the poet's standing. Yet we do not have specific information about
how much of the vast body of poetry that was produced in this period
was performed aloud and how much was even read at all. Similarly,
Hindi literature had an important place at court, especially in musical
assemblies, but we do not know how Hindi poets interacted with Persian poets, especially those who were émigrés. There was a conspicu-
ously active interaction between the Persian and Indian traditions
as exemplified in the collaborations between Persian and Sanskrit
scholars on various official translation projects from Sanskrit to Persian under Akbar for instance, but in the end these are only a miniscule part of the totality of literary works composed in this period.

Audiences at poetic assemblies were sophisticated and well versed
in one or more literary traditions. The Mughal gentleman, whether
nobleman or prince, known as *mirza*, combined the characteristic of
a flaneur and aesthete who took poetry seriously: "Poetry appreciation and patronage was one of a Mughal amir's pre-eminent cultural
occupations. . . . Patronage of poets was a status symbol for a cultivated Mughal nobleman, and the expense incurred was well-justified
in his view, since his mansab and estate was not hereditary; he tried
to spend his wealth as lavishly and as elegantly as possible during his
lifetime."[89] By the seventeenth century there was a growing number
of young princes, sons of the nobility from diverse backgrounds, and
a new bourgeoisie that needed to be trained in the culture of *adab*
and *sha'iri*—composing and assessing good poetry. A revealing story
is told that Emperor Humayun was conversing with his general,
Bairam Khan, one evening as the latter was nodding off. When the
king spoke sharply to him, Bairam Khan said, "Indeed, my King, I am
present, but since I have heard that in the service of kings one should
watch one's eyes, among dervishes one should watch one's heart,
and among scholars one should watch one's tongue, I was won-
dering which one I should watch since you are a king, dervish, and
a scholar."[90] Humayun was happy with this response. Being skilled
in repartees while staying within the bounds of *adab* was a major
skill required to flourish in this culture.

Listening to stories was one way of learning about the past and about the rich cultural traditions of India that the Mughals encountered. In fact, unlike his father and grandfather, Akbar preferred this form of entertainment to the poetic *musha'ira* in which love lyrics were sung. He was fond of stories from both the Perso-Islamic and Indian past, and he was also somewhat of a storyteller himself. It is through listening to these texts that Akbar sought to educate himself and the court about the mythology, history, and religious beliefs of the Hindu majority population. The still popular accounts of the witty exchanges between Akbar and his minister Birbal may not have been completely based on historical record, but the spirit of the anecdotes shows the emperor had a lively nature and was constantly engaged with men of all backgrounds. Said to be illiterate, Akbar was equally comfortable with the sophisticated and rich classical Persian literary tradition. According to his biographer Abu al-Fazl, he used to recite fluently from the *Masnavi* of Maulana Rumi and the *divan* of Hafiz. People like Akbar and 'Abdur-Rahim who were multilingual and negotiated the nuances of different cultures with ease, feeling equally at home with Persian poets and Hindu musicians, provided models of what it meant to be a Mughal in the cultural sense.

One of Akbar's favorite narrative works in Persian was the popular romance of Amir Hamza, the uncle of the prophet Muhammad, a work that also enjoyed immense popularity in Urdu literary culture in later centuries. Such tales provided entertainment and relaxation not only when the court was in residence in the capital, but also while it was on campaigns or other trips. Abu'l-Fazl writes that during a hunting expedition in Malwa in 1564, Akbar took pleasure in listening to Darbar Khan's recital of the story of Amir Hamza, an early Muslim protagonist of heroic tales. The emperor was said to have been so fond of this text that he would recite the story himself in the manner of the professional storytellers. It was the extreme delight and enjoyment in listening to and performance of this narrative work that led to his commissioning a lavishly illustrated manuscript of the *Hamzanama*.[91] The extremely large paintings from this manuscript depicted fights between heroes and demons in some extremely gory scenes and were used as visual aids while a storyteller narrated the dramatic tale. The best storytellers (i.e., those who had the most desirable voice and pronunciation) were native Persian speakers. In fact, one such person at Akbar's court, Darbar Khan, was the son of Taklu Khan, who had been a storyteller for the Safavid Shah Tahmasp.[92] There were other individuals who were part of the cultural network connecting the two courts.

The polymath 'Abdur-Rahim shared Akbar's catholic tastes in the arts and was also described by Nihavandi as having an avid interest in storytelling in several languages: "He also knows the stories and traditions of the Turks better than those people such that he likes to listen to tales and stories to induce sleep; sometimes they are recited in his presence in Turki, sometimes in Hindi, sometimes in Persian."[93] The traditional Mughal art of storytelling known as *dastango'i* has recently been revived in India, quite successfully, and in addition to Urdu, Hindi is also used to reach a wider audience. In Iran the storytelling tradition, called *naqqali,* and almost exclusively used for the telling of epic tales from the *Shahnama* (Book of kings), never fully died out and has opened up to women practitioners today.

Although Jahangir was fond of travel and spent a great deal of his life first as prince and then as ruler in various provinces, he appears to have liked to enjoy his literature in private sessions. More than listening to stories, Jahangir's favorite mode of relaxation was to listen to poetry in intimate interactions with performers who sang *ghazal*s and discussed them with him. Anecdotes recorded in texts from his period reveal the eclectic range of his interests and his insatiable curiosity to learn about all aspects of poetry. The courtier 'Abdus-Sattar Qasim of Lahore, in his *Majalis-i Jahangiri* (Assemblies of Jahangir), a detailed and intimate record of sessions with the emperor dating from November 2, 1608, to November 24, 1611, noted that at bedtime all kinds of singers and musicians (*qavvalan va kalavantan va digar guyandagan*) gathered around the ruler as he drank wine.[94] Singers would perform a single poem for hours as the emperor enquired about its author and discussed its meaning. Jahangir once asked the assembled people in his chamber who was the greater poet of the two classical masters: Sa'di or Hafiz, not in terms of mastery over the *ghazal* because he knew it was the former, but in terms of mysticism (*darvishi*) and piety (*khudaparasti*).⁹⁵ These aspects of courtly life show the importance of poetry in the sustenance of a vibrant literary culture.⁹⁶ There must have been similar scenes in the Mughal harem with singers and storytellers hired to entertain the women, as well as female *musha'ira*s, but sources are silent on such matters.

In 1627, the last year of Jahangir's life, another author made a transcript of his private sessions with the emperor providing intriguing glimpses into his keen poetic sense. A visitor from Samarqand in Central Asia to the Mughal court, Mutribi Samarqandi, described the emperor's continuing interest in poetry and curiosities of all kinds. His work was an addendum to a larger work called *Nuskha-yi ziba-yi Jahangiri* (Jahangir's beautiful book) composed in 1625. During one of their sessions, Emperor Jahangir asked the seventy-year-old Mutribi to sing, which the latter did reluctantly, and then a theoretical discussion on music ensued. In another meeting the emperor told Mutribi that "the sweet-voiced nightingale Fasih Khan has been reading your book to us for hours. We enjoy it very much."⁹⁷ At a subsequent meeting, the emperor informed Mutribi that Fasih Khan had finished reading his anthology and he had ordered the book to be placed in the royal library. Jahangir also advised Mutribi that his own anthology, compiled when he was a prince, could easily be incorporated into the poet's work, to which the author could not but acquiesce.⁹⁸ These vignettes illustrate the way that texts were not always fixed and could be enlarged and adapted to suit a particular set of circumstances. In their last meeting, Jahangir wanted Mutribi to accompany the court to Kashmir, but the poet had been homesick for some time and received permission to return to Samarqand, laden with ample gifts that he had received from the emperor.

While oral performance of poetry was instrumental in the dissemination of poems and stories, a flourishing culture of producing books—from lavish manuscripts used in gift-giving to quotidian reading copies—also played a significant role in the circulation of literary works. In keeping with their Timurid heritage, the Mughals paid a great deal of attention to "the collection, preservation, and production of books—bibliophilism."⁹⁹ The Mughal imperial library's most valuable treasures were those manuscripts that had been owned by and passed down from their illustrious ancestors, such as a prized copy of the classic Sa'di's *Gulistan* (Rose garden) that was cherished from one generation to another. Seals and inscriptions on these manuscripts attest to the value they had for their owners or readers and also reveal the relationships that individuals had with physical books and the sometimes unexpected ways in which these objects circulated. Mughal copies of the Persian classics were given distinct features, such as paintings in the more realistic Mughal style to illustrate the old narratives. Gifts received from Safavid and Ottoman rulers and nobles were also treasured but more likely to be parted with in a regifting process.[100]

The Mughals were particularly interested in caring for the Indo-Persian literary past. When it was discovered that the imperial library did not have a complete copy of Amir Khusrau's last historical verse narrative, *Tughlaqnama*, which in fact had not survived in a single complete copy by the late sixteenth century, Jahangir commissioned the poet Hayati to complete the missing sections with a careful eye to the original style. Poets compiled their own *divan*s and sometimes wrote introductions to them, while others wrote laudatory prefaces for their friends' collections of poetry. Such books were passed around among the educated classes and copies were often presented to the emperor or a provincial governor. Two types of books are particularly helpful for us in understanding the literary and artistic tastes and preferences at different moments in time. One is the *bayaz* or *safina* (literally "boat," so-called because of its long shape), a notebook in which an individual jotted down favorite or popular verses, often a hemistich from a *ghazal* heard in salons. The album, *muraqqa'*, was another prized object in the book culture of Persianate courts, and for the Mughals it became a way to showcase the best and innovative examples of paintings, calligraphy, portraits, verses, as well as the binding itself. Albums depicted the aesthetic concerns of a courtly culture in a microcosmic fashion.[101] The so-called Salim album focused on the diverse religious figures of India such as yogis and dervishes, thus providing a kaleidoscopic view of Mughal society. Many albums had a short introduction penned by various authors and dis-

tinguished figures, such as the one Prince Dara Shikoh made for his
wife, Nadira Banu.[102]

Bibliophiles such as Faizi, who owned around 4,600 books, 'Abdur-
Rahim Khankhanan, and Prince Dara Shikoh were known to have
impressive libraries, none of which survive as collections today. It was
Akbar who had established the imperial atelier (kitabkhana) where
an army of calligraphers, painters, bookbinders, and other craftsmen
skilled in the book arts were employed.[103] The emperor's or other
highly placed patron's aesthetic tastes guided the choice of subjects
of works that were copied anew or refurbished, whether from the
classical canon of Persian literature or a corpus of new literature that
came to be composed in a Mughal sociopolitical context. Some projects were ambitious and took several years to complete, the best
known of these is the illustrated copies of the Hamzanama and the
Hindu epic Ramayana, while single-page works, such as portraits and
calligraphic panels, were executed quickly. Of the two major translation initiatives that sought to bring Sanskrit texts to a Persophone
audience, the first one under Akbar was literary in its orientation,
though not without its political underpinnings, while the second, undertaken half a century later under Shah Jahan's son Prince Dara
Shikoh, was philosophical and religious, and ultimately gave Europe
the first translation of the Hindu philosophical work, the Upanishads,
by way of a Persian version. The Persian translation of the autobiography of the first Mughal ruler, Baburnama, carried out by none other
than 'Abdur-Rahim, was an important founding text and copies were
distributed to many courtiers. A few decades later Shah Jahan, who
was obsessed with historical texts especially of his own time, commissioned multiple histories of his reign. One of the chronicles of his
age, the Windsor Palace Padshahnama, was written by 'Abdul-Hamid
Lahauri. It included forty-four realistic paintings of court scenes and
battles that were executed by the best Mughal artists, such as Bal-
chand, Payag, and Bishandas. These images bring the court and its
activities alive before our eyes today. The incomplete work was presented to George III by the Nawab of Awadh in 1799 and ended up in
another imperial library.[104] What was left of the Mughal imperial library
after a succession of plunderers in the eighteenth and nineteenth

centuries was taken to London in 1858 and is now in the British Library.

After Akbar's large-scale projects of translation and production of books ended, many artists from the imperial atelier began to work on a freelance basis. Artists and poets found patronage under provincial governors, and the level of bibliographic activity was robust away from the capital city in places such as Ahmedabad, Burhanpur, as well as at the Deccan courts. The short-lived rebellion of Prince Salim, who would soon be Emperor Jahangir, led him to set up his own workshop in Allahabad and the production of several rare works that survive in manuscripts. From the late Akbar period, as members of the Mughal nobility and mercantile classes began to emulate the Persianate way of life to become *mirza*s schooled in *adab,* they created a demand for cheap copies of literary works with less lavish paintings.[105] This led to a thriving industry of the production of non-imperial copies of the Persian classics, such as the *Shahnama,* among other texts, with the artists who created them often having apprenticed at one time in the Mughal atelier.

We have seen how closely knit Safavid and Mughal literary cultures were, but by the turn of the sixteenth century Ottoman Turkish literati began to enthusiastically receive Persian texts, chiefly poetry of the fresh style, from the Mughal court. The scholar of Ottoman music and literature, Walter Feldman explains this phenomenon: "By the beginning of the seventeenth-century Ottoman poets were becoming aware of the poetic revolution being effected by the Persian poets of Iranian, Transoxanian or Indian origin writing in the Mughal court." The two star poets of Akbar's court, Faizi and 'Urfi, were particularly influential among Ottoman literati for whom Delhi and Lahore were the vibrant centers of poetry. Feldman adds, "The frequent references to the cities or regions of nuclear or 'greater' Iran, such as Shiraz, Kashan, Isfahan, or Shirvan are usually connected with past ages, going back to Firdausi . . . while Hindustan is linked with the names of several recent poets:

The writings of my pen
Turned Rum into Lahore

It hurled into obscurity
Fayzi, ornament of Hindustan.
In truth through the beneficent shadow
Of the Khan of Rum
The volumes of heart-attracting writings
Equal those of Hindustan."[106]

For the Ottoman poet Naili who wrote these lines, Iran was connected to a cherished but dead past, while Mughal India represented
the dynamic present, the home of wonders and riches. The exotic aspects of India were packaged in Indo-Persian narrative tales that enjoyed a wide circulation.

Along with *ghazal*s, verse romances, known as *masnavi*s for their
use of rhyming couplets, on subjects drawn from Indian lore or environment were immensely popular among audiences in the Safavid
and Ottoman realms. It was through these works that Mughal Persian poets distinguished themselves from those who wrote poems
on traditional Perso-Islamic themes such as Laila-Majnun, Khusrau-
Shirin, and Alexander the Great (Iskandar), in imitation of the three
classical masters of this form, Nizami, Amir Khusrau, and Jami. Mughal Persian poets, whether Iranian or Indian, consciously drew inspiration from Indian legends and storytelling traditions in crafting
a Mughal literary corpus. Faizi composed the romance of Nal-Daman,
based on the Sanskrit story of Nala and Damayanti from the Sanskrit
epic *Mahabharata*, while another poet, Masih, versified the tale of Ram-
Sita based on the *Ramayana* that was also widely available in the
vernacular languages of the time.[107] The Iranian poet Nau'i wrote an
original romance, *Suz u gudaz* (Burning and melting), a story of two
ordinary Hindu lovers in which the female protagonist commits *sati*
after her fiancé dies. Such romances were instantly popular with
Persophone audiences. Since the project of forging an Indo-Persian
identity in the larger Persian literary world was something the Mughals took seriously, for this they often looked to the works of the
earlier poet Amir Khusrau of Delhi as models. An engagement with
this poet's works also conveniently served the empire's propaganda
needs, both within the realm and outside, since Amir Khusrau was

an accepted canonical poet in all Persophone societies. A robust market already existed for packaging India's exotic features in literature and the other arts.

What was the history of the received view regarding India, variously as the land of wonders and diversity of flora and fauna, a refuge and paradise, and how did this change in the Mughal period to shape the idea of Arcadia? With geography, travel, and topography combining to make the land a reality, but with the persistence of strong tropes that emphasized its wondrousness in Mughal Persian literature, it would be worthwhile to map the shifting view of India in the wide range of literary genres available to authors who came from different backgrounds and ended up in imperial service. Although Iranian and Indian-born Mughal poets had different views of place, there was more complexity to the literary culture than a dialectic tension between two social groups whose common aim was the production of a new body of literature that was fitting for their patrons at a particular moment in history.

The Mughal Discovery of India

ↄ: *Veni, vidi, amavi* :ↄ
I came, I saw, I fell in love

In the premodern period, India and the Indian Ocean world had a long history in the imagination of people of the Near East and Europe as being a place of marvels, wonders, exotica, and riches.[1] The textual genre of wonders (*'aja'ib*) in Perso-Arabic and *mirabilia* in European literary traditions routinely included sections on India describing the strange and bizarre, ranging from the diversity of its flora and fauna to the customs of the people.[2] This tradition originated in the geographical and pseudoethnographic descriptions of the ancient Greek historian Herodotus and other classical writers such as Pliny the Elder and share features with the Old English *Marvels of the East*. In the tenth century, Persian sea captain Buzurg ibn Shahryar wrote an Arabic work, *Book of the Wonders of India*, that described strange phenomena witnessed on land and sea in the Indian Ocean world. Compiled from tall tales he had heard from travelers or based on personal experiences, the subject matter of Buzurg ibn Shahryar's work includes social practices such as *sati* and cremation, as well as a story similar to Odysseus and the Cyclops.[3] Persian translations of Arabic cosmographical works, such as one widely read by medieval scholars in the thirteenth century and later, Zakariya ibn Muhammad Qazvini's

'Aja'ib al-makhluqat va ghara'ib al-maujudat (Wonders of creation and the oddities of existence), also included sections about India that added to the knowledge of the region and its diverse cultures. Numerous travel accounts and narrative tales such as those in the *Thousand and One Nights,* whose origins are partially in the storytelling tradition of the subcontinent, as well as the popular Alexander romance, drew on these traditions and exploited the trope of wonders to represent India as a place of magic and adventure. When it came to the Persian world, its views of India had been formed both through the Islamic tradition and from experiences of conquest and cultural encounter. The binary images of the dark Hindu and the fair-skinned Turk were commonplace in classical Persian poetry, as were those of Brahmins, idols, and temples.

One of the earliest scientifically detailed studies produced by a Muslim writer on pre-Muslim Indian civilization was Abu Raihan al-Biruni's eleventh-century encyclopedic work in Arabic, *Tahqiq ma li'l Hind,* but commonly referred to as *Indica* or his India book. The Persian-speaking al-Biruni was in the service of the eleventh-century Turkish Sultan Mahmud, who ruled a mighty but short-lived empire from Ghazni, in present-day Afghanistan. al-Biruni's India book is genuinely impressive in its scope for its time. It ranged from philosophy and astrology to death rituals and festivals and deepened the state of knowledge, but also the sense of otherness, about Indian civilization. Works like these further fueled the trope of wonder in the imagination of authors writing about India for centuries to come. As al-Biruni states at the outset of his endeavor, "For the reader must bear in mind that the Hindus entirely differ from us in every respect, many a subject appearing intricate and obscure which would be perfectly clear if there were more connections between us."[4] This feeling of otherness defined the representation of India in a diverse range of literary and historical works and had a strong hold on the Persian imagination. At the same time, it must be remembered that the Indo-Persian author Amir Khusrau propagated the view of India as a refuge and paradise in his poetic works. Therefore, in the late sixteenth and early seventeenth centuries, it was somewhat ironic that the chief centers of Persian literature were squarely in a place that was more part of the imagination and at the fringes of the central Islamic lands.

The Timurids, the descendants of Timur or Tamerlane predecessors of the Mughals, who ruled and lived in Herat and other parts of Central Asia and Iran, learned about India from an additional source: a fascinating account by the court functionary Kamaluddin 'Abdur-Razzaq Samarqandi in 1442, who traveled as an emissary to Calicut and the kingdom of Vijaynagar in south India.[5] Abdur-Razzaq wrote with keen interest on the court life he witnessed, while drawing on the trope of marvels. His work is contemporaneous with the European age of exploration of the region, and his gaze takes in many of the same aspects of subcontinental life and culture that Europeans did in this period. The Italian Ludovico de Varthema's book, *Itinerario de Ludouico de Varthema Bolognese*, published in 1510 in Rome and dubbed the first bestseller on India,[6] documents the author's extensive travels, accompanied by a Persian merchant, in the Middle East, India, and Southeast Asia. The ethnographic component of de Varthema's book, replete with illustrations, is in the same spirit of works by Muslim writers who were fascinated by local cultural practices, especially political and religious aspects of the peoples with whom they came into contact. In this regard, the Ottoman historian Giancarlo Casale offers the compelling comparison of the European and Ottoman ages of maritime exploration as both responding to "a starting point of relative geographic and cultural isolation" coupled with imperial ideologies and commercial interests.[7] Although different from these vast endeavors of maritime history, the Mughal discovery of the cultures of India nonetheless offers a narrative that begins with a body of knowledge about marvelous creatures and weird practices in a magical land, and then moves on to the recording of actual history and scientific ethnography. The spread of the Persian language and Persianate cultural practices were defining features of this particular discovery.

One of the most expansive literary articulations of a cosmographical view of the Persian world is found in an ambitious work written under the Mughal emperor Akbar around 1593–1594: *Haft Iqlim* (Seven climes), by Amin Ahmad Razi, whose origins were in Iran.

The work presents the political and literary history of Persophone societies through a geographical matrix, recording the contributions of notable people from every region and period relevant to Persianate culture. This work has been regarded chiefly as a compendium with useful life accounts in the *tazkira* (biographical dictionary) genre, but it is much more than that, especially in terms of dynastic histories of some of the places. The world, according to Razi, is divided into seven climes that encompass the inhabited lands. In his scheme, most of the Indian subcontinent falls in the second and third climes. The second clime includes Persianate India other than the north: Deccan, Ahmednagar, Telangana, Ahmedabad, Somnath, Nagaur, Bengal, and Orissa along with the Arabian cities of Mecca and Medina. The third clime includes the area of western Iran, that is, Iraq-i 'Arab: Baghdad, Kufa, Najaf, Basra, Yazd, Fars, and Sistan along with Qandahar, Ghazni, Lahore, Sirhind, Delhi, Agra, Lucknow, and Awadh. The fourth clime is entirely Iran: Iraq-i 'Ajam, including Khurasan, Balkh, Herat, Mashhad, Nishapur, Sabzavar, Isfahan, Kashan, Qum, Sava, Hamadan, Ray and Tehran, Damavand, Astarabad, Tabaristan, Mazandaran, Gilan, Qazvin, Azarbaijan, Tabriz, Ardabil, and Maragha. The fourth clime, from which perspective Razi views the world, represents moderation in all things. There was a long history behind the division of the known world into climes. Muslim geographers had grafted this schematic division that ultimately goes back to the Ptolemaic tradition to ideas from Iranian cosmology and administrative divisions.[8] The underlying idea was "that the external, natural cosmos influenced the formation of ethnic, cultural, and geographical identities."[9] Europe is absent in Razi's configuration, although its existence was known about, largely because it did not have any cultural or historical connections with Persian civilization. In earlier models of the seven-part system division of the world according to climes, such as one in al-Biruni's work, India falls entirely in the first clime. In the writings of Babur, about half a century before Razi, Hindustan was distributed in the first, second, and third climes.[10] As India became increasingly Persianized, parts of it were conceptualized as being closer to the central fourth clime.

In his introduction, Amin Razi states that it took him six years to complete his work, which was a result of his research into the lives of the nobles and notables undertaken on his own initiative as well as at the behest of friends. It comprises poetry (*ash'ar*), reports (*akhbar*), anecdotes (*hikayat*), and works (*asar*), which makes it an anthology par excellence. Each section begins with a description of the major centers of literary production in that region followed by a who's who of scholars, Sufis, and some poets, with samples of their poetry. The selection of poets is not exhaustive—there are many noncanonical names associated with a place—and actually covers a broader social range than found in some courtly works.

The encyclopedic *Haft Iqlim* was produced at the height of Mughal power at Akbar's court, around the time when other works were produced to mark the end of the first millennium of Islam, and remains somewhat unique in its universal vision and ordering of the world with distinct Persianate literary spaces. This work inspired a number of geographical works later, though no other text combined its breadth with a history of literary production. The encyclopedic work *Shahid-i Sadiq* (Truthful witness), by Muhammad Sadiq Isfahani, was completed a few decades later in 1648 at Shah Jahan's court. It included the earliest Mughal map of the world, along with geographical tables and lists and a division of the cities of the world in alphabetical order identifying their climes and citing verses by poets associated with them where appropriate.[11] As India increasingly became more than an imagined place for many people in the Persophone world, though never losing its older and more potent designation as land of wonders, the role of poetry in the production of scientific knowledge and as a civilizational gauge gained in importance.

Even before the Mughal age, a project of documenting the uniqueness of Indian cultural traditions and its astonishing diversity in every aspect of life in a poetic vein had been initiated by the poet Amir Khusrau in the latter half of the thirteenth and early fourteenth centuries. Of mixed Turkic and Indian heritage, like some rulers of the imperial Mughal family after Akbar, Amir Khusrau took immense pride in the land of his birth, which, he believed, deserved to be included as a core part of the Muslim world. His designation of India as a "refuge" and "paradise" would crop up again in the early Mughal period, thus indicating the long genealogy of this idea. Amir Khusrau's poetic descriptions of imperial architecture and people of the city of Delhi would be picked up by later poets across the Persianate world and manipulated in endless ways to praise different imperial centers. However, his influence on the literature of and presence in the life of the Mughal period has yet to be studied in all its dimensions though there is ample evidence of it. Outside the world of texts, he was very much part of the life in Delhi. The shrine complex with the tombs of Amir Khusrau and his Sufi master Nizamuddin Auliya held a great significance for the Mughals and has continued to be the setting for the performance of devotional poems in Persian, Hindi, and Urdu in the form of *qawwali*s in a continuous tradition from medieval times. The practice of royal visits to these graves continued, and in the eighteenth century these and other shrines were also popular sites with pilgrims as well as holiday makers.[12]

HINDUSTAN BECOMES HOME

The very first Mughal text, the autobiography of the dynasty's founder Babur, *Baburnama,* written in Chaghatai Turkish and later translated into Persian, drew to some extent on the age-old trope of wonder about India. This mode of writing would be seen in varying degrees in the writings of Mughal poets and historians until the very end of their rule. Ironically, it became so well established that even Hindu writers of Persian turned their gaze on their own community to record what would have been familiar practices to them through a Persianate eye and represent themselves as wondrous and strange. The intended audience here was always the putative Persophone Muslim reader, whether in India or outside, who may have been knowledgeable about the world with respect to empirical facts but never lost his sense of wonder and curiosity about the exotic cultures in it, especially those of the subcontinent. One consequence of this was that Mughal poets no longer felt constrained in describing idealized gardens and assemblies that were frozen in time, for not every garden in the Persianate world was the proverbial rose garden inhabited by nightingales. They frequently wrote about spaces and people in actual time and place. Especially in the seventeenth century, the fauna of the subcontinent that was already being recorded in ethnographic texts is increasingly described in more lyrical forms.

Babur confessed in his memoirs that he had "craved Hindustan" ever since he conquered Kabul, and he realized his dream about twenty years later in 1526.[13] Even when he first stepped foot on the threshold of the subcontinent in Nangarhar, he wrote that "a new world came into view—different plants, different trees, different animals and birds, different tribes and people, different manners and customs. It was astonishing, truly astonishing."[14] We read earlier his observation on the diversity of languages in these parts of the subcontinent as well. When he entered the land as a conqueror, his reaction to the new landscape reads like it was taken from a book of wonders. "It is a strange country. Compared to ours, it is another world. Its mountains, rivers, forests, and wildernesses, its villages and provinces, animals, and plants, peoples and languages, even its rain and winds are altogether different."[15] And this was only after his first introduction to the northern areas that are culturally and geographically similar to the world he was leaving behind, in and around Kabul.

A few days after Babur had captured Agra, the capital of the Lodhi ruling house he had defeated, and became ruler of the kingdom of Hindustan, his troops were restless and longed to return home to Kabul and Ghazni. One particular person who was fighting with Babur, Khvaja Kalan, was not enamored of the new land, despite the riches it offered in contrast to his poor homeland, and was impatient to go back. Babur relented and gave him permission to return home. Before leaving Khvaja Kalan penned this verse on the wall of his place of residence in Delhi: "If I cross the Indus in safety, may my face turn black if I ever desire to see Hindustan again." Recording this incident, Babur wrote in an indignant tone in his memoirs, "To compose such a facetious line and write it was inexcusable. That he left was one reason to be cross with him; such nastiness gave me another reason. I too composed an extemporaneous quatrain, and sent it to him:

Give a hundred thanks, Babur, that the generous Pardoner of all has given you Sind and Hind and a vast kingdom.
If you cannot endure the heat and say, 'I would see the face of cold,' there is Ghazni."[16]

Ghazni would not have been a prize in Babur's view because he had written about this city that it was "a truly miserable place. Why kings who hold Hindustan and Khurasan would ever make such a wretched place their capital has always been a source of amazement to me."[17] His dreams were pinned on making Hindustan a fit place for himself and his family and people.

The urge to go back after seeing and conquering the new place afflicted more than one individual. In 1527, Babur wrote about the desire of one of his men Turdi Beg Khaksar "whom I had persuaded to leave off being a dervish and made a military man," to return to his old life back in Khurasan. Babur was reminded of a poem he wrote the previous year:

> O you who have gone from this country of India feeling pain and
>   distress,
> You thought of Kabul and its wonderful climate and hotly left India.
> There you have apparently found pleasure and joy, and many good
>   things.
> Yet we have not died, thank God, although we have suffered much
>   pain and untold grief.
> You have no more physical distress, but then neither do we.[18]

These lines show a remarkable degree of resilience. Although Babur made a commitment to remain in India, it did not prevent him from penning some candidly negative observations about the land. In these oft-quoted lines he sounds like an ugly tourist who refuses to have an open mind because the place he is visiting is not like home. Perhaps he was having a bad day and was feeling nostalgic for home:

> Hindustan is a place of little charm. There is no beauty in its people,
> no graceful social intercourse, no poetic talent or understanding, no
> etiquette, nobility, or manliness. The arts and crafts have no harmony
> or symmetry. There are no good horses, meat, grapes, melons, or
> other fruit. There is no ice, cold water, good food or bread in the
> markets. There are no baths and no madrasas. There are no candles,
> torches, or candlesticks.[19]

In actuality, many of his later positive observations contradict these pronouncements. One must keep in mind that there was already a highly developed Persianate society with all its trappings for several centuries in north India before Babur arrived on the scene, therefore his words must be taken with a grain of salt.

Even if Indian cities did not compare to Kabul or other places he had left behind, this was balanced by his appreciation of and delight in the new world he has discovered. When he declared, "The cities and provinces of Hindustan are all unpleasant. All cities, all locales are alike. The gardens have no walks, and most places are flat as boards. . . . there is little running water aside from the great rivers,"[20] this would seem to be another of his spontaneous categorical reactions that was tempered when he became acquainted with real places over time. He seemed to have softened his attitude, for instance, when he praised the town of Chanderi. "Chanderi is a superb place. All around the area are many flowing streams. The citadel is located atop a hill, and inside it a huge reservoir has been carved from rock. . . . The lake, called the Betwa, three kos from Chanderi, is renowned throughout Hindustan for its good, sweet water."[21] Babur comes across as a regular person here, though he was conqueror and traveler together, whose emotions and reactions to the beauties of a new landscape varied depending on the moment of time and quality of the experience. By the end, it would seem that Hindustan was not all that unpleasant and he came to love many aspects of life there, especially things like the monsoon season and mangoes—though this fruit was not superior to the melon back home!

Being a traveler allowed Babur to survey the land of which he had become ruler. He was particularly attentive to distances between places and their topographical features. In and around Gwalior, he visited various buildings, including a palace, madrasa, temples, all of which he described in some detail. The highlight of this trip was an excursion to a waterfall where he and his companions in a blissful state sat on the rocks and "had some ma'jun."[22] There were musicians and singers with the party to create a spontaneous *majlis,* the natural setting and good company being the height of pleasure for a man of his background.

The sections in the *Baburnama* on the flora and fauna of India reveal a mixture of scientific curiosity and amazement at the sheer variety found in the natural environment of the subcontinent, observational qualities that would be passed down to some of his descendants. The metaphor of Hindustan as the emperor's garden is reflected in his laying out of several gardens and love of the outdoors. This was also later articulated by rulers such as his grandson Akbar and great-grandson Jahangir, as the family's hold on and attachment to the land became deeper.[23] Babur's memoirs break off abruptly a little over a year before he died. If he had lived, he would have recorded many more aspects of the life and cultures of the subcontinent.

Babur's younger first cousin, Mirza Dughlat, was familiar with his intrepid relative's memoirs and they were a model for his own work, a historical chronicle in Persian, which has much more of an official quality than the intensely personal *Baburnama*. In his work, Mirza Dughlat occasionally described places in a similar manner, and his description of the mountainous region and valley of Kashmir, one of the favorite places in the empire for the Mughal imperial family in the early seventeenth century, is the earliest of any Mughal account.[24] Mirza Dughlat ruled the valley of Kashmir on behalf of Babur's son and successor Humayun for a decade from 1541 to 1551, almost half a century before Mughal forces would annex the kingdom as a province. In his history, he devotes several pages to writing about the beautiful region. "Kashmir is among the well-known countries of the world. It is famous throughout the world for its various delights, even though no one knows it as it really is, and in ancient books not even a summary of its conditions is to be found." He goes on to praise the natural landscape there, including the trees and lakes: "The greenery of the fields with their flowers and trees withers the pre-eminence of paradise and the Garden of Iram." He adds, in a rhapsodic vein that would become characteristic when writing about the valley, "In sum, for the delightfulness and verdure of its gardens, meadows, and mountains, for the pleasantness of its weather throughout the four seasons, and for perfect temperateness, no place like Kashmir has ever been seen or heard of." The chief among the wonders are the 150 idol temples. The author is at pains to assert that his is the first true description of the land, a major leap from an imagined place to reality. He states that the earlier historian of the Timurid period, Sharafuddin Ali Yazdi, in his *Zafarnama* (Book of victory), had described Kashmir, "but it is not accurate because the mawlana [master] did not see Kashmir. He merely asked travelers about it and wrote what they reported. Those people did not have a proper regard for veracity. That is why the mawlana's report is not accurate."[25] This is followed by a short account of the coming of Islam to Kashmir and its first Muslim rulers. A few decades later, this early report of the region would prove to be an important account as Mughal armies prepared to take over the valley.

With the expansion of the empire through conquest and the growing consciousness of the translocal spread of Persianate culture, writers of both prose and poetic works from the late sixteenth century began to celebrate local places in regional histories and biographies of notables, in an effort to integrate them into a larger narrative of Muslim history of India. We saw that this was the impulse behind the most universal of all works, the *Haft Iqlim*, whose author displayed an equal enthusiasm for the universal and local, describing a particular place's past history, customs, and renowned sons of the soil. Other works written around the same time attempted to treat parts of the subcontinent as discrete areas with multiple local histories and cultures. The best known of these was Abu'l-Fazl's encyclopedic gazetteer, *A'in-i Akbari*, which provides detailed information on the different provinces (*suba*) of the empire. Other historians of this period, such as Nizamuddin Ahmad in his *Tabaqat-i Akbari*, devoted space separately to each of the empire's major provinces. Historical works occasionally contained some information on the topography of the regions, and once part of the empire, Kashmir was especially praised for its climate and geography. It is worthwhile to examine some of the official descriptions of Kashmir since they are closely tied to imperial ambitions and court poetry composed about its landscape.

Kashmir was taken from the Chak dynasty by the Mughals in a relatively quick military operation in 1586. After it became a province of the empire, several factors played a role in its playing a symbolic function in the propagation of the idea of Mughal Arcadia. In the *A'in-i Akbari*, Abu'l-Fazl provides both geographical and cultural information about Kashmir:

> The country is enchanting, and might be fittingly called a garden of perpetual spring (*bagh-i hamisha-bahar*) surrounding a citadel terraced to the skies, and deservedly appropriate to be either the delight of the worldling or the abode of the dervish. Its streams are sweet to the taste, its waterfalls music to the ear, and its climate is invigorating. The rain and snowfall are similar to that of Turkestán and Persia and its periodical rains occur at the same season as in Hindustán. The lands are artificially watered or dependent on rain for irrigation. The enchanting flowers fill the heart with delight. Violets, the red rose and wild narcissus cover the plains. To enumerate its flora would be impossible. Its spring and autumn are extremely beautiful.[26]

He goes on to focus on one class of people in the valley with admirable qualities. "The most respectable class in this country is that of the Brahmans, who notwithstanding their need of freedom from the bonds of tradition and custom, are true worshippers of God. They do not loosen the tongue of calumny against those not of their faith, nor beg nor importune. They employ themselves in planting fruit trees, and are generally a source of benefit to the people. They abstain from flesh-meat and do not marry."[27] Abu'l-Fazl's admiration for the simple qualities of the natives is a central characteristic of pastoral literature that would later feature in court poetry about Kashmir.[28]

Abu'l-Fazl's partly ethnographic description of Kashmir can be read in tandem with his account in his chronicle *Akbarnama*, which describes Akbar's first visit to the valley in 1590, a few years after its annexation:

> Since the wonder of destiny increases farsighted thoughts, he was constantly thinking of Kashmir and imagining its delightful climate. When the incomparable deity brought that beautiful region into the imperial realm, it increased the emperor's desire to tour that land of perpetual spring (*hamisha-bahar*). As much as the chatterers at court represented that it was not wise for a monarch to abandon such a vast

expanse and go off to a corner without an important reason of state, the emperor refused to agree, saying, "The divine Bestower gives me no choice in this desire, and furthermore Jannat-Ashyani [Humayun] took this wish to the grave with him. Our expedition there will be the fulfillment of his desire."[29]

In this euphemistic vein, the conquest and possession of Kashmir by the powerful and wise king was described as predestined.

At the same time, Abu'l-Fazl's brother and poet-laureate Faizi commemorated the event in a panegyric ode (*qasida*), representing the military operation more akin to a pleasure trip:

> *hazar qafila-i shauq mikunad shabgir / ki bar-i 'aish gushayad bi-'arsa-i Kashmir*
> *tabaruk Allah azan 'arsa'i ki didan-i u / varaq-nigar khiyal ast u naqshband zamir*
> *hava-i u mutannavi' chu fikrat-i naqqash / zamin-i u mutalavvin chu safha-i tasvir*
> *bi-tarzha-i guzin karkhana-i abda' / bi-naqshha-i 'ajab karnama-i taqdir*[30]

> A thousand caravans of desire travel through the night to deliver their loads of luxury to Kashmir.
> Praise God for that land for viewing it the imagination is the calligrapher and the heart the painter.
> Its climate is diverse like the fancy of a painter; its earth is multicolored like a page of painting.
> Creation's workshop with its choice ways, fate's model with its wondrous forms.

In this celestial setting, Faizi refers to Akbar as the Sufi master, *murshid* and *pir*, to the people of the land, imbuing the monarch-subject relationship in a spiritual light. Going even further, Faizi refers to the administration of the city in utopian terms, boasting that if the mountain springs do not gush forth, "the Muslim scholar hauls them before the judge of the city, and the inspectors of the province reprimand them" (*agar na mufti-i u mikashad bi-qazi-i shahr / kunand muhtasiban-i vilayatash ta'zir*). In this way, a Persianate Shangri-La was created. Not surprisingly, his rival 'Urfi also came up with his own *qasida* on Kashmir.[31] 'Urfi's poem is a more lyrical panegyric to place and ruler, describing the valley as an enchanting paradise (*Kashmir bihishti ast faribanda*). From reading their poems, one cannot tell whether Faizi or 'Urfi had visited Kashmir.

Abu'l-Fazl drew on not only Mirza Dughlat's descriptive prose on the valley of Kashmir, but also the one found in the twelfth-century Sanskrit text, Kalhana's *Rajatarangini*, a chronicle of the kings of the region, that was translated into Persian at Akbar's court. The ancient text describes the place in this way:

> Kashmir is studded with high cliffs, and cannot be conquered even by the strength of a good army; and the people are afraid of nothing but of the future world. In winter there are hot baths by the river, in the summer the cool river-banks; and the rivers are calm, and not infested with water animals. It is a country where the sun shines mildly being the place created by [the sage] Kashyapa as if for his glory. High school-houses, the saffron, iced water, and grapes, which are rare, even in heaven are common here. Kailasa is the best place in the three worlds, Himalaya the best part of Kailasa, and Kashmir the best place in the Himalayas.[32]

From a sacred space for Hindus, the same features of its geography and topography enabled the Mughals to appropriate Kashmir for their own use. Over time, due to its Sufi connections Kashmir also came to be regarded as Muslim sacred space, even as it continued to be an important pilgrimage site for Hindus. Writing on Sanskrit texts about Kashmir, Ronald Inden explains that there were two concurrent practices at play here: one of *imagining* Kashmir as a paradise, and the second of *making* it into one. In his view, "Textual practices were crucial to the making of Kashmir into a paradise," along with "careful settlement and cultivation of the countryside and the construction of a beautiful capital."[33] Although reflecting a similar phenomenon in Sanskrit literature in the pre-Mughal period, the process of describing Kashmir as paradise was an equally central concern for many Mughal historians and poets. The inscription of Kashmir as paradise in the seventeenth-century Mughal propaganda machinery relied heavily on the image of the empire as garden and paradise, as well as a fitting home for Persian culture and literature. Kashmir became a microcosm of the vast empire, right from the moment of conquest of the valley and continued into Jahangir's reign when the new emperor and his wife fell in love with the actual place. Jahangir describes his feelings about the valley, along with other places in the empire, in his own words in his memoirs.

BETWEEN TOWN AND COUNTRY

The autobiography of Emperor Jahangir, in the form of memoirs in Persian, is known by the titles *Tuzuk-i Jahangiri* or *Jahangirnama*. These titles consciously connect the text to the author's great-grandfather Babur's work, and it is one of the most readable works from the early modern period. In comparison to Babur's memoirs, Jahangir's work offers a more settled view of the Mughal world, and also one that is more focused on emotions than actions. We have seen the curiosity in Jahangir's nature when it came to poets and poetry; this extended to the whole world around him, from precious objects to natural phenomena. Ebba Koch explains that "the Mughal *padshah*'s interest in the natural world was far more scientific than that of any of his counterparts in the Muslim world, and he comes closer than any European ruler to Sir Francis Bacon's (1561–1626) ideal of a prince as a learned observer and investigator of nature."[34] Like his father, Jahangir had a menagerie and aviary to house the various specimens of birds and animals that were trapped for or gifted to him. Some historians have dismissed him as a weak and dissipated ruler, due to his addiction to wine and opium that resulted in him ceding virtually all power to his wife Nur Jahan, whom he married in 1611. But he was a man of many sides who maintained interest in the empire until the end of his life.

Jahangir, or Prince Salim, had been a precocious child in many respects. He was born of a Hindu mother after Akbar was blessed by the spiritual master Salim Chishti with the prediction that the childless emperor would have three sons. As a spiritual exercise Akbar had also made the pilgrimage barefoot to the Sufi shrine in Ajmer. Salim rebelled against his father as a young man and set up his own court in Allahabad from 1600 to 1604. On November 2, 1605, he became emperor, taking the name Jahangir (world conqueror) and ruled for twenty-two years. A painting in a royal copy of Jahangir's memoirs shows the public celebrations in the city of Agra that marked his accession to the Mughal throne (see Figure 2). Painted by the artist Abu'l-Hasan about a decade after the actual event, the work is similar to visual depictions of the city with throngs of happy people of diverse social and ethnic backgrounds during the reigns of Akbar and Shah Jahan. This vignette of the bustle of urban life against the backdrop of monumental architecture showcases the cosmopolitanism of the Mughal capital. The image is dominated by the archway, which itself has a Persian inscription and smaller images from the story of Laila-Majnun.[35] The populace was composed of every variety of skin color, headdress, and social position, including a Jesuit from Europe. Such scenes became commonplace in the paintings done for Jahangir and Shah Jahan, coinciding with the high point of poetry on places. The emperor is not shown in the painting but his presence is implied as the courtiers look to the top left of the scene, presumably up at the *jharoka* window or other elevation.

The literary culture at Jahangir's court, or at least what can be pieced together from the sources, indicates that although it was not a dry period by any means, the age was devoid of the brilliance and spectacle of literary production that marked both his father's and later his son's reigns. Poetic culture was the mainstay of court life, of course, and there was no shortage of good poetry or poets at his court. Its performance was not monumental and public, but rather a private activity. His reign also saw a further participation of Hindi and Sanskrit men of letters, as Mughal culture in the arts began to take on a distinct form. The various sources for literary history of this period are largely anecdotal, including Jahangir's memoirs, where one is provided a glimpse into the same aesthetic engagement with a verse or poem that marked the emperor's fondness for exotic and luxury items. Just as wondrous objects, gems, or animals fascinated him,

FIGURE 2 Celebrations at the accession of Jahangir

poets from Iran, Central Asia, or different parts of India all evoked a sense of curiosity and pleasure in him. Jahangir's court was as vibrant as Akbar's had been, with Iranian émigrés prominent in all areas of administration, religion, and literature. His Iranian wife Nur Jahan's extended clan played an important role in the administration of the empire during these years. Jahangir did not commission any large-scale projects of translation or history writing as compared to his father and then his son. His frequent travels with Nur Jahan resulted in Jahangir describing a variety of landscapes and places in a poetic-ethnographic vein. It was also due to their zeal and efforts that Kashmir became a regular imperial retreat for the court for the next half century.

Jahangir was aware of the ethnographic and wondrous mode of writing about India because right in the beginning of his memoirs, after he gives some details about his birth and the capital city of Agra, he includes sections on the descriptions of Indian fruits, flowers, and trees, in a more poetic style than Babur had done. This vein of description runs throughout the memoirs. At one point he remarked on his own strong sense of the visual element of things. "Although His Majesty Babar wrote in his memoirs of the shapes and forms of some animals, apparently he did not order the artists to depict them. Since these animals looked so extremely strange to me, I both wrote of them and ordered the artists to draw their likeness in the Jahangirnama so that the astonishment one has at hearing of them would increase by seeing them."[36] Sharing his patron's obsession for details, the court painter Ustad Mansur documented the vast range of flora and fauna and completed a series of paintings that were scientific in detail, yet delicate in the way they were executed. Mansur, who also specialized in the illumination of manuscripts, was familiar with and influenced by botanical works and florilegia from Europe. His extraordinary talent led the emperor to bestow on him the lofty title "Wonder of the Age" (*nadir al-'asr*).[37]

Jahangir was also a keen observer of topographical features of places. In 1618–1619, after spending time in central India, he decided that he would go to Gujarat where he would be able to see the ocean. His nine-month sojourn in Ahmedabad, the provincial capital, was filled with new experiences, though the dusty terrain and a prolonged illness prompted him to dismiss the city, "I have already called Ahmadabad *Gardabad* (Dustburg). Now I don't know what to call it *Samumistan* [land of pestilential wind], *Bimaristan* [land of the ill], *Zaqumzar* [thorn-patch], or *Jahannamabad* [hell-ville] since it has qualities of all of them. Were it not for the monsoon, I wouldn't stay in this abode of tribulation for a single day but would get on my flying carpet like Solomon and fly away, delivering my men from this pain and tribulation."[38] In contrast, British visitors at this time, Sir Thomas Roe and Sir Thomas Herbert, found much to admire in the city.[39] Jahangir did appreciate the figs in Gujarat, and was also delighted to see that roses could grow in this arid climate.

The romantic streak in Jahangir was in harmony with his high aesthetic standards. On one occasion he visited the Gulafshan garden in Agra on the bank of the Jamna River that was in the charge of a Khvaja Jahan. A heavy rain shower had freshened the atmosphere and he was pleased with the ripe pineapples before him. The scene with its verdure and flowing water so moved him that he recalled the verses of the classical twelfth-century Persian poet Anvari:

> It is a day for enjoyment and revelry in the garden; it is a day for a
>   market of flowers and herbs.
> The earth gives off an aroma of ambergris; rose water drips from the
>   breeze's skirt.
> From encountering the zephyr the face of the pond is as jagged as a
>   sharpened file.[40]

These verses invoke the imagery of an ideal Persian garden that could be applied to any felicitous place in which one read or recited them. But there was nothing like a real place matching the description cherished in the poetic imagination.

It was in Jahangir's reign, and continuing into the first part of Shah Jahan's, that Kashmir became a fashionable haunt of the court and visiting it developed into, as one scholar calls it, an "imperial pursuit."[41] The empress Nur Jahan was single-handedly responsible for changing the shift in "the physical mobility of the court, which under her guidance traveled increasingly for leisure's sake."[42] Did Kashmir represent for Nur Jahan a suitable substitute for the land of

her birth, which she never actually saw, having been born in Qandahar
while her family was en route to India? In any case, the tradition of
visiting Kashmir and beautifying its natural landscape with ordered
gardens and pavilions would continue for several decades. The frequent trips to Kashmir had important consequences for the harem.
"As women now went out more often for their own amusement . . .
rest stations and gardens began to proliferate to the far reaches of the
Mughal countryside in order to accommodate the expanding needs
of the harem."[43] Scores of women from princesses and concubines
to servants would have made the trip to Kashmir, but their narratives of travel have not come down to us.

Nur Jahan's name is connected with several gardens in Agra, Lahore, and Srinagar. The Shalimar bagh, the jewel of the gardens of
Kashmir, is made up of two gardens: the Farahbakhsh, built by Jahangir in 1620 for her, and the Faizbakhsh, constructed by his son
Shah Jahan in 1634. Jahangir described the site in his usual lyrical
mode reserved for picturesque landscapes: Shalimar is "adjacent to the
lake and has a beautiful water channel that comes from the mountain and empties into Dal Lake. My son Khurram ordered it stopped
up to create a waterfall one might enjoy. This spot is one of the scenic
delights of Kashmir."[44] The second largest garden and perhaps even
more charming than the Shalimar is the Nishat Bagh, built by the
empress's brother Asaf Khan in 1625. Nur Jahan also patronized the
construction of the Achabal or Achval and Jharoka gardens, among
others, in and around Srinagar. One of the most stunning gardens,
Verinag, was a site originally connected with Hindu pilgrims due to its
natural spring. It was transformed by Jahangir, even before he married
Nur Jahan, because it lay on the road from the valley to the plains. A
painting of the Verinag garden (see Figure 7) from Shah Jahan's
reign shows how such spaces were used by the court.

In the middle of a lengthy ethnographic description of Kashmir,
Jahangir lapses into praise of the stunning landscape of this land:

> Kashmir is a perennial garden and an ironclad bastion. For mon-
> archs it is a garden that delights the eye, and for poor people it is
> an enjoyable place of retreat. Its lovely meadows and beautiful
> waterfalls are beyond description. Its flowing waters and springs

are beyond number. As far as the eye can see there is greenery
and running water. Red roses, violets, and narcissi grow wild;
there are fields after fields of all kinds of flowers; and the varieties of herbs are too many to count. During the enchanting
spring, mountain and plain are filled with all sorts of blossoms;
gateways, walls, courtyards, and roofs of houses come ablaze
with tulips. What can be said of the plateaus covered with
refreshing clover?

The coquettes of the garden displayed themselves, cheeks adorned,
each like a lamp.

Buds give off the fragrance of musk from beneath their skin, like
musky amulets on the arm of the beloved.

The melody of the dawn-rising nightingale sharpens the desire of
wine-drinkers.

At every spring a duck puts its beak to drink—like golden scissors
cutting silk.

A carpet of flowers and greenery laid out in a garden: the lamp of the
rose lit by the breeze.

The violet has twisted the ends of her locks, tying a tight knot in the
heart of the rosebud.[45]

This poetic effusion combines realistic imagery with traditional garden
imagery of classical Persian literature that is an experiential reaction
to a place, rather than a purely aesthetic one. Along with the proverbial nightingale of the Persian garden, there is also the more
quotidian duck. But in effect, this was an important moment in the
development of the Mughal conception of their land as Arcadia
because Jahangir, like others with a keen poetic sensibility who experienced Kashmir with him, would have realized that this landscape
was the actualization of what was celebrated in Persian garden poetry. If it took a bit of the leap of imagination to conjure up a Persian
garden in other lovely spots, being in Kashmir did not require any
such effort. The whole place was one big garden that was the apt setting for a *majlis* of friends and courtiers.

Jahangir's poet laureate Talib accompanied Jahangir on one or
more of his trips from Lahore to Kashmir, whence he drew inspiration
to compose two poems that mention the difficulties of the journey

and praise for the land with eulogistic verses on the emperor. Talib hailed from Mazandaran, a province in the Caspian litoral coast in Iran, whose verdant and watery landscape, though not its humid climate, is similar to that of Kashmir. Indeed, the similarity in terms of the landscape would not have been lost on the poet. After trying rather unsuccessfully to make it as a court poet in Isfahan and Marv, Talib had arrived in India when he was in his late twenties. During his first appearance before Jahangir at court he remained tongue-tied, not a promising sign in a professional poet, due to the opium he had taken to calm his nerves. In 1616 he succeeded in gaining royal favor and in 1619 was appointed the Mughal poet laureate. He was to hold this post only for about seven years during which time he accompanied Jahangir on his travels through the empire. In his last years Talib was afflicted with mental illness. Talib was close to his elder sister, Sittiunnisa, who also made a successful career in Mughal India as tutor to the royal princesses and a supervisory role in the harem after the death of Empress Mumtaz Mahal in 1632. Sittiunnisa's tomb is in the larger complex of the Taj Mahal, not far from where the emperor and empress are entombed.[46]

Talib's two poems on Kashmir are in the formal *qasida* form, the same that was used by Faizi in his poem to commemorate the Mughal annexation of this region. In the manner of court poetry in almost any literary tradition, these poems are essentially paeans celebrating Jahangir's rule and the pax mughalica. The description of a journey to Kashmir merely provides the exordium for launching into a full-blown panegyric of the emperor, but the fact that Talib chose this subject suggests the importance of these journeys. In Talib's first poem, the poet boasts that Jahangir's rule has eased the difficulties of the difficult path to Kashmir that is "more delicate than the arrow-like eyelashes" of the beloved and on which "the traveler clings as a feather to an arrow" (*rahi bariktar az tir-i mizhgan / bar u chasbida rahrau chun par-i tir*).[47] After describing the difficult path in a dozen or so rhetorical ways, the poet concludes that "the mountainous region is a garden made by God that is renovated by the architect of its spring" (*yaki baghist izad-saz-i kuhi / ki mi'mar-i baharash karda ta'mir*). At the end of the road is a garden with streams and a variety of flowers and fruit trees, peopled with nightingales and ring doves singing melodiously.

The picturesque quality of the place overwhelms the viewer and one's vision (*nazar*) cannot get enough of this sight. Talib's poetic talents are insufficient to describe this "divine garden" to the point that the limits of speech are stretched. After having set the appropriate scene, more than half of the poem is then devoted to praise of Jahangir.

In his second, more hyperbolic, poem, Talib makes a case for Kashmir as a special locale and invites his readers to enjoy the pleasures of the place:

> *nava-yi murgh-i tarab in buvad bi-gah-i safir / ki bada bada-yi Hind ast u gul gul-i Kashmir*
>
> *zi Hind garchi gul u bada nadir-and u mufid / mai-yi 'Iraq u gul-i Fars ra bi-muft magir*
>
> *chu majlis az mai u saqi tamam-i asbab ast / bigir kam-i dil az 'ishrat u bahana magir*
>
> *mara ki surat-i bagh-i bihisht dar nazar ast / sazad ki taza kunam ruh-i bulbulan bi-safir*
>
> *chu vasf-i gulshan-i Kashmir mikunam farz ast / ki shuyam in dahan-i talkh ra bi-shikar u shir*
>
> *zahi maqam-i salamat kaz i'tidal-i hava / bi-'umr-i Khizr nagardand sakinanash pir*[48]

> When the trumpet blows [on the day of resurrection], may the song of the joyous bird be:
> 'The wine cup is the wine cup of India and the rose is the rose of Kashmir.'
> If the rose and wine in India are rare and efficacious, then don't take the wine of 'Iraq and rose of Fars for free.
> If an assembly with wine and a saqi are all one needs, take your heart's pleasure and don't make an excuse!
> It is fitting that I who have the garden of paradise in view revive the spirit of nightingales with a trumpet.
> Bravo to a salubrious place whose mild weather keeps the inhabitants from getting old, like Khizr.

The religious overtones of these lines—references to the day of resurrection and the legendary prophet-guide Khizr whose secret of eternal youth was that he had discovered the fountain of life—sets up Kashmir as a replica of paradise on Earth: "If a houri sees this sample of paradise in a dream, / Its heart would be sated from the pleasure of traveling through it" (*gar in namuna-yi jannat bi-khvab binad hur / dilash zi lizzat-i sair-i bihisht gardad sir*). In one particular line he cautions readers not to shut their eyes on this scene or even sweep their houses, for the earth here is light and the dust elixir (*ma-push dida dar an mulk u niz khana marub / ki khak-i u hama nurast u gard-i u aksir*). But more than anything else, Talib is entranced by the climate of the valley that defeats weariness and nurtures the lovely flowers and fruits of the land. In a few lines Talib lists the fruits of Kashmir: cherry (*shah-alu*), fig (*anjir*), pomegranate (*nar*), apple (*sib*), grape (*angur*). As in the memoirs of Babur and Jahangir, the poetic and ethnographic elements here are intertwined closely in what was becoming an almost clichéd mode of describing India and its different regions. In the panegyric part of the poem, Talib expresses the wish that Jahangir's justice should be like the eternal spring in the garden of Kashmir.

The excitement of traveling in Kashmir is communicated in a contemporary painting made for an album (see Figure 3). The scene seemingly depicts Jahangir, although a miniscule inscription by the kingly figure says "Akbar," with a large entourage in seven boats, sailing on what is thought to be Lake Wular. This is clearly a pleasure party that would have included hunting as well, given the presence of three men with falcons. Wular is located northwest of the capital Srinagar and is the largest lake in Kashmir. In his memoirs Jahangir describes the island, visible in the painting, with buildings constructed by previous rulers of the valley, the finest of them called Zain Lanka built in the time of pre-Mughal ruler Sultan Zainulabidin. The gray mountains in the background indicate that this landscape is unmistakably Kashmir. Poet and artist both manage to convey in their own way the palpable sense of adventure in exploring the many corners of the mountainous province.

Jahangir visited Kashmir more times than any other Mughal ruler, and more than other parts of the empire aside from the capital cities. As emperor, he sojourned in the valley in 1607, 1619–1620, 1622, 1624, 1625, 1626, and then the fateful trip in 1627 when he died

FIGURE 3 Jahangir on Lake Wular

on the way back to the plains. He stopped recording his memoirs in 1622 and thus he does not describe all the trips undertaken during the last years of his reign. In the spring of his last year, Jahangir had gone to Kashmir to recuperate from an illness and a few months later, at age 58, on October 28 he passed away in Rajauri, one of the stations on the so-called Mughal Road connecting the valley to the plains. His body was eventually brought to Lahore and buried in a garden owned by Nur Jahan on the banks of the Ravi River. Nur Jahan virtually disappeared from the scene in the following years, though she supervised the building of and lived near her husband's tomb until 1642. There were no great poets left to compose elegies on Jahangir's death; even his poet laureate had predeceased him by a few months.

The Kashmir poems by Faizi, 'Urfi, and Talib were the precursors to a literary phenomenon that flowered in the 1630s and 1640s among Shah Jahan's court poets, a period when the frequent trips by the court and imperial family to the valley continued as a ritualistic practice. Even more than Emperor Shah Jahan, it was his offspring and courtiers who were the primary agents in making Kashmir not only a resort but also a spiritual center that marked the apex of Mughal cultural life in this period. But in order to understand the different textual streams that contributed to the making of the literary phenomenon of the Kashmir poem, it is necessary to first focus on other relevant aspects of Mughal literary culture, and specifically on the flourishing genre of topographical poetry on cities. Court poets were so much more accustomed to writing about cityscapes that they viewed the countryside through an urban lens. Kashmir was to become a focal point of the imperial poetic gaze on the model of its celebrated urban centers.

THREE

Celebrating Imperial Cities

⌐ Urbs in horto, hortus in urbe ↝
A city in a garden, a garden in a city

Mughal Persian court poets and historians of the sixteenth and seventeenth centuries paid special attention to praising the cities that
they inhabited and the places that they occupied for ceremonial or
private use, such as palaces and pavilions, bazaars, and gardens, reveling in the here and now. This new awareness of place in the early
modern period was linked not only to the actual expansion of territories, but also to the opening up of the aesthetic parameters of the
Persian literary language to include metaphors and images that entered the tradition through a familiarization with new regions and
people, even languages, as they were appropriated into the imperial
orbit. The transition from purely Persian to Persianate literature can
be mapped through the spatial consciousness of poets who were no
longer constrained to describing idealized gardens and assemblies
that were connected with specific spaces in actual time. Poets writing
in Delhi, Bijapur, or Istanbul used established poetic forms and genres
to write about these topics in Persian but also in local languages such
as Dakhni and Turkish, in a way that would have been both familiar
but also strangely new. In fact, the binary of the cosmopolitan center
versus provincial periphery, as well as the urban-rural binary, was
challenged by some works produced by Mughal poets.

The three early modern Muslim empires shifted their capitals several times in response to political and environmental exigencies. The
Ottoman capital was briefly in the cities of Bursa and Edirne in addition to Istanbul. The Safavids began in Tabriz, closer to their ancestral city, then moved to Qazvin in 1548, and finally to Isfahan in
1598. Mughal rulers inhabited Agra, Delhi, Lahore, and Fatehpur
Sikri as the seat of power at various times, though Delhi as Shahjahanabad became the more or less permanent Mughal capital in 1648.
The reigns of Shah Jahan (r. 1628–1656) and Iran's Safavid Shah
'Abbas II (r. 1642–1666) are similar in terms of the rulers' passion
for the arts, architecture, and history. Topography played an especially important role in the lives of all the rulers that resulted in a
striking representation of buildings and landscapes in texts and paintings of the period. While Shah 'Abbas's Safavid capital Isfahan was
beautified with gardens and new buildings such as the Chihil sutun
pavilion, Shah Jahan beautified Agra and then built the capital city
of Shahjahanabad. Although many of the great poets had left for
India before Shah 'Abbas II began his rule, there was an impressive
array of men of letters in his court. A mutual awareness existed in
Persianate societies of the many construction projects and splendors
of each other's cities through poems and reports by travelers and am-
bassadors. Poems on all these cities were written at various times and
in different poetic forms. While Ottoman poets wrote poems about
dozens of cities across their empire, Safavid and Mughal poets primarily wrote on the capital cities and less often about provincial
capitals. The scholar Paul Losensky uses the useful term "urban-
topographical" for this category of poems, which include versified
travelogues and the *shahrashub* "with its playful inventories of the
urban marketplace with all its commercial wealth and winsome
shopkeepers."[1]

The *shahrashub* poem in a few lines is in effect a building block for
longer poems and Ottoman, Safavid, and Mughal poets used it differently to suit their own purposes.[2] In the Ottoman case, "famous
beloveds were catalogued in verse, city by city" in this kind of poem,[3]
and "poets extolled the virtues of drinking, taverns, coffeehouses,
and young male and female beauties."[4] In Safavid poems the idea

was to showcase the practice of poetry among all classes of people and the connection to guilds and Sufi orders was strong. Mughal poets focused on the social and religious diversity of their society, reveling in the variegatedness of creation and culture. Although Safavid poets did not focus on ethnic or religious diversity in their poems to the extent that Mughal and Ottoman poets did—their concern was more the power of poetry and the poet's love for the various beloveds to form an urban network of professionals—this sentiment occasionally shows up, as in one Safavid historical chronicle. On the construction of Farahabad, a summer palace in Mazandaran that was begun by Shah 'Abbas I in 1611, the Safavid historian Iskandar Beg Munshi writes,

> Each garden in the grounds has its own mansion, and the palace
> complex includes bathhouses, markets, and pleasure gardens.
> Because it is such a beautiful place, the bourgeoisie and artisans
> aspired to reside there. Over the years, thousands of houses belonging
> to Muslims and non-Muslims from all parts of the empire sprang up
> in the palace grounds. Today, it is doubtful whether there is another
> city of its size within the confines of the Islamic world.[5]

Shah 'Abbas himself wrote to Jahangir about how pleased he was with the town of Farahabad in paradisial Mazandaran, and asked his fellow monarch to send some specifically Indian items, such as indigo, rice seeds, a bullock cart, and buffaloes of both sexes.[6]

Imperial architecture was an essential part of courtly ceremonial practices and allowed the proper distance to be maintained between ruler and subjects. As Akbar's kingdom was fast becoming an empire, the lifestyle of his father and grandfather, who preferred to conduct much of their daily lives in garden settings, was in need of modification. According to the art historian Sussan Babaie, the circumstances in India differed from the other empires that shared other courtly traditions and practices. "Windows and the performance of the daily and perpetual framing of the sun or the eye, however, scarcely convey the palpable immediacy that the feasting rituals of the Safavids did. Moreover, and like the Ottomans, Mughal emperors did not attend the kind of large banquets that the shahs in Isfahan hosted." Indian society with its different classes and religious groups required a different kind of set-up: "eating in the company of mere mortals did not suit the Mughal discourse of kingship—so painstakingly refined and articulated, by the emperors Jahangir and Shah Jahan in particular during the first half of the seventeenth century—which positioned the emperor, the sun-king, the light of God, in a transcendental realm."[7] The *jharoka* or viewing of the emperor's person was a ritual that was faithfully maintained, just as gardens and pavilions provided a private setting for feasts and other gatherings. Poets at court who witnessed the use of these spaces by the emperor, princes, and nobles wrote about them as paradisial spots. It would seem that every inch of imperial space was paradise.

Despite the existence of extensive literature about places that was fit to be illustrated, visual representations of Safavid cities are almost non-existent as compared to the Mughal or Ottoman ones. Safavid poets relied almost exclusively on the verbal form to highlight architectural and topographical details. Their artists were skilled in presenting idealized scenes, some of them more emblematic of an aesthetic ideal than a specific context and therefore more rooted in a long classical tradition. By and large, although Mughal artists also developed their own aesthetic ideals, they were directed by patrons to focus on the present moment, as did the poets. Drawing from a shared classical poetic tradition, in each court poets used their talents in different ways.

A poet's attachment to a particular place, whether stemming from an affection for his native land or because he was paid to praise it by a ruler or governor, was expressed through a range of emotions. The *shahrashub* was one of several ingredients in Mughal Persian poems, the others being descriptions of architectural monuments, nostalgia for a past that survived in the cultural memory of a people, and the euphoric glorification of the positive qualities (*faza'il*) of a place. Plural of the word *fazila, faza'il* refers to "a definite category of literature . . . [that] exposes the excellences of things, individuals, groups, places, regions and such for the purpose of a *laudatio*." It can also include the praise of "profane" things such as the herb basil and coffee.[8] In the

Indian context the most frequently praised items are the mango, betel-leaf (*pan*), and sugarcane. This type of poetry had a long history in the classical Arabic and Persian literary tradition in which poets flattered a ruler or prince through the beauty of the city and its glorious past, its learned and pious inhabitants, as well as its natural and man-made topography. The virtues of a city, *faza'il*, could also be described in prose texts such as chronicles and local histories.[9] Literary representations of cities can be conceptually linked to imaginations of utopias as described in Islamic philosophical texts, such as in al-Farabi's ninth-century Arabic treatise on the *Madina-yi fazila* (The virtuous city), in which he says, "The excellent city resembles the perfect and healthy body, all of whose limbs co-operate to make the life of the animal perfect and to preserve it in this state."[10] He later describes the organic role of the inhabitants of the city: "they are not parts of the city by their inborn nature alone but rather by the voluntary habits which they acquire such as the arts and their likes."[11] For this reason verses in the *shahrashub* mode appear in poetry about cities. In the early modern age of Persianate culture when there was tremendous building activity in old cities and new capitals, poetry praising cities proliferated in many diverse forms, mainly in the verse *masnavi* since it allowed the poet to create a narrative around topographical themes. The various manifestations of the topographical genre must then be studied in the context of the broader category of *faza'il*, described earlier. Palace architecture, gardens, bazaars, and individuals inhabiting these spaces are put together in a single imperial frame in multiple ways, as each author privileges some parts over others.

Amir Khusrau's poetic oeuvre in praise of Delhi and India was discussed in Chapter 1. As early as in the literature of the Timurid court in the late fifteenth century, Amir Khusrau's verses about Delhi's architectural wonders were recycled to describe the city of Herat and other places in Mu'inuddin Muhammad Zamchi Isfizari's historical work *Rauzat al-jannat fi ausaf madinat-i Harat* (Gardens of paradise in praise of the city of Herat). Since there was a generic quality and timelessness about the verses, in Akbar's time Razi, in the *Haft Iqlim*, also chose several apt quotations from Amir Khusrau's poems written almost three centuries earlier. For instance, in describing the mild winter season in Hindustan, he quotes three lines from Amir Khusrau's *masnavi Nuh sipihr*, and then while praising the betel leaf (*pan*) he quotes ten lines from the *Qiran al-sa'dain*. Amir Khusrau's influence on early modern Persian poets writing in this genre has been largely unnoticed.

Even before Mughal poets composed original poems on cities, in the Deccan the Iranian émigré poet Zuhuri, who gained renown without moving on to Mughal lands in the north, made a big splash with an innovative literary work. Zuhuri was a professional poet, first at the Nizamshahi court in Ahmadnagar and then at the Adilshahi court in Bijapur, both vibrant centers of the arts. The rulers of the Deccan sultanates had close political and cultural connections with Iran, mainly due to being Shia as well, but they were too small to hold out against the Mughals who over time absorbed the five kingdoms. Zuhuri's poetry exerted a great influence among poets of the larger Persianate world, and he was on friendly terms with the Mughal poet laureate Faizi. His poetic *masnavi, Saqinama* (Book of the cupbearer), which praised the city of Ahmadnagar and parts of which he later recycled for praise of Bijapur, exploited the combination of architecture and topography, along with *shahrashub* elements, in an Indo-Persian context. This work was in turn read and served as a model for poems by many Mughal poets.[12]

Detailed poetic representations of new architectural projects and capital cities of the Safavid realm first appeared when the court poet of Shah Tahmasp I, 'Abdi Beg of Shiraz, wrote a quintet of *masnavi* poems titled *Jannat-i 'Adn* (Garden of Eden).[13] These poems celebrate the construction in 1558–1559 of the new palace complex Sa'adatabad near the capital, Qazvin. In his detailed analysis of these poems Paul Losensky cautions us that "for all its documentary value, *Jannat-i 'Adn*, is first and foremost a work of literature, and its factual content is organized and inflected by a complex poetic construct."[14] In one of the poems a list of eighteen varieties of fruits is later followed by a 120-verse paean to the melon of which nineteen varieties are described! For poets the melon was to Iran what the mango was to India (or sometimes the sugarcane or betel leaf). There is no evidence that 'Abdi Beg's quintet of poems directly influenced any Mughal poet for nothing so extensive was composed about an Indian city, with the exception of Zafar Khan's poems on Kashmir that are discussed in Chapter 4. Mughal poems on cities were shorter and all date from the seventeenth century.

We may also ask why certain cities became the subjects of poems at a particular time and what determined the choice of poetic forms, such as giving up the more formal *qasida* form, as in classical poetry, to the *masnavi*. A close reading of key texts in the context of the lives of their authors reveals that topographical poems, like all court poetry, essentially functioned at a metaphorical level to espouse an imperial ideology through hyperbolic praise of the ruler's just disposition. It is true that poets did have some degree of freedom to choose their own topics for praise poems. Despite the flurry of construction in Akbar's time, such as the building of the city of Fatehpur Sikri and then other building projects in Agra, no poetry was composed about these activities. However, some manuscripts for the chronicle of Akbar's reign, *Akbarnama*, do include paintings on the subject, one of which shows the emperor himself supervising the construction work (Figure 4). Under Jahangir there was a nascent phase of Mughal topographical poetry, with *qasida*s on Kashmir, Kabul, and Lahore composed by the poet laureate Talib, but the genre of versifying the city and countryside flowered only during Shah Jahan's reign.

The various ingredients that were brought together in the genre of urban poetry—*faza'il, shahrashub,* architectural descriptions—were repackaged by poets to describe the countryside and led to the appearance of a variety of bucolic and courtly pastoral poetry describing nonurban spaces such as the landscapes of Kashmir and Bengal. The ultimate aim of this poetry was to showcase the appropriation of far-flung places into the imperial domain with praise for the building projects sponsored by various rulers and governors. Literary and cultural developments away from the imperial centers were also important factors in shaping the particular way that Mughal poets wrote about place, both the city and countryside, and for that the life of one particular individual, 'Abdur-Rahim Khankhanan, whom we have encountered earlier as a patron and poet of Hindi, is important.

RECREATING IRAN IN INDIA

The Deccan region in central and south India with Muslim states of different sizes had been a lively center of Persian literature and received men of letters from Iran even before the Mughals and continued to be so until it was annexed to the northern polity in the seventeenth century.[15] For those who came by the sea route from Iran and disembarked at Surat, the first stop would usually be one of the Mughal cities in Gujarat or Khandesh—Ahmedabad and Burhanpur—that were often governed by literary-minded officials, or the Deccani courts at Ahmadnagar, Bijapur, and Golconda, where employment could be found with the sultans. Some people would remain in the Deccan, others would move on to the north to serve in the capital cities of the Mughal empire. People arriving by the land route could find employment in one of the Mughal provinces, such as Kabul, Sindh, or Lahore, which were closer or contiguous with Safavid territory, or then travel all the way to the east in Bengal. These poets regularly crossed the boundaries between Mughal and non-Mughal territories and experienced the variety of life in different parts of Persophone India.

Although there were many master poets in this period who achieved a canonical status, perhaps the brightest among them in the Persian literary world of the seventeenth century was the Iranian poet Muhammad 'Ali Sa'ib, a larger than life figure whose influence was felt for generations.[16] Like scores of other poets he made the decision to make the journey to India; one could imagine that he wished to see for himself the riches and new experiences that the place had to offer, but, unlike most of his peers who did that, he returned to Iran and never left it again. He went on to become the poet laureate of the Safavid Shah 'Abbas II during the middle decades of the seventeenth century in Iran, a time when he was prolific in his poetic output. Therefore, his fame largely rests on his career in Iran, but his brief sojourn in India was an eventful period that he describes in his verses.

Sa'ib had arrived in Kabul in 1624–1625 at the end of Jahangir's reign, where he forged a personal and professional relationship with two Iranians in Mughal service, Zafar Khan and his father, Khvaja Abu al-Hasan Turbati (*rukn al-saltanat,* "Pillar of the State"). Father and son were both responsible for governing Kabul and then Kashmir. After spending seven years with them in Kabul and other parts of India, Sa'ib returned home when the father-son duo moved to Kashmir to govern that province. Originally a Turkish speaker from Tabriz, the young Sa'ib appears to have been a charming and affable person whose company was much sought after. For family reasons he was compelled to return to Iran and, as fate would have it, build a long career employed by the Safavid court and not the Mughal. Coincidentally he left India just before the two senior poets Kalim and Qudsi arrived at Shah Jahan's court. Although primarily a poet of the *ghazal,* some of Sa'ib's historical poems written later in his career have a bearing on Mughal life. The modern edition of his collected works comprises six thick volumes, a daunting prospect for scholars of Safavid and Mughal literature, for it is almost impossible to date most poems and pinpoint them to his Indian phase. Despite his gigantic stature in the early modern period, Sa'ib is not as well-known to the larger world as the classical poets Rumi and Hafiz are; such has been the fate of court poets of this period. Poets like Sa'ib did not compose Sufi poetry, at least not in the overtly mystical style that has found appeal among readers around the world today, and he remains to be discovered among a wider audience. Moreover, his role as a major practitioner of the "fresh style," which was condemned by many modern literary historians, has meant that he disappeared from the poetic canon. The people of Isfahan remember him to this day and with some regularity a poetry reading takes place at his tomb every Friday morning.

In Kabul, Sa'ib composed a poem on the city that was also beloved by the Mughals.[17] The striking topographical feature of this city is the mountain range framing it, as noted by Sa'ib:

khusha 'ishrat-sara-yi Kabul u daman-i kuhsarash
ki nakhun bar dil-i gul mizanad muzhgan-i har kharash
khusha vaqti ki chashmam az savadash surma-chin gardad
shavam chun 'ashiqan u 'arifan az jan giriftarash

So splendid is the pleasure palace of Kabul and its mountainous range
That the eyelash of every thorn scratches the heart of the rose.
Happy the moment that I laid eyes on it,
I become infatuated with it like lovers and wise men.

As Sa'ib admires the Judas trees there, he lists the main topographical attractions of the city such as the Pul-i Mastan, and Shahrara and Jahanara gardens. As in such poems, the beauty of its inhabitants gets a brief mention: "Who can count the number of beauties on the rooftops? Two hundred suns have appeared at the base of the walls" (*hisab-i mahjabinan-i lab-i bamash ki midanad/du sad khurshid ru uftada dar har pa-yi divarash*). The water of the streams in this city has the quality of bestowing eternal life, the poet declares, but it was thanks to the just administration of Zafar Khan that Kabul was such a splendid city.

When he passed through Lahore or another city in Punjab, Sa'ib composed a lyrical poem on the celebration of *basant,* the north Indian spring festival, that is unusual for using the non-Persian word for the festival as the rhyme. This spring poem is, of course, a variation on the popular genre of spring poetry (*bahariya*) that marks the Persian new year (*nauruz*) and is dedicated to his friend Zafar Khan. It represents perfectly the mingling of Persian and Indian traditions in a spirit of wonderment. Struck by the joyousness of the festival, Sa'ib celebrates the riot of floral colors. Basant is related to the other Indian spring festival of Holi where colors are central to the celebration of the season: "The autumn has passed and colors have burst forth; the colorful new spring of Basant has arrived" (*guzasht fasl-i khizan shikast rangiha/rasid mausam-i rangin-i naubahar-i basant*).[18] Invoking the literary image about the blackness of India, the colors come as a surprise: "The blackness/land of India that appeared as a crow became like a peacock's feather from the spring of Basant" (*savad-i Hind ki chun zagh amadi bi-nazar/shuda ast chun par-i ta'us az bahar-i basant*). This festival would remain memorable for Sa'ib, as would the friendship of Zafar Khan and his time in India: "Since bright companionship never leaves one's memories, Basant remains in my heart" (*chunan ki suhbat-i rangin namiravad az yad/hamisha dar dil-i man hast khar khar basant*). Sa'ib also visited the Deccan briefly where he met 'Abdur-Rahim Khankhanan in his last years. Few men matched the generosity and hospitality of this man who welcomed visitors from Iran, but in a show of loyalty to the friends he made earlier in his travels into India, Sa'ib singled out Zafar Khan over the Khankhanan in terms of being a generous patron, as he declares in this verse: "Sa'ib, I have seen the Khankhanan in feast and battle; [but] in generosity and bravery there is none like your Zafar Khan" (*Khankhanan ra bi-bazm u razm, Sa'ib, dida'am / dar sakha u dar shuja'at chun Zafar Khan-i tu nist*).[19] During his subsequent long years of professional service at the Safavid court, Sa'ib turned out a sizeable body of topographical poetry, on the river Zayanda in the capital Isfahan, as well as buildings, gardens, and bridges that were newly constructed.[20] We will return to Sa'ib's memories of India later on.

'Abdur-Rahim was active during the reigns of Akbar and Jahangir and his career overlapped with that of Zafar Khan by only a few years. Both shared several features in terms of their lives and personal characteristics: primarily Mughal administrators and pillars of the state, both were patrons and poets in their own right (writing under the pennames Rahim and Ahsan, respectively), both had fathers who arrived from Persohphone lands to serve under the Mughals and were linked to the imperial family by marriage alliances ('Abdur-Rahim's daughter Jani Begum was married to Akbar's youngest son Daniyal, while Zafar Khan was married to Buzurg Khanum, Nur Jahan's grand-niece), and both cared deeply about the places they governed. In fact, both had some similar physical characteristics, described as short-statured men by their biographers. 'Abdur-Rahim is virtually a household name in India today, not only due to his fame as a poet of Hindi but also his lavish patronage of men of letters and artists. His reputation was widespread and the reach of his activities so wide that the French historian Corinne Lefèvre observes, he "possessed a certain fluidity in identity that has by and large failed to be addressed in scholarship."[21] In contrast, Zafar Khan is almost entirely unknown except to scholars, and even in Srinagar, Kashmir, there is no cultural memory of him, not in the least because he was a poet of Persian, not of Kashmiri or Hindi. We will return to

Zafar Khan again later in the discussion of his Kashmir years under Shah Jahan.

'Abdur-Rahim was born in 1556 the year that Akbar took the Mughal throne at age thirteen. His father Bairam Khan, who also held the title "Khankhanan," was of Kurdish origin and had served the Mughals faithfully. After falling into disfavor he was packed off to perform the hajj, but was assassinated on the way in Patan, Gujarat, in 1561. The five-year-old 'Abdur-Rahim was brought up by Akbar as a younger brother. After a glorious life that included military conquests, several governorships, and even years of being out of favor with Jahangir, he died in 1627. The life and achievements of 'Abdur-Rahim were immortalized in a work called the *Ma'asir-i Rahimi* (Achievements of Rahim). An unusual work in the Mughal archive, this massive text is a history and biography authored in 1616 by 'Abdul-Baqi Nihavandi just two years after coming from Iran into the circle of the general. Its inspiration came from several texts: most immediately, the celebratory biography of Akbar by Abu'l-Fazl, *Akbarnama,* and perhaps also the biography of the fifteenth-century Timurid patron-poet 'Ali Shir Nava'i by Ghiyasuddin Khvandamir, *Makarim al-akhlaq* (Laudable qualities of virtues). Nihavandi spent the entire duration of his Indian career under the patronage of 'Abdur-Rahim, whose court, first in Ahmedabad and later in Burhanpur, was as appealing as the imperial court for many new arrivals to India. It was no wonder that he was called a "maker of Hindustan into Iran" (*Hindustan-i Iran-saz*) because he recreated the literary and hospitable atmosphere of Iran right in the heart of India, not to speak of his lavish bequests to poets.

Among many poetic works in Hindi (i.e., Braj-bhasha and Avadhi) attributed to Rahim, one is a work reminiscent of the Persian *shahrashub*. This is the *Nagar-shobha* (City beauty), a collection of couplets (*doha*) that comprises a catalogue of sixty-six women from different castes and communities, in the way that Persian poems wrote of male youths. This work, then, can "be approached as both a vehicle for Persian sensibilities and a sincere attempt to participate in local literary culture."[22] The women, who range from a Brahmin woman (*brahmani*), betel-leaf seller (*tamolini*), dancer (*domni*), to a washerwoman (*dhobin*), are described in a flirtatious manner with wordplay on various aspects of their professions. This particular classification of the women can be thought of as a novel way to list heroines (*nayik-abheda*), a staple of Sanskrit and Hindi literatures, though given the cultural milieu and 'Abdur-Rahim's knowledge of Persian, there is no reason to believe that he did not have the Persian genre of such verses in mind. For instance, his verse on a female *pan*-seller is strikingly similar to a Persian poem that is attributed to Amir Khusrau:

> *surang baran bar-in bani nain khavaye pan*
> *nisi din pherai pan jyon birhi jan ke pran*[23]

> Dressed in red, the *tamolini* feeds *pan* with her eyes.
> Daily she fans the leaves, doing the same to the hearts of her lovers.

The verses that go by the name of Amir Khusrau essentially depict the same scene of the *pan*-seller and object of affection occupied in his daily work:

> *tanboli-yi man dush 'ayyari mikard / khush khush bi-dukan barg-shumari*
> *   mikard*
> *u barg bi-khalq misipurd u hama kas / dar pish-i dukanash jan-sipari*
> *   mikard*[24]

> Last night my *pan*-seller was up to his tricks
> As he slowly prepared *pan* leaves in his shop.
> As he gave the people in his shop their leaves,
> In return they surrendered to him their lives.

In keeping with the respective literary conventions, Rahim's poem relies more on the alliteration and assonance, while the rhyme and the fourth being the punch line provide aesthetic pleasure to the reader.[25]

As with the Persian genre, a cycle of such poems conveys the idea of a joyous city where the beautiful inhabitants are playfully engaged in their trade as inhabitants of a metaphoric city of love. There are no immediate precedents for these poems in Mughal literature, either in Hindi or Persian, as most of them were written after Rahim, but he would have known the ones from the classical Persian tradition and very likely even those written by Safavid poets. Rahim displayed his poetic skills in transferring the genre into the female-centered Indian system of aesthetics. This is not to say that there was only Persian influence at work here, rather there is the balance of Persian and Indic elements that fits in with the poetic genius of Rahim and his awareness of his position in multiple traditions. Away from the Persocentric culture of the north, the Mughals in the provinces, as well as patrons and poets of the Deccan courts, were relatively freer in experimenting with mixing different linguistic registers and literary traditions, ranging from themes in individual poems to poetic vocabulary. One striking example that is close in spirit to Rahim is Muhammad Quli Qutb Shah, the sultan-poet who ruled the Qutb-shahi state based in Golconda-Hyderabad from 1580 to 1611. Just as Rahim composed a cycle of poems on women of different backgrounds and professions, the poet Quli wrote a number of *ghazal*s in Dakhni on the beauties of his court. Celebrating the diversity of female beauty, as Persian did with male beauty, Quli refers to them by playful names such as Dusky, Lovely, and Cheeky (*sanvli, pyari, and chhabili*). 'Abdur-Rahim would have known some of these poems, along with the works by other poets of the Deccan.

'Abdur-Rahim's biographer Nihavandi devotes several pages to the topography of the places that his patron governed, describing the new architectural projects and renovations that he supervised. The capital of Gujarat province was Ahmedabad, the richest city in the empire and one of the earliest to be conquered under Akbar. 'Abdur-Rahim resided there as governor of the province from 1584 to 1589, and this is where he began to recreate the imperial assemblies of the north. Due to his efforts and the geography of the city, Ahmedabad became a major center of Persian literary activity in the early seventeenth century, though sadly one would not know this today with the virtual invisibility of Mughal artifacts. This is also because of the endurance of a more dominant pre-Mughal sultanate character in the old city and relatively shorter period of Mughal rule as compared with places like Lahore and Delhi. Ahmedabad's proximity to the port city of Surat, in Gujarat today but a separate administrative unity in Mughal times because of its importance for hajj traffic, made it a bustling place. The western region of the subcontinent was a busy crossroads of cultural traffic, especially in terms of its connections to the Arab and Iranian lands. Pietro della Valle, the Italian visitor to the city between 1623 and 1625, described it as "one of the four cities, amongst all the others of his dominions, where the Grand Moghol by particular privilege hath a palace and a court; and accordingly, he comes sometimes to reside there."[26] Jahangir, who had a love-hate relationship with the city, had made a prolonged stay here that was discussed in Chapter 2. Gujarat was the threshold to the Mughal North and the Deccan. Among the Iranian poets who spent substantial parts of their lives there were Naziri Nishapuri, Taqi Auhadi, and Muhammad Sufi Mazandarani, who chose it over other cities in the empire. The case of Naziri, who ranks among the premier Persian poets of the Safavid and Mughal periods, is an example of someone who took an unusual career path: he had come to India in the 1580s and was initially attached to the circle of 'Abdur-Rahim Khankhanan. In addition to continuing as a freelance poet, Naziri was also a merchant who set himself up as a gentleman farmer in Gujarat. Summoned to Agra by Jahangir in 1610, he did not live long in the capital and died back in Ahmedabad, where he was buried. Given its importance at the time, how did a place such as Ahmedabad figure in the oeuvre of Mughal poets?[27]

Writing almost three decades after 'Abdur-Rahim resided in the city, Nihavandi described his continuing legacy in Ahmedabad, which included a garden named Fath Bari, the site of the decisive military victory in 1573 over Sultan Muzaffar Shah III that won Gujarat for the Mughals, and various charitable works. In customary fashion and since the generic quality of the poetry allowed it, Nihavandi's rhapsodic description of the city is augmented with five lines from a *qasida* by the classical poet Azraqi: "Its trees are aloe and their leaves emeralds; its foundation is of enamel and its earth ambergris" (*dirakhtanash az 'ud u barg az zumurrud / binayash zi mina u khakash zi 'anbar*).[28] Echoing Razi's praise for the city's bazaar and people in his

Haft Iqlim, another poet from Iran named Salik Qazvini, who visited various Safavid and Mughal cities in the 1640s, called Ahmedabad the best city of the world, singling out its merchants for their business savvy and inhabitants for their beauty.[29] Expressing himself in a purely lyrical vein, Salik does not seem to have noticed any particular details of the topography of the place.

Salik visited Burhanpur next, the second city that had benefited from 'Abdur-Rahim's attention and one with a rich cultural legacy. Burhanpur is now a provincial backwater that is not often connected to the grandeur of the Mughals. As the capital of the small province of Khandesh, today part of the modern state of Madhya Pradesh, Burhanpur was taken by the Mughals quite late, in 1601, as part of a campaign led by Akbar himself to conquer the Deccan sultanate of Ahmadnagar. Soon after this, 'Abdur-Rahim was appointed governor and made the city his home, expending great resources on beautifying it. The Englishman William Finch visited the city at this time and had a mixed reaction to it, "This citie is very great, but beastly, situate in a low, unholsome air, a very sickly place, caused especially by the bad water."[30] However, this is not the impression we get from reading Nihavandi who wrote in a flowery vein. Burhanpur is also remembered as the place where during a military campaign in 1630 Shah Jahan's beloved wife Mumtaz Mahal passed away.

The Burhanpur garden of the previous rulers, the Faruqi sultans, was renovated under 'Abdur-Rahim's supervision as a venue for both private assemblies and for the use of local people.[31] Nihavandi rhapsodizes that it is such an enchanting place with flowers, birds, fruits from Hindustan, Iraq, and Khusrasan, that heaven has appeared on Earth (*bihisht ru-yi zamin namudar*), a rather clichéd metaphor of this time. The lofty fortress of Burhanpur is described in hyperbolic terms and in a language especially used for architectural poetry. Apart from quoting a few lines of his own, Nihavandi includes a twenty-eight line *qasida* by a poet named Mulla Shirazi Hamadani, not a particularly famous poet, which includes a chronogram. The first line is: "What a building it is that intoxicates the heart and stuns the vision! If I don't err, it is the manifestation of paradise" (*chi manzil ast ki dil mast u dida hairan ast / agar ghalat nakunam jilvagah-i janan ast*). And in another line he again employs the paradisal metaphor: "It seems that the moon and Jupiter from the constellation have moved to the heavenly garden" (*gu'i ki mah u mushtari az burj-i asman/tahvil karda and bi-bagh-i khudaygan*). A *hammam* in the city that was built under 'Abdur-Rahim's public works patronage and that eased the life of the city's inhabitants is mentioned but not praised in poetry. A description of the pool (*hauz*) of the congregational mosque is illustrated with one line from Amir Khusrau's poem, *Qiran al-sa'dain*, on Delhi, and seven further lines that includes a chronogram by a Maulana Fariduddin Munajjim, who was also a relatively minor poet in the circle of 'Abdur-Rahim. The cultivation of the best melons in the area is attributed to the care and attention of the great patron.

A garden called La'l Bagh was constructed some distance from the city in which a pond with lotuses was the most exquisite sight that, according to Nihavandi, was not something to be found in Iran. The pond is described by quoting six lines from a *qasida* by Azraqi, who seems to be one of his favorite poets when it came to poetry about buildings. The traveler Finch also had a positive impression of this garden, "Some two cose forth of the citie is Can Cannans garden, called Loll bage, the whole way thereto being under shadie trees, very pleasant. Within it are divers faire walkes, with a stately small tanke standing square betweene foure trees, all shaded and inclosed with a wall."[32] To the west of Burhanpur a new exclusive suburb named Jahangirpura was founded in the name of the emperor. It had the best of everything, from bazaars to buildings, in the entire land.

Nihavandi also interspersed his panegyric prose on buildings and gardens with his own verses, as well as some by his contemporaries, but more often quotes from classical Persian poets, conveying a sense of the timelessness of the experience of visiting the places. At the end of the topographical section of his biography, Nihavandi also briefly describes the contributions that 'Abdur-Rahim made to the four major cities of the empire: Lahore, Agra, Surat, and Delhi. Thus, in about a dozen pages, written in a lyrical style that is poetic prose, Nihavandi records the aspect of the cultural legacy of 'Abdur-Rahim that is linked to his attachment to the places he lived in, as well as those that showcased the glory of the Mughal Empire. These were important episodes in the idea that parts of the empire were akin to paradise or Arcadia, which would culminate in poetry about Kashmir under Shah Jahan.

POETRY AT SHAH JAHAN'S COURT

The literary output of Shah Jahan's reign shows that poets had a greater zeal for writing about places than those in the Jahangir period. Shah Jahan was a major patron of monuments, paintings, and words. Buildings such as the Taj Mahal and so much of old Delhi that we recognize and know today were his creation, as were scores of other buildings and gardens across the empire. He also commissioned more chronicles and histories than any other Mughal ruler, including two verse epics about his glorious reign. In addition, scores of paintings of courtly scenes, battles, and individual portraits from this period attest to his obsession with recording important events. When the prince Khurram was to take the throne as Shah Jahan, it was widely broadcast that he was going to be special in many ways for, in the words of Ebba Koch, "the new emperor would end a period of chaos and religious decline, meaning the reign of Jahangir when imperial power had been in the hands of a woman, Nur Jahan. A new era had begun under the second Timur, who had been born at the beginning of a new millennium and thus could claim to be a *mujaddid,* a religious renewer, a *mahdi,* who would bring a new golden age to mankind and a new spring to Hindustan."[33] It was also to be a new era for Persian poetry.

Ironically, unlike the first four emperors, Shah Jahan did not seem to possess a particularly keen literary bent or a highly aestheticized sense for poetry, therefore it is not surprising that he is the only great Mughal ruler who did not pen any poetry or prose himself.[34] Rather, he was interested in collecting the best men of letters at his court, just as he was interested in art objects. One of his historians chronicled his regular activity in the hall of private audience: "A part of the time His Majesty spends in inspecting the works of exalted magical artists such as lapidaries, enamelers, and others. At other times, the superintendents of construction of royal buildings, in consultation with the wonder-working architects, lay before the critical eye designs of proposed edifices. The royal mind, which is illustrious like the sun, pays full attention to the planning and construction of these lofty and substantial buildings."[35] It may not be far-fetched to imagine that he would have been actively involved in suggesting topics for historical and panegyric poetry to his court poets. Shah Jahan's taste in bedtime listening was also different from that of his grandfather or father, as one historian writes, "So that His Majesty may fall into a sweet sleep, the eloquent members of the assembly read behind the veil works on biography and history, containing accounts of prophets and saints as well as events of the reigns of former kings and emperors—which are memoirs of vigilance for the blessed who take warning and reminiscences of pardon for the enlightened who are fortunate." His favorite works were the memoirs of his ancestor Babur and the *Zafarnama*, a history about another distant ancestor Timur."[36] After all, like the latter he also held the title *sahib-qiran*, Lord of the Auspicious Planetary Conjunction.

If one were to judge the literature of Shah Jahan's age in terms of the number of court poets and historians, the sheer volume of literary texts produced, and the grand scale in which the arts were patronized, this period undoubtedly appears as the highpoint of Mughal culture. The court's efforts to create utopian notions of just rule and a happy society was encapsulated by the inscription on the hall of private audience (*divan-i khass*): "If there is a paradise on earth, it is here, it is here, it is here" (*agar firdaus bar ru-yi zamin hast / hamin ast u hamin ast u hamin ast*). The triple reiteration of the phrase "it is here" emphasized the present moment and place, and this became a mantra for several poets who traveled to and described different corners of the empire. But it was not just in the Agra or Delhi of Shah Jahan that paradise was recreated, but any spot in the empire that could be described in poetry. Art historians have studied the metaphor of paradise in this period, when it comes to the construction of gardens, palaces, carpets, and the Taj Mahal, but when it comes to textual production, this image is applied to almost every place or space that a court describes: the phrases *jannat-nishan, jannat-nazir, iram,* and *firdaus,* among others, became clichéd due to the frequency of their usage. But the point was that one had to have a firm belief in the idea that the empire and court really was a paradise on Earth.

The histories chronicling Shah Jahan's reign are many and confusing because some bear the same or similar titles and others were left incomplete. There are many narrative poems on historical themes from this period as well. The image that the chronicles present of the emperor, and for that matter of others, according to historians Begley and Desai, was "entirely externalized—the literary equivalent of the rigidly formal portraits which were executed with fastidious detail by painters in the imperial atelier, and designed for inclusion in elegantly calligraphed royal manuscripts."[37] Yet, more often than in Safavid or Ottoman paintings of individuals, behind the formalized representation the individuality of these people stands out and they become real. Biographical accounts about such people, or memoirs, produced in the Mughal realm convey the same impression, and we are drawn to a particular person over another one because of a certain anecdote that reveals a quirkiness or a humanity that transcends time and space.

Poetry about place clearly became a serious preoccupation for poets at Shah Jahan's court, and Agra was one of the first cities to be praised in verse by two senior poets of his court, Kalim and Qudsi. The lives and career trajectories of these two poets are of relevance here because they set a trend that would continue for more than two decades. Their city poems are of interest also because they both subsequently wrote similar poems on Kashmir, creating a related genre of bucolic poetry. The phenomenon of the composition of a large body of topographical poetry in this period was surely, to a large degree, in response to the emperor's own aesthetic preferences, in tandem with the frenzied pace of historical writing and painting of historical scenes. But the poets of this period also had before them works by recent authors, not to speak of the classical ones, that would have provided inspiration. These range from the poems of 'Abdi Beg on Safavid Qazvin, Zuhuri's *Saqinama*, Talib's *qasida*s, Nihavandi's biography of 'Abdur-Rahim Khankhanan, the memoirs of Babur and Jahangir, as well as the looming presence of Amir Khusrau's works. Shah Jahan's court, thus, proved to be the ideal time and place for the development of a new kind of poetry.

Shah Jahan's poet laureate, Abu Talib Kalim Hamadani, first came to India around 1601 as a young man and found employment as a poet in the court of the 'Adilshahis in Bijapur, one of the Muslim kingdoms in the Deccan that the Mughals would eventually conquer.[38] Kalim then returned home to Iran for two years, where he failed to make a successful career in the Safavid capital Isfahan, so in 1621 he made up his mind to try his luck again in India. For a few years he served as panegyrist in the entourage of the general Mir Jumla Shahristani "Ruh al-Amin," himself an expatriate Iranian and poet who was first at the Qutbshahi court and then in Mughal service.[39] Eventually Kalim managed to enter the highest circles at the Mughal court by praising Asaf Khan, the new emperor Shah Jahan's brother-in-law. Until his death in 1651 in Kashmir, where he had retired toward the end of his life, Kalim was the most prestigious poet of the court, who was acknowledged far and wide as a master of the *ghazal* in the fresh style. He had an eye for the unusual and his poetic style is imaginative and succinct, something that he has been faulted for by critics but has been much more appreciated in modern times. Kalim's poetry was innovative in several respects: he was among the first Mughal poets to use Hindi words, mostly botanical terms, in his poems; his chronograms and historical poems in various forms together narrate the history of Shah Jahan's reign; and most importantly, he wrote about actual places that were central to the cultural life of the court, such as Agra, Lahore, and Kashmir. Overall, there is an elegance and finesse in his diction that sits well with his humanistic outlook on his world.

Kalim's literary output was in harmony with Shah Jahan's larger project of documenting his reign for posterity. Leafing through Kalim's *divan* is like experiencing the daily rituals of life at Shah Jahan's court through poetic vignettes that range from the usual official verses to mark the Muslim holidays, birthdays of the emperor and princes, weighing ceremonies, elegies, but also the documentation of the production of luxury objects and architectural monuments.[40] In the hands of Kalim, the poetic *masnavi* especially became a malleable form that was a suitable vehicle for all kinds of subjects. Objects that were part of court life such as a sword, gun, throne, ring, and binding of the magnificent *Padshahnama* manuscript all became topics for his poetry. Kalim described in topical poems the terrible famine of 1630–1632 in the Deccan and Gujarat, as did other poets at court, the recovery of Princess Jahanara on November 25, 1644, from serious burns she sustained when her dress caught fire from a candle after an evening gathering in March of the same year, Prince Aurangzeb's fight with an elephant in a mini-epic, as well as other sundry topics. On a more personal level, poems on his feeling the ill effects of old age, the snow and mud on a bleak winter day in Kashmir, or breaking a leg while returning home from a party make him appear real for us. In the opening line of a *ghazal* Kalim declares that, "I have no sorrow of a home or worry about my place of origin. / It's not strange if I have *no* place in my heart" (*gham-i maskan u fikr-i ma'va nadaram / 'ajab nist gar dar dili ja nadaram*).[41] In this line, he professes to be sated with life, perhaps mirroring his own contented state. Kalim breathed his last in Kashmir, where several of his compatriots had retired from active court life. In many ways, the death of Kalim marked the end of an era.

In contrast to Kalim, the other senior poet of Shah Jahan's reign, Qudsi, came to India late in life and his reason to migrate was much more dramatic and touching. For many years he was the treasurer of the holiest Shia shrine of Imam Riza in the city of Mashhad, as indicated by the large number of poems he dedicated to the eighth imam. His patron was Hasan Khan Shamlu, governor and *beglarbegi* (Beg of begs) of the province of Khurasan, based in nearby Herat, who had a fine circle of literati around him.[42] Due to financial problems connected with his official position at the shrine and then the death of his adult son, Qudsi decided to emigrate to India in 1632. In several of his poems, the fear and hesitation about making such a big move at his age and leaving his beloved homeland behind is palpable. He would not regret this decision for he attained great glory among the Mughals, his fame then traveling back to Iran, but his last days were not entirely without worry. In fact, his own compatriots were the source of much of his worry: people he thought were his friends but who were ruthless about achieving fame and fortune in India. In one poem he admits that he came to India to make his fortune but bemoans the state of his life now:

Ilahi tu dardam bi-darman rasan / mara bar-i digar bi-Iran rasan
bi-vasl-i Khurasan dilam shad kun / zi Hind-i jigar-khvaram azad kun
sazavar-i bakht-i arjumandi niyam / hamin 'aib-i man bas ki hindi niyam
darin mulkam i'zaz u ikram hast / mara ham bi-qadr-i hunar, nam hast[43]

God, find a cure for my pain and take me to Iran once again.
Gladden me by union with Khurasan, free me from the liver-eating
    Hind.
Am I not worthy of a lofty fortune? My one fault is that I am not
    Indian.
I have honor and respect in this land; I also have a reputation in
    keeping with my rank.

Qudsi's death from dysentery in 1646 in Lahore, while returning
from Kashmir, was memorialized in a moving elegy by his friend
Kalim. Superior to Kalim in the eyes of some critics, Qudsi was not
particularly known for his *ghazal*s, but rather for the heavier and
solemn *qasida*s and *masnavi*s. Like his compatriot Kalim, Qudsi experienced and wrote about some of the most beautiful spots in the
Mughal empire.

THE PLEASURES OF AGRA, DELHI, AND LAHORE

Agra remained the official Mughal capital for over a century, until
Shahjahanabad in Delhi replaced it in 1648. Akbar and Jahangir spent
long periods of residence elsewhere, especially Fatehpur Sikri and
Lahore. Muhammad 'Arif, one of Akbar's historians, emphasizes the
cosmopolitan character of the capital city Agra's population as early
as 1564: "The multitude of foreigners from all sorts of nations, from
the corners of the four sides of the world, have gathered, for trade
and fulfillment of necessities, in such a country that the capital city
of Agra has become all of India."[44] The local had quickly become a
microcosm of the world. Abul-Fazl, chronicling the reign of Akbar,
echoes the same view regarding the capital in his section on the
province (*suba*) of Agra, "It is filled with people from all countries and
is the emporium of the traffic of the world."[45] The celebration of the

pax mughalica was echoed time and again by the professional poets under Akbar, Jahangir, and Shah Jahan. Kalim praised Shah Jahan's Agra in the following lines from a poem on the city:

chunin shahri bi-'alam kas nadida ast / ki dar vay haft iqlim aramida ast
zi har kishvar dar u khalq aramida / ta'adi ra na dida na shanida[46]

Nobody has seen such a city in the world
In which the seven climes repose.
People from every country reside in it,
They have never seen any harm here.

The positioning of the city vis-à-vis the seven climes, which meant the whole world, though hyperbolic and not at all unique in this period, is a significant reference.

European visitors were routinely awed by the city of Agra and remarked that as the emporium of the world, it was even larger than London or Isfahan. In a letter to a friend the French traveler François Bernier describes it using a European frame of reference: "Agra has more the appearance of a country town, especially when viewed from an eminence. The prospect it presents is rural, varied, and agreeable; for the grandees have always made it a point to plant trees in their gardens and courts for the sake of shade, the mansions of *Omrahs, Rajas,* and others are all interspersed with luxuriant and green foliage, in the midst of which the lofty appearances of old castles buried in forests. Such a landscape yields peculiar pleasure in a hot and parched country, where the eye seeks in verdure for refreshment and repose."[47] Shah Jahan's Agra indeed appeared as one big garden to the people of his age, such that, in the words of one of the emperor's historians, Muhammad Salih Kambo, "the desire to stroll in the garden of Paradise is completely erased from the page of memory."[48] The many lovely gardens of Agra, especially, were the feature of the city that would remind people of paradise. This is not the state of the city today, of course, but the vestiges of past grandeur are clearly there even without the Taj Mahal.

From Babur's time in Agra formal riverfront gardens had been cultivated along the Jumna (or Yamuna, in Persian Jaun), and when he

CELEBRATING IMPERIAL CITIES   **113**

had beautified an ungainly area with greenery and running water, it came to be called Kabul. This was one of the earliest attempts to make a small part of Hindustan resemble the Persian world. As the Mughals would have done, Agra's architectural and verdant splendor would best have been appreciated from a boat as one came down the river. Texts and images both indicate that Agra was seen as a city of riverfront gardens with walled enclosures, and boats plying the Jumna provided the best view. Ebba Koch's masterly studies of Mughal Agra and the reconstruction of its spaces indicates that it had "a suburban character" and "reflected the concept of the garden as primordial residence of the Mughal dynasty and, in a wider ideological sense, served as a symbol of the flowering of Hindustan under the just rule of Shah Jahan."[49] Gardens had always been central to Persian and Persianate court cultures, but now they were imbued with a new meaning.

In his biography-chronicle on Akbar's reign, Abu'l-Fazl in his typical fashion provides useful details about construction in the capital city of Agra in 1566.

> An imperial decree was issued for the removal of the old fortress, which was located on the banks of the Jumna to the west of the city and the foundations of which had begun to deteriorate due to the vicissitudes of time, and for the construction in its place of a mighty fortress and unassailable bastion of hewn stone that would be as stable as the basis of this dynasty's fortune. Therefore, at an hour auspicious for permanence of labor and founding of fortresses, expert geometers and architects laid out the foundations of the great building, and the seven layers of the earth were dug for the foundations. The thickness of the wall was fixed at three imperial ells, and the height reached sixty ells, including four gates opening felicitously to the four corners of the earth.

After the elaborate planning of the construction projects, the actual work began: "Every day three to four thousand spry builders, strong-armed laborers, and other construction workers toiled. From the foundation to the crenellations hewn stones of a fiery red color, each of which was a world-revealing mirror of purity and of the rosy hue of the cheek of fortune, were so fitted together that not a hair would fit in the joint. This lofty bastion, the likes of which the architect of the imagination had never seen, including crenellations, breastworks, and loop-holes, was completed over the course of eight years."[50] Several Mughal paintings depict the busy construction sites where traditional building techniques were used, sights that are still familiar in South Asia. In a painting from a copy of the *Akbarnama,* the viewer's attention is drawn not just to the architectural details but also the diversity of craftsmen and activities, as in the image where Akbar is depicted supervising the manual labor in the construction of Fatehpur Sikri (see Figure 4). With all the new construction of cities in Akbar's reign and with precedents for this in Timurid and Safavid literature, it is somewhat surprising that no poetry about these spaces was composed. Akbar's court poets were occupied with producing other kinds of literature, and it would be the poets of the monumentalist ruler Shah Jahan who were innovators in the genre of poetry about places.

About twenty-three miles (37 kilometers) from Agra, the indefatigable Akbar built and occupied Fatehpur Sikri in 1571–1585. This Xanadu-like capital's architecture perfectly suited his lifestyle. It was located near the shrine of the Sufi Salim Chishti whose blessings rewarded him with the birth of his first son. The planned city's designated buildings such as for musical assemblies, interfaith dialogues, and a library, were symbolic of the vision of a utopian community. Visitors from abroad expressed a preference for one or the other: the English traveler Ralph Fitch wrote that Fatehpur Sikri was "greater the Agra, but the houses and streetes be not so faire." Both cities appeared to him to be greater than London and the twelve-mile road between the two was "a market of victuals and other things, as full as though a man were still in a towne, and so many people as if a man were in a market."[51] Fatehpur Sikri was abandoned, it is believed, because of water problems, and it is possible that Akbar moved on to Lahore rather than Agra or Delhi to create some distance between his court and his architectural wonderland.[52]

At the very beginning of Jahangir's memoirs, the emperor takes Agra as the starting point to launch into more general descriptions

طرح تقسیمی علل بندی چرهٔ های ساحوخورد   ۱۲۷   ۱۷۳   ۹ ۱۶

FIGURE 4 Akbar inspecting the construction of Fatehpur-Sikri

of India. Calling it "one of the ancient and large cities of Hindustan," Jahangir concedes that from the point of view of climate it is not ideal, but its fruits and flowers are out of this world. As for the people of the city, they are "quite industrious in acquiring skills and learning. Various classes of every religion and sect have taken up residence in this town."[53] These are the people that we saw in the painting earlier depicting the public celebrations on Jahangir's accession (see Figure 2). Shah Jahan changed the official name of Agra to Akbarabad in memory of his grandfather and it was this city that was the subject of so much literature in verse and prose.

Echoing the enthusiasm for the capital city in his time, the poet Qudsi gushes over the charms of Agra in a short poem:

bi-mulk-i digar khatiram shad nist / bihishti bih az Akbarabad nist
darin gulshan-i 'aish u dar-i surur / bi-har gusha'i jush-i ghilman u hur
zi sabzan-i shirin-shama'il mapurs / lab-i pur namak bin u az dil mapurs[54]

> My heart doesn't rejoice in any other place—there is no better
> paradise than Akbarabad.
> In this garden of pleasure and abode of joy, there is a bonanza of
> *ghilman* and houris.
> Don't ask about the dusky beauties—look at their cute lips and don't
> ask about their hearts!

He goes on to admire the narrow waists and indifferent attitude of the beautiful creatures, both boys and girls, who conjure up visions of the beauties in paradise. Qudsi's poetic effusion is not original in any sense; he is clearly employing a formulaic description to represent the typical attractive beloveds in an urban setting. However, it is the time and place that make his words meaningful. In another poem he describes the Jahanara garden in Agra, before which Herat and Kashmir, both celebrated for their natural gardens, would be ashamed. In fact, it is so lush that the differences between the sweet-talking parrot and ugly crow disappear.[55]

Kalim also wrote a poem on Agra emphasizing its urban qualities. The verse panoramic tour of the city, for which he uses the official designation of Akbarabad, includes a description of its magnificent architecture, gardens, and bazaar and is the equivalent of what painters of this time were doing with images. Kalim begins his poem by praising first the land of Hindustan (some of these lines are quoted earlier in this chapter) and then the city of Akbarabad, which is so vast that a thousand Egypts exist in every street. His guided tour of the bazaar of Akbarabad, where he encounters various young and beautiful boys, is in the *shahrashub* mode and follows 'Abdur-Rahim's similar catalogue of women. Kalim's gaze takes in an *'attar* (druggist), *bazzaz* (cloth-seller), *sarraf* (money changer), *jauharfurush* (jeweler), *khayyat* (tailor), *zargar* (goldsmith), *shaikhzada* (shaikh's son) and *sipahzada* (soldier boy). In keeping with the Indian landscape, there are specifically local tradesmen for which Hindi words are used, such as *mahajan* (merchant), *tanboli* (*pan* seller), and *dobi* (washerman), as well as specific social groups such as Shaikhs, Rajputs, and Pathans. This is not a random selection of people. Each was carefully chosen to represent the cream of the population of the Mughal Empire. As in Kalim's poem, several other poems of place in the *masnavi* form in this period employ the combination of *shahrashub* with other popular topoi.

As he moves from the bazaar to the garden, Kalim is amazed by the Jumna River, the boats on it, and the lofty buildings alongside it. He exclaims: "A city on two sides and the river in between; on the seashore [but] a sea without shore" (*du janib shahr u darya dar miyana / kinar-i bahr, bahr-i bi-kirana*) and proposes a ride on the river. The third section of the poem is on the Jahanara garden in which he lists some specifically Indian flowers, such as *champa, maulsri,* and *keora,* in order to emphasize its Indo-Persian quality. At the end of the poem Kalim declares that although the previous owner of the garden, Mumtaz Mahal, is in paradise (*jannat*), she left *this* particular paradise to her daughter Jahanara, after whom the garden was named. Kalim's poem was meant to highlight the magnificence of the Mughal capital in the time of Shah Jahan for an audience beyond the limits of the Mughal lands. In his verses, nature complements the cityscape and is contained within a walled garden in the city, with everything in its proper place. This would be the starting point for him to write about nature and the countryside.

The Taj Mahal is, of course, the main attraction in Agra today and marketed as the most famous memorial of love and imperial splendor, commissioned by Shah Jahan for his deceased wife Mumtaz Mahal. Constructed during the 1630s and 1640s, this building did not get much attention in Mughal poetic texts because funerary monuments were not celebrated in the same way as other grand architecture. In the court poetry of the time, it was only described in the epic poems of Kalim and Qudsi in brief sections using the customary language of the genre of architectural poetry. Qudsi hails the monument as a sacred spot:

zahi marqad-i pak-i Bilqis-i 'ahd / ki banu-yi afaq ra gashta mahd
munavvar maqami chu bagh-i bihisht / mu'attar chu firdaus-i 'anbar-sirisht[56]

Hail to the pure tomb of the Bilqis of our age,
for it has become the heavenly lady's cradle.
A luminous spot like the garden of paradise,
perfumed like the ambergris-scented heaven.

The tomb also found a European admirer in the Frenchman François Bernier who wrote in 1663, "It is possible I may have imbibed an Indian taste; but I decidedly think that this monument deserves much more to be numbered among the wonders of the world than the pyramids of Egypt, those unshapen masses which when I had seen them twice yielded me no satisfaction, and which are nothing on the outside but heaps of large stones piled in the form of steps one upon another."[57] We will read about Bernier's experiences in Kashmir later.

Other Mughal poets and historians wrote about Agra, such as Munir Lahauri, who described the gardens of the city, as well as the historian Kambo in his prose work *Bahar-i sukhan* (Spring of poetry), both works still unpublished in our times. In the context of vernacular literary culture, a Jain poet named Lakshmichandra composed a topographical poem on Agra in the Rajasthani-Hindi register that was in dialogue with the Persian poems of the age.[58] Lakshmichandra particularly praises Agra's bazaars and then compares the city to the heaven inhabited by the Hindu gods:

Akbaravad hai aisak, lakhiyai Indrapur taisak
sab gun shahar hai bharpur, dekhat jat hai dukh dur

Akbarabad is as they describe the city of Indra to be.
It's a city full of all virtues; beholding it removes all sorrows.

As we have seen, the virtuous nature and beneficial effect of a well-governed city is a common trope in Persian poetry as well. Agra and its monuments, however, fade in Mughal Persian literature when Shah Jahan built his magnificent capital in Delhi that provided the backdrop for tremendous cultural achievements and witnessed many historical upheavals in the ensuing three centuries.

For over a millennium Ajmer and Delhi have been cities that were designated as Muslim holy space early in the history of Islam in the Indian subcontinent, sometimes even being regarded as a second Mecca. Delhi was where the tombs of scores of Sufis dotted the landscape. Some still exist, the most sacred among them being those of the Chishti masters Nizamuddin Auliya and Qutbuddin Bakhtiyar Kaki, both special to the Mughals at different times. In the complex of the Chishti shrine and near the burial place of Nizamuddin Auliya was also the tomb of Amir Khusrau, who as we have seen was held in high regard in the early modern period as the architect of Indo-Persian poetry. Razi in his *Haft Iqlim* has an appropriately reverential attitude regarding Delhi. He describes it in glowing terms, especially praising its architectural splendors and gardens. Not surprisingly he begins with two verses from Amir Khusrau's oft-quoted poem on the city: "Delhi, refuge of religion and justice, long may it endure since it is a heavenly paradise." He goes on to say, "Since Delhi has always been the home of saints and pious ones (*mahbat-i auliya va atqiya*), truly, he whose extended scroll of life is decorated with a final signature is buried in that pure land."[59] Thus, it is no surprise that the first personage among the few chosen to represent this city is Nizamuddin Auliya, followed by other Sufi figures like Amir Khusrau and Hasan Dihlavi, the favorite disciples of the Chishti master.

Before Razi lists the notables of the city, he praises it in a mixture of prose and verse, especially focusing on its architectural marvel, the

Qutb minar, one of the earliest monuments of Islamic architecture in Delhi. While describing this wondrous tower, he quotes these lines from Amir Khusrau's *Qiran al-sa'dain*, which were originally not written for this victory tower but could be easily reused due to their generic quality:

> *shikl-i manara chu sutuni zi sang / az pay-yi saqf-i falak-i shisha-rang*
> *ta sarash az auj bi-gardun shitaft / gunbad-i bi-sang-i falak sang yaft*
> *mah nakhuspad hama shab ta sahar / kaz sar-i sikhash khala darad bi-bar*[60]

> The minaret's form is a stone pillar
> reaching out to the glass vault of heaven.
> With its top stretching into the sky,
> the stoneless dome of heaven got a stone.
> The moon does not sleep all night until dawn
> with its [the minaret's] peak poking its breast.

These verses on another minaret in Delhi sufficed to convey the grandeur of the Qutb minar, a monument that had stood strong for centuries and was a recognizable feature of Delhi for people in Mughal India. The old Delhi gave way to the coming up of a grander one in the mid-seventeenth century.

The new capital of Shahjahanabad in the north of Delhi was officially inaugurated on April 18, 1648. This was a tense time in the empire because the Mughal armies were in the middle of a difficult campaign to defend the frontier fortress of Qandahar from the Safavids, the complete story of which will be described later. In the annual Jesuit report for 1648–1649, there is an account of a peculiar occurrence around the composition of a poem at the festivities.

> The King at great expense had built a most magnificent city to which he gave the name Shahjahanabad; in praise therefore of the vast city he had founded, the King asked Mirza [Zul-Qarnain], by far the best poet of these Regions, to write a suitable piece of poetry. Mirza summoned up all the power of his talent; he wrote in verse that was perfect; but in it he sang, not the praise of the King, but the power of

God alone. Mirza's only object was to show the King that the glory of the city and its perfection was attributable to God alone. The King, who in his greed for flattery, expected his own praise, indignantly rejected the panegyric. Afterwards, he substituted his name where that of God came in, so that what was said to God's praise would be attributed to him. In this you see how the Mirza's intrepid piety came into conflict with the intolerable arrogance of the King.[61]

If this story is true, it was indeed an inauspicious start to the inauguration of the new capital. The poet mentioned here, Mirza Zul-Qarnain, an Armenian Christian, is actually not mentioned as a poet in Persian literary sources, but almost everyone at court composed one or more line of poetry. In any case, with other matters demanding his attention, Shah Jahan spent less than a year in Shahjahanabad, moving to Lahore where he could monitor the tense situation on the border. This may explain why there were no individual poems composed on Shahjahanabad on this momentous occasion. In addition, by this time most of the Iranian poets of Shah Jahan's early years had passed away or retired from active service. But this was only the beginning of a new phase of this city's greatness. Shahjahanabad was praised in Persian and Urdu literary texts in the subsequent two centuries, both as the jewel of the late Mughal Empire and for its long history as a center of power and spirituality.[62] In the late Shah Jahan and early Aurangzeb periods, the historians Muhammad Varis and Kambo, the *munshi* Chandarbhan Brahman, described it in a highly poeticized language. Among the poets, Zafar Khan's son 'Inayat Khan "Ashna" composed verses on it that are found in his unpublished *divan*. It was no coincidence that several of these men had their origins in or around Lahore, whose history had always been connected with that of Delhi.

Going back in time again, we learn that Akbar had left Fatehpur Sikri and shifted the entire court to Lahore, located in the heart of Punjab, in 1584 where the court was based for the next fourteen years. According to the urban studies scholar William Glover, "Throughout Akbar's reign, court nobles were encouraged to build palaces, gardens, and religious institutions in and around the city, and Lahore grew rapidly, both in extent and population."[63] Like Agra, it was also called the emporium of the world. The imperial attention to Lahore coincided with it becoming the base for Qadiri Sufi *pirs* such as Shah Abu'l-Ma'ali during the reigns of Akbar and Jahangir. In Jahangir's time, during 1613–1627, Lahore again became the favorite imperial city, especially since it was a convenient embarkation point for his frequent Kashmir trips. Poems to the city from this period by court poets such as Talib Amuli and Munir Lahauri demonstrate the gradual way in which the city found a place in the Mughal poetic imagination as a place of pleasure and spirituality, even before any similar poems were written on the other older capital cities of Agra or Delhi.

At Jahangir's court, the poet Talib wrote two poems on Kashmir. He also composed a short poem, this one also a *qasida,* in twenty-three lines, with the refrain "Lahore."[64] This poem celebrates the city that was loved by Jahangir and Nur Jahan and houses both their tombs. The very first line of the poem proclaims that Lahore's pleasant atmosphere and abundant water obey the inclination of old learned men as well as the young (*khusha Lahaur u faiz-i ab-i Lahaur / bi-ta'at-i mail-i shaikh u shab Lahaur*). Lahore was in competition with the larger and perhaps more cosmopolitan city of Delhi, for Talib declares, "All the tools of play belong to Delhi, all the means of pleasure belong to Lahore" (*hama alat-i lahv alat-i Dihli / hama asbab-i 'aish asbab-i Lahaur*). He is enamored of this city because even the non-Muslims would be able to point out where the *masjid* and *mihrab* were located (*zi taq-i abru-yi zunnariyan purs / ki nishan-i masjid u mihrab-i Lahaur*). The inhabitants of Lahore appear to be beautiful in character (*khalq*) and appearance (*chihra*). At the end of the poem Talib confesses that the reason he is describing the wonders of Lahore is because his spiritual master (*pir u murshid*), Shah Abu'l-Ma'ali, who is one of the spiritual axes (*qutb*) of the city, resides there.[65] Talib's poem moves from celebrating the more superficial aspects of the city's charms to its inscription as a sacred space. His own relationship to it is mediated through the spiritual aura of his master who would have been alive when this poem was composed. Although he was not a native of the city, Talib displays great affection for it.

Several other poets and historians of Shah Jahan's court described Lahore in their works. One of these was Munir, a native of the city, who felt a kinship with other Indo-Persian poets of the past, especially the early poet Mas'ud Sa'd Salman whose loving paean to twelfth-century Lahore would have been known to him. Whereas the city was a beloved for the classical poet, it is a munificent patron for Munir in whose wine party the poet receives his rightful appreciation. Munir's poem is in the form of a long *saqinama* (address to the wine server), which was a popular genre of poetry at this time used for a whole range of topics.[66] In keeping with this poetic genre, Munir sustains a series of oenological metaphors, as if the city is the setting for an exhilarating celebration. Munir declares that fragrant Lahore is undistinguishable from Shiraz so that even Kashmir, already celebrated at this time as the paradise on Earth, is its servant (*chun gulzar-i firdaus-i pur-rang bu-st / ki Kashmir az khana-zadan-i u-st*). Going even further, Munir inverts the usual binary trope of skin color by declaring that the dark-skinned Lahauri beauties put the fair-skinned Kashmiris to shame (*zi khubi-yi husn-i siyahan-i u / safidan-i Kashmir bi-abru*). Significantly, Munir does not see Lahore in isolation but as part of the larger Mughal imperium, for it is a part of the heart of Hindustan (*jigar-gusha-yi mulk-i Hindustan*). Going even further, he likens the clear water of its river to his own verses (*ravan ab-i safash chu ash'ar-i man*), validating his right to praise the city.

One expects to see fleeting references to Lahore's buildings and gardens in Munir's poem, if not in the one by Talib, but there are none. Lahore was beautified by its governor Vazir Khan, a native of the province, in the 1630s, and also by Shah Jahan, who commissioned buildings such as his father Jahangir's tomb and the Shalimar garden.[67] Based on the literary sources, Lahore was not usually viewed as a city of gardens or architectural marvels, as Srinagar or Agra were at this time.[68] Another feature that is absent in these two poems on Lahore is a description of the city's bazaar and individual craftsmen or sellers, which are found in poems about some other Mughal cities. Rather, Lahore is consistently described the way Ahmedabad was, in generic terms as a thriving commercial center, land of beautiful people, but also as the abode of holy men and the seat of imperial power.

As with the Hindi poem on Agra, there exists one on Lahore written during Jahangir's reign by a Jain poet named Jatmal. The poem is in a register that combines Rajasthani and Braj-bhasha. Jatmal is aware of the city as a Mughal achievement—"There [rules/resides] the king Jahangir whose father was lord Akbar; Babar laughingly founded the dynasty; having routed his enemies, he exiled them" (*tihan hai patisiyah Jahangir, jako bap Akbar mir/Babar vans upjyo hans, bairi mar kiye nirbans*)—and also as a home to Sufis and the gateway to the divine Krishna. Unlike the Persian poems of this time, this one mentions several specific neighborhoods and areas of Lahore by name, along with praising its imperial architecture.[69] As in the Persian poems of this genre, Jatmal lists some of the chief professions practiced by men, as well as the local flora and fauna, and using a feature of the Indic literary tradition there is also a description of the beautiful women there who are compared to the damsels in Indra's celestial city.

Ironically, in the post-Shah Jahan period, when Lahore and Punjab emerged as subjects for praise poems out of pride by local poets, they "reverted to a declining provincial status."[70] In the first part of the seventeenth century, Lahore served as one of the imperial capitals after Agra and Delhi because of its geographic location as the starting point for the court on its journey to the mountains and the ultimate destination of Kashmir. As poetry about cities flourished in this period, Kashmir, both the city of Srinagar and the valley, became a fashionable subject for court poets for the next few decades. Kashmir was the ideal balance of city and countryside and could be described in innovative ways in the Persian poetry of this period.

FOUR

Mughal Arcadia

ﮯ *Et in Arcadia ego* ﯼ
I too am in Arcadia

MUGHAL PASTORAL

In the early years of Shah Jahan's reign, an Iranian poet named 'Ali Quli "Salim" of Tehran arrived in Agra. During his presentation at court, Salim declaimed a poem before Emperor Shah Jahan praising the natural beauty of the valley of Kashmir, the jewel in the Mughal Empire. At this point, the poet laureate Kalim, also originally from Iran, came forward and informed the emperor that Salim had previously presented the exact same poem about Lahijan, a city in northern Iran, when he was employed at the Safavid court. He had merely substituted Lahijan for Kashmir and the poem was not an original composition. Apparently, Shah Jahan was put off by this trickery and rejected the poem and poet. Salim was forced to look for employment with another patron.[1] Did the topography of Kashmir, a place he may not have seen when he just arrived in India, really remind Salim of Lahijan, or were these poems so generic that they could be applied to any place indiscriminately?

This anecdote, recorded in several early modern Persian historical sources, can be dismissed as literary gossip, and there were many such factual and fictitious vignettes that filled the pages of *tazkira*s, the increasingly popular anthologies-cum-biographical dictionaries among the literati, to provide entertainment and edification for readers. But it does illustrate some important points that were central to Mughal literary culture: the position of Iranians as arbiters of the Persian language and the way a poem was a commodity that poets could use to further their chances of social mobility (and even recycle some verses for another occasion). The reason that Salim chose a poem on Kashmir to ensure his entry to the court and gain Shah Jahan's favor was because composing poems on this topic had recently become a literary fashion.

We learned how the province of Kashmir had become the summer retreat of the imperial family under Jahangir and Shah Jahan, and during this time it also came to be regarded as the manifestation of cherished cultural and aesthetic ideals. The valley of Kashmir had a long history of being celebrated in Persian historical texts. In poetry, it was celebrated in the conventional manner for its elegant cypresses and graceful inhabitants, but at the same time it came to be regarded as a more felicitous space than the typical Persian garden. The valley lent itself perfectly to being viewed as a Persianate Arcadia for Mughal poets and others, especially given its salubrious climate, serene gardens that skillfully combined the natural and artificial, and a seemingly bucolic way of life, all of which exemplified perfectly what the empire stood for. In the reign of Shah Jahan, from being an imperial retreat during the summer months, it gained significance as a Sufi center for his children and as a colony for some his senior court poets. The memory of this imperial connection still lingers in the ruins of Mulla Shah Badakhshi's Sufi lodge, as well as the now impossible to find cemetery of Mughal poets (*mazar-i shu'ara*) that contained the graves of the major poets of Shah Jahan's court—Kalim, Qudsi, and Salim among others—once located on a romantic spot by the Dal Lake in Srinagar.[2] Although the main Mughal gardens in Srinagar are maintained for tourists, others are now virtually impossible to locate, and we only know of them from the poetry and chronicles of the period.

For Iranian émigrés, Kashmir, the land of flowers and springs, was "Little Iran" (*Iran-i saghir*) for mainly two reasons: first, because it was the actual manifestation of an idealized Persian garden fixed in poetic geography, and second, because of the number of Iranians residing there in the seventeenth century for whom its cooler climate was more bearable than the searing heat of the Indian plains. The valley of Kashmir bears more than a superficial resemblance to the landscape of the northern provinces of Gilan and Mazandaran in Iran, the narrow strips of land that hug the southern shore of the Caspian Sea: both regions are mountainous, lush with greenery, and are marked by the presence of large bodies of water. That is why the poet Salim would have been able to exploit the situation and pass off a poem about the Iranian region as being about Kashmir, if the event occurred at all. Although poems in a generic vein with the usual stock images and metaphors—after all, one garden was quite like any other in Persian poetry—were composed by several poets of this period, there was also a discernable shift in the way they represented the topography of this region. At first glance, Kashmir was another Mughal province that had been beautified with neatly laid-out gardens, fountains, and pavilions, but here there was also nature in its pristine form, with no walls to separate the hostile desert from the oasis. Poets reacted to this new environment in individualistic and creative ways.

The province of Kashmir was described by a large number of poets and historians of the seventeenth century, most of them of the Shah Jahan period, perhaps more than any other place in the Mughal Empire, including the imperial capitals. As men from the provinces increasingly made contributions to the literature of the period, and provincial governors created mini-courts to attract talented men of letters to their circles, there was also an interest in the celebration of nonurban places. Cosmopolitan cities were no longer the only places that resembled paradise. The unspoiled landscapes of some of the provinces were actually closer to an Arcadia. Poets of the Shah Jahan period adapted the city poem that had been in vogue and modified it to describe the valley. The Kashmir poems by Jahangir's poet laureate Talib also served as models for the flowering of this genre. In the Shah Jahan period *masnavi*s on Kashmir, poets described both man-made spaces and natural formations such as mountains, water-falls, streams, and saffron fields, as well as gardens of course. The image of garden as paradise is as old as Persian poetry itself, with "a constant interplay between the real world and the ideal."[3] The art historian Monica Juneja argues that nature in Mughal culture "was far from being benevolent, it was not a space of innocence, of harmony, sufficiency or unrestrained abundance." Rather, it was "conceived of as uncontrolled, potentially inimical and destructive—as a force which needed to be domesticated and 'civilised' through superior human intervention—through the laying down of formal gardens and the erection of buildings. Its ferocity was to be vanquished through the hunt, an activity valorized and encoded as a practice signifying courtliness."[4] But it was in the process of domesticating nature that the potential for a new kind of poetics emerged in the 1630s and 1640s, which would transform the representation of natural landscapes in Mughal court literature.

The similarity of Kashmir and the province of Mazandaran in northern Iran in terms of their topography was remarked upon earlier. Although a fad similar to the Kashmir poem did not develop in the case of Mazandaran, some poets versified the region's beauty as a setting for the Safavid court's retreats. The poet-historian Vahid described the Caspian province's landscape in his chronicle:

> *hast bi had u bi kiran saidash / az zamin ta bi-asman saidash*
> *hamchu darya hava zi sair-i abist / dar hava abr, bal-i murghabist*
> *hast bar said, tang dam nigah / gar farazad bi-asman khargah*
> *khail-i urdak bar asman bi-had / chun sutur-i kitaba bar gunbad*
> *takht su-yi gavazn hargah shah / bisha'i har taraf fitad bi-rah*
> *kam kasi dida az saghir u kabir / bisha'i ra ki ram kunad az shir*[5]

There's no limit or end to the game there.
Game abounds there from earth to sky.
The air is as thick with moisture as the sea.
Clouds in the air are waterfowl on the wing.
If he raises his pavilion to the sky,
the net of its gaze falls tight over the prey.
The endless flocks of ducks around the sky
are like the lines of an inscription around a dome.

Whenever the king charged forward toward deer,
a jungle set off running every which way.
Young or old, few people have seen
a jungle that runs away from a lion![6]

In these lines, the natural landscape is the royal hunting ground and one of the several spaces for the staging of courtly activities. It was only the rare court poet who could transcend this frame of viewing and describing the landscape.

Classical poetic traditions in Arabic and Persian shared many conventions, especially in the early years of the latter tradition, and these comparative aspects can provide an understanding of the history of poetry about nature. Writing on classical Arabic literature, Salma Khadra Jayyusi, remarks on the absence of pastoral poetry in Arabic, "In Abbasid and Andalusi [Arabic] nature poetry, orchards, flowers, fruits, fountains, trees and flowing streams became not only common images but direct objects of description, together with the man-made creations of palaces, ponds, orchards and shady arbours." But, it seems that "some poets developed the usage to real heights of metaphorical sophistication, both in the East and in al-Andalus. However, it was to external nature that the poet addressed himself, to an aesthetic element of his experience; his relationship with nature was not normally one of challenge and necessity. Nature, to this urban poet, was never wild and awesome, but friendly and accessible, humanized and under the poet's control. What the poet usually saw in nature was its external, pleasant and passive qualities."[7] Although pastoral poetry composed in a romantic mode was also not all that common in classical Persian literature, the Mughal poets' relationship to nature underwent a change in this period.

With its origins in classical Greek and Latin literatures, the pastoral poem celebrates the pristine countryside, in opposition to the corrupt city. In the context of Renaissance literature Raymond Williams explains how the meaning of "pastoral" underwent a profound change: "Its most serious element was a renewed intensity of attention to natural beauty, but this is now the nature of observation, of the scientist or the tourist, rather than of the working countryman."[8]

This certainly seems to have been true in the Mughal Persian case, especially since almost all of the poems were produced by court poets visiting Kashmir. The images of nature in classical Persian literature that included gardens, mountains, lakes, waterfalls, deserts, and other topographical features were described with the use of long established and somewhat overused metaphors for the most part. The imagery of ideal gardens, with roses and nightingales in the season of spring, was a system of complex metaphors for a range of courtly and mystical practices and are almost never to be taken as literal representations.[9] Some Mughal Persian poets began to view nature differently in the seventeenth century, as is reflected in the largely unexamined corpus of poems on Kashmir and other places, using a courtly pastoral mode of writing.[10] They became aware of not just the picturesque elements of nature, but also its awesome and sublime aspects. In terms of aesthetics, this is similar to the poetics of nature in Sanskrit and Hindi poetry, as discussed by Valerie Ritter, where often objects from nature "are linked, not uncharacteristically, with the trappings of court."[11] A similar turn toward realism in the use of actual places as settings also finds a parallel in Mughal period Persian and Hindi poetry. It was as if the poets were looking at the same topography through the filters of their respective traditions and coming up with a new and mutually appreciated aesthetic.

A fundamental challenge for the premodern Persian poet was the anxiety about being an original poet. With a few restricted poetic forms at their disposal, but somewhat more freedom in mixing what we would today call genres of poetry, a poet had to be truly innovative to get noticed. Imitation in the *ghazal* allowed for a potentially infinite number of permutations on a single image or metaphor because the brevity of the lyric form or the quote-worthiness of a single distich or line meant keeping or losing the attention of a reader or listener. To do this in narrative poetry had its own challenges. For instance, with the existence of scores of versions of the romance of Laila and Majnun in classical Persian literature, several of them of fine quality, students today are only familiar with and refer to the original version by Nizami. Mughal Persian poets, whether Iranians or Indians, had the advantage of drawing on the culture and geog-

raphy of the places they were writing about, rather than simply re-
lying on a fixed repertoire of imagery, to introduce innovative elements in their verses. When it came to the Kashmir poems of Shah
Jahan's age, poets first of all had to follow the standards set by the
senior poets at court, Kalim and Qudsi, who took the initiative in this
literary flowering. Reading the poems of poets who followed them,
it is difficult to conclude whether they had really been to Kashmir or
just obtained their sketchy topographical information from people or
books. Most of these poets described the difficult path to the valley,
then the gardens and pavilions built by the imperial family and governors, but beyond that there is little geographical specificity in their
poems. However, despite appearing to be staged and courtly, new images and tropes are found in several of these poems, which adds to
an understanding of the development of a literary genre. Then there
were also few poets who had an eye for the unusually pristine nature of the landscape.

Since imperial propaganda for Shah Jahan exploited the use of botanical imagery, as was the case in Agra's riverfront garden city, in
pietra dure floral motifs in architecture, and ornamentation in manuscripts, it was natural that his court poets would be drawn to the
possibilities that the Kashmiri landscape offered. Jahangir's nature
artist Mansur was commissioned to produce a series of paintings on
Kashmir's flora and fauna.[12] In her study of Mughal art and architecture, Ebba Koch explains the significance of botanical imagery for
this ruler: "The image of the garden and its flowers was the main
metaphor of Shah Jahan's imperial symbolism: it stood not only for
the emperor himself and his good government but also for his court
and his family."[13] Floral images are found on so many objects in Mughal art and architecture, just as the metaphors of garden and paradise
were applied to almost every place in Persian historical and poetic
texts of this time, that one is a bit stumped by their clichéd connotations. But in the age of Shah Jahan, these images gained subtler and
more complex meanings.

In contrast to European pastoral poetry, the Persianate ruler was a
gardener rather than a shepherd, a metaphor used for all the early Mughal rulers. In retreat in the deep valley of the mountainous region,

or even down in the plains, Shah Jahan's poets and historians could portray the emperor as tending the garden that was the vast empire, and Kashmir was the Arcadia, an unspoiled space, where the city and countryside blended harmoniously. This idea would be eclipsed by major historical events and then other literary trends by the end of his reign. Of course, from the vantage point of today's world, where the decades-long violent conflict in the region of Kashmir remains unresolved, and there are deep wounds that Kashmiris of all faiths have sustained, the idea of the region as Arcadia is fraught with irony. But the literary and historical realities of the seventeenth century were quite different.

THE ROAD TO KASHMIR

During his thirty-year reign, Shah Jahan made four trips to Kashmir: in 1634, 1640, 1645, and 1651; fewer than his father, but all of them were ceremonial and included a large part of the imperial household. The trip during the summer of 1634 took place three years after the death of his beloved wife Mumtaz Mahal when Kashmir would have been the ideal change of scene for the grieving husband. A painting from a Mughal album shows Shah Jahan inspecting jewels on a terrace by Dal Lake in Srinagar (see Figure 5). The emperor and his four attendants are all dressed in white, perhaps still in mourning for the empress, but the color also reflects the pristine quality of the Kashmiri landscape in the background with the lake, boats, inhabitation, and mountains. The court poets were in turn occupied with transferring this tranquil experience to the verbal form.

Among the hundreds of courtiers, attendants, and family members who accompanied Shah Jahan were the two poets Kalim and Qudsi, who would in all certainty have been visiting the province for the first time. The two senior court poets were aware of Shah Jahan's interest in poetry about places and the way that imperial cities provided the backdrop for the staging of some of the court's most important rituals. They would also have known of the earlier writings on Kashmir in Persian, in prose works by Mirza Dughlat, Abu'l-Fazl, and Farishta, who had all mentioned the bucolic quality of the

FIGURE 5 Shah Jahan examines jewels by Dal Lake

countryside with all urban features virtually absent. They would also have been aware of poems by Faizi, 'Urfi, and Talib. Following in their footsteps was one of Shah Jahan's secretary-poets, Chandarbhan Brahman, who in his *Chahar chaman* (Four meadows) lists the different provinces of the empire with short descriptions of each one.[14] He has the following to say about Kashmir:

> Kashmir is one of the charming and enticing provinces with a pleasant climate. This land reigns over others due to its gardens. It can be called a second paradise because of its paradisiacal gardens, lovely buildings, wide meadows, flowing waters, pleasing leisure spots, and lush fields full of greenery, herbs, variety of flowers and all kinds of fine and special qualities. Although the extremely difficult crossing of the stations on this path involves tall sky-reaching mountains, and the bird of the imagination cannot unfurl the wings of its desire around them, a trip to paradisiacal Kashmir and viewing its gladdening atmosphere and experiencing its gentle climate removes the rust from the heart.[15]

Although there are distinct poetic features in Chandarbhan's prose, it is also clear from his tone that he is writing about a real place. Not only would he have visited the place but he would have witnessed an over two-decades-long phenomenon of composing poems about the beauties of the valley.

The poet laureate Kalim initiated the fad of writing poems about Kashmir at Shah Jahan's court. Kalim's polished verses make up a rhapsodic paean to the distinct place of the valley compared to the rest of the subcontinent. Similar to his Agra poem, he begins this *masnavi* with the epiphany that Kashmir is more than a garden: "I spoke in error; not just a fragrant garden or rose garden, it is the abode of spring, a place of beauties, a paradise" (*ghalat guftam—chi bustan u chi gulzar / baharistan, nigaristan, iram-zar*).[16] The climate here is its most enticing feature, with no sign of the hot summer of the plains, and the clouds in the sky like a lover roaming in his beloved's lane. The topography of this land is so unique that it is garden, sea, and city all at once. Kashmir refers to both the province and city:

"Few cities such as this are seen in the world that are garden, sea and city" (*buvad zin guna dar afaq kam shahr / ki ham bagh hast u ham darya u ham shahr*). This is a deliberate and harmonious blurring of the division between the urban and rural binary. The sea of course refers collectively to the various lakes, streams, and rivers around Srinagar.

Employing intricate puns and rhetorical figures, Kalim takes note of the two main bodies of water here: the Bahat (Jhelum river), like the Nile, and the other Dal Lake, make one's heart (*dil*) restless. He then invites the reader to take a ride on the water, as he had done in his Agra poem: "Come for a trip on the Dal, what's a rose garden? Collect flowers on a boat, what's a skirt?" (*bi-sair-i Dal biya, gulshan chi bashad? / bi-kishti gul bibar, daman chi bashad?*). As Kalim becomes the guide on the boat, he is struck by the fact that this is a garden of paradise on a green sea. The lotuses on the water (*kaval*) are like the lips of a beloved red with chewing *pan* and plucking them is like applying henna to one's hands.

Specific sites that are visible from the lake are pointed out: Takht-i Sulaiman (Solomon's Throne is the hill where the Shankaracharya temple is located), the gardens of Bahrara, 'Aishabad, Farahbakhsh (Shalimar), Hari with its avenue of *chinar, bid, majnun,* and *safida* trees, the royal canal, and the Nishat garden with its lofty buildings that match the mountains behind it and its nine fountains. At one point Kalim notes that with so many gardens in this country, which one should he be the nightingale for in his praise! Nature here is all contained within the limits of the city and lives in harmony with man-made architecture. It is both wild and cultivated.

The last quarter of the poem is a panegyric to Shah Jahan who is praised for his just rule and his support for upholding Islam in India. He is the "refuge of the seven climes" (*panah-i haft kishvar*) for those who have given up hope; he takes the hand of those who have been knocked over by fate. Kashmir is only a patch in the garden of his temperament, while the fingers of his hand are the five rivers of Punjab that irrigate the world. Kalim ends with a benediction on Kashmir:

bi-khubi ta shavad Kashmir mazkur / bi-'alam nam-i nikash bad mashhur
kunad daryuza kuh-i Pir Panjal / zi chatr-i daulatash rif'at hama sal

As long as Kashmir is mentioned with good words, may it be renowned in the world.
The Pir Panjal mountain begs that in its shade, Kashmir's fortune be
exalted all year.

With this reference to the mountain range in the last line, the poet
leads the reader on the way back to Hindustan. In using the template
of the city poem on Agra, Kalim makes equivalences between different parts of the empire, urban and rural, at the same time paying
attention to topographical specificities of different places. Together
these spaces allow the professional panegyrist to showcase the
Mughal Empire's diversity and vastness. Kalim's poem is carefully
crafted, especially when one keeps in mind that he is performing his
role as poet laureate not just for the court but also the larger Persianate world. Kalim's poem was such a success that almost every
major poet in Shah Jahan's reign who came from Safavid Iran wrote
a similar work on the province.

The Kashmir poem by Qudsi, the other senior poet at Shah Jahan's court, contrasts with Kalim's but also complements it in several
ways. Qudsi's narrative is longer and more conventional in form.[17]
The court chronicler 'Abdu'l-Hamid Lahauri mentions Qudsi as composing poetry while on the court's 1634 trip to the valley. Qudsi
begins and ends with eulogizing the emperor whose entrance into
the province is like the coming of spring to a rose garden, and with
prayers for the success of his poem so that it can remain evergreen
like Kashmir. For him, the valley is a paradise nestled in a rocky citadel that is difficult to reach. A section in the poem on the "Difficulties of the way to Kashmir and the Pir Panjal mountain range" shares
the experience of the arduous journey with his readers. Scaling the
dizzying heights of the formidable barrier of the mountain range is a
daunting experience that brings a person close to the skies, although
many have also plunged to their deaths below. At the end of the long
hike, one comes upon a heaven on Earth. The journey itself becomes
part of the quest for this paradise. At the end of the tour of Kashmir,
Qudsi brings us back to the Pir Panjal pass, ready to cross over into
the Punjab plains.

In terms of poetics, Qudsi's poem uses several devices effectively, although his description of the topography is entirely an exercise in rhetorical skills with stock, and oftentimes tedious, metaphors. Throughout the poem, Qudsi assembles a catalogue of places in the Islamic world to which Kashmir matches up in every respect. Its superiority in climate is acknowledged by places such as Khurasan, 'Iraq, Isfahan, Azarbaijan, Shiraz, Syria, Egypt, and the Hijaz, the presence of water year round puts the Iranian desert cities such as Yazd and Kashan to shame, its apples outshine those of Samarqand and Isfahan, the mountains around it are taller than Alvand and Damavand in Iran. Unlike Kalim, he does not remain in Srinagar looking at the city's sites from Dal Lake, but gives us a grand tour of various sites in and around the city, often alluding to figures from the Perso-Islamic classical tradition to make his point. He finds Farahbakhsh garden, the earlier section of the Shalimar complex, to be superior to the others, just as the young and handsome Yusuf was the best among his brothers. Crossing the Pir Panjal is like being Farhad, the ardent lover of Shirin. Among the gardens mentioned are Farahbakhsh and Faizbakhsh that form the Shalimar, Shahzada, Nishat, Jahanara, Sadiqabad, Nasim and 'Aishabad, Ilahi, Nur, Bahrara. The lake at Safapur, known for its lotus pond, is inhabited by nymphlike fair beauties on boats. In the gardens of Achval and Verinag, fed by natural springs, he mentions Sikandar and Khizr in the search for the water of life. Begumabad, Asafabad, and Koh-i Maran are also included in his list of places to be visited.

The clever use in multiple contexts of all the words connoting paradise, *bihisht, firdaus, jinan, Iram, rizvan,* and *khuld,* show Qudsi to be a master poet who is in control of his language. Whenever water is mentioned there are references to the fountains of paradise or holy springs, *zamzam, tasnim,* and *kausar,* while boats on the lake are the peacocks of paradise. Using a relatively novel image in Persian poetry, near the end of the poem Qudsi declares that if one day he found himself here again, he would use spectacles (*'ainak*) to view the landscape! The Kashmiri shawl is also an unusual image that he picks up from the local culture. Given their fine achievement, both Qudsi and Kalim provided a new context for poetry on Kashmir in epics written for Shah Jahan.

Both Kalim and Qudsi in their capacity as the chief poets at court wrote epics on the model of Firdausi's *Shahnama* that are known by various grand titles, *Padshahnama, Shahanshahnama,* and *Shahjahan-nama*.[18] It was a common practice among the Timurids, and to some extent among the Safavids and Mughals as well, for kings to have their court poets compose epics with themselves as the heroes. Poems were produced for the Safavid rulers Shah Isma'il and Shah 'Abbas I, although the Mughals had preferred the autobiography and biography mode of recording life history. The *Timurnama* by the poet Hatifi was an epic on the legendary founder of this dynastic house and enjoyed great popularity. Such works overlapped several traditions and were the result of the synthesis of a literary tradition marked by a high degree of intertextuality. Poets wrote in various poetic forms and experimented with mixing genres. Like the Safavids, Ottoman verse histories also flourished earlier than they did with the Mughals, the fifteenth and sixteenth centuries being the great age for this type of writing, and significantly, Iranian émigrés played an important role in this endeavor.[19]

The significance of including accounts of Shah Jahan's trips to Kashmir and a description of the Mughal monuments in the valley is obvious in the broader context of the emperor's life and deeds. Mughal presence in Kashmir marked the apex of Shah Jahan's power, the attainment of a physical paradise that was merely a metaphor in the urban setting. The difficult path to the valley and visiting its ordered gardens became an allegory for the Mughal achievement in both the cultural and political spheres. Kalim also praises Agra and Lahore, and as in Qudsi's narrative, his work includes a section in praise of Kashmir. These portions in both epics were reworked or in some cases directly taken from independent poems in their *divan*s, including the *masnavi*s that they composed. Especially in the case of Kalim, writing such an ambitious work in his twilight years in Kashmir, he would have gone through the output of a lifetime to reuse material for a mosaic of Shah Jahan's life and career.

It is not possible to date the Kashmir poems that were written by other poets of this period, but given the historical context and the time when these men were active, they were written during or around Shah Jahan's trips to the valley. The poet Salim Tihrani had spent the best years of his professional life in Bengal and not in the central court, so perhaps the story that he had written his poem on Lahijan in Iran, which he then changed to Kashmir, was true after all. He may have accompanied the imperial court there in 1640 or 1645, for he died in 1647. In any case, in his fine description of the difficult road to Kashmir, which Salim cleverly likens to the night journey (*mi'raj*) of the Prophet Muhammad,[20] he employs a multiple array of images to build up the scene:

rahi bar inchunin kuh-i durushti / bi-ham pichida mar u sang-pushti
rahi pichida hamchun qufl-i vasvas / mashaqqat-khiz chun ayam-i iflas
rahi bar pa-yi dil zanjir-i anduh / rahi hamchun sida pichida dark kuh
rahi az zulf-i khuban pichash-afzun / azin rah gashta kaj-raftar gardun

A path across such a harsh mountain;
A snake and tortoise all twisted together.
A winding path like lock of temptation,
Causing hardship in a time of penury.
A path that shackles the heart like an ankle,
A path like a sound echoing in the hills.
A path like the curls of beautiful creatures,
Fate is off course because of this path.

Salim's metaphors convey well the dizzying experience of travel through the mountains. About the place of Kashmir within the empire he declares: "The beauty of Hindustan is the rose garden of brilliance; upon it, Kashmir is Laila's beauty mark" (*jamal-i Hind gulzar-i tajalli ast / bar-u Kashmir khal-i sabz-i Laili ast*). And individuals are like trees:

chinar u sarv u bid azadagan and / tuhi dastan-i bagh u bustan and
sanubar niz az sahib-dilan ast / 'alamdar-i saff-i bi-hasilan ast

Noble plane trees, cypresses and willows,
are empty-handed in the gardens and orchards.

The pines are like the mystics,
staff bearers of the unattached.

Salim's description of Kashmir though not completely free of the traditional imagery of gardens is truly bucolic. He is also conscious of the historical cultivation of the province by the Mughals, as when he narrates hearing about Jahangir first falling in love with the place, and how it became his beloved for whom he died, perhaps referring to the emperor's death on the Mughal road. Kashmir blossomed with the presence of the emperor who stumbled upon the spot that would become the Shalimar garden. Shah Jahan was a young prince then and in turn strove to complete his father's vision.

Descriptions of Kashmir are also found in poems that are not solely on the beauties of the valley, such as the verse travelogues of the poets from Iran, Bihishti Hirati and Salik Qazvini, in which their Persianate peregrinations in Iran and India culminated in Kashmir. Bihishti's description of Kashmir comes after that of Hindustan and like it is succinct and includes the usual topographical highlights, each deserving just a phrase or a couple of verses.[21] He says it was his fate that brought him here:

sali ki qaza bi-hukm-i yazdan / avard mara bi-Hind az Iran
zan rah kardam bi-bal-i taqdir / parvaz bi-sair-i khuld-i Kashmir[22]

The year that by God's command fate brought me from Iran to
   India,
I flew on the wings of fortune from there to visit the paradise of
   Kashmir.

Salik's descriptions of places are much more detailed and concrete. He also includes panegyrics to his accomplished compatriots Qudsi, Kalim, and Mir Ilahi, who all made their careers with the Mughals, and a personal and warm account of meeting Jalala Tabatabai, a retired historian from Shah Jahan's court. A section of his poem discusses the good and bad qualities of the local population in Kashmir. Refraining from the usual hyperbolic descriptions, he cautions in a philosophical vein:

Kashmir parivashist maghrur / afganda zi husn dar jahan shur
darad bad u nik u zisht u ziba / darad gul u khar u la'l u khara[23]

Kashmir is a conceited fay, whose beauty has captured the world.
It has bad and good, ugly and beautiful; it has roses and thorns,
    rubies and rocks.

He then set off for Multan with Prince Murad-bakhsh, the youngest son of Shah Jahan and Mumtaz Mahal. Kashmir was not the ultimate destination for some poets, but because it was a meeting place of princes, nobles, and poets, it was a place for networking where useful connections could be made, if one chose not to live there permanently.

A minor poet Sayyid 'Ali "Saidi" (his penname means "Prey") left an incomplete poem on Kashmir,[24] as well as three other short poems on the gardens of Sahibabad, Shalimar, and Faizabad. Saidi resided in India during the years 1653 to 1658, primarily enjoying the patronage of Shah Jahan and his favorite daughter Jahanara. In Iran he had written poems in praise of the Prime Minister Saru Taqi "I'timad al-daula" and his brother Mirza Qasim. Saidi's connection in India was Taqarrub Khan, a physician of Shah 'Abbas I who had arrived at the Mughal court in 1644, just in time to treat Princess Jahanara when she was badly burned in an accident.[25] Like many an Iranian who had come to Mughal India to make his fortune, Saidi died young in Delhi in his forties. Choosing brevity over what was becoming a verbose and florid genre, Saidi says: "Poetry describing Kashmir is out of place; shut your mouth here and open your eyes" (*sukhan dar vasf-i Kashmir ast bija / zaban inja biband u dida bugsha*). Yet, this does not seem to restrain Saidi from exercising his rhetorical skills. In one poem he transfers the Perso-Islamic mythical world and geography of Iran to praise Shah Jahan in Kashmir:

sar-i Zahhak zulm-afkanda-yi u / Faridun-i 'adalat banda-yi u
bi pish-i dushman-i Ya'juj lashkar / ghubar-i maukabash sadd-i Sikandar

Zahhak's head is one of his noble deeds;
Faridun is his slave in justice.
Before the inimical troops of Magog,
the dust raised by his mount is the wall of Alexander.

Zahhak was the evil Arab king in the Persian epic, *Shahnama*, who was dethroned by the heroic Faridun. Shah Jahan is thus even superior to this Persian hero. In the poem on the Sahibabad garden in Kashmir, belonging to Princess Jahanara, Saidi again praises Shah Jahan:

ki dargahash jahan ra qiblagah ast / khala'iq ra zi har afat panah ast
azin 'asl dirakht-i padshahi / ki sarsabz ast az lutf-i ilahi
chu paivandash bi-nakhli vajib amad / nukhustin miva begum sahib amad[26]

His court is the qibla of the world where people have refuge from
    every trouble.
From this origin the tree of kingship is lush due to God's kindness.
The best fruit from the garden of Shah Jahan was Begum sahib!

Begum sahib, as the poet's audience would have known, was the eldest daughter of the emperor, after whom the garden was named. Princess Jahanara had taken over as first lady after her mother's demise.

Although today we can only imagine the way the Kashmir poems would have been read, discussed, critiqued, and imitated by the poets of Shah Jahan's court, and then in the larger world of Persian literature, it is certain that they created an excitement that permeated other spheres of Mughal literary culture. Audrey Truschke discusses a short Sanskrit text on Kashmir by the poet Jagannatha that would have been written around the same time, in the 1630s.[27] The work, *Asaphavilasa* (Play of Asaf Khan), is a panegyric piece in mixed prose and poetry written in praise of the high-ranking officer and the Mumtaz Mahal's uncle Asaf Khan, who accompanied Shah Jahan to Kashmir. Jagannatha praises the beauty of the region and the Himalayas along with the virtues of his patron. Although it is unclear whether the subtleties of the composition were appreciated by Asaf Khan or other nobles, it was almost certainly composed in response to the Kashmir fad among the Persian court poets. This poem seems to be one of a kind, unlike the Persian ones that were part of a longer phenomenon, though others, whether in Sanskrit, Hindi, or even Kashmiri, may be uncovered at some point in the future.

ZAFAR KHAN'S KASHMIR

We return to Zafar Khan, who appeared earlier as the premier patron of poets only second to 'Abdur-Rahim Khankhanan. His association with Kashmir began when he was appointed governor of the province after his father's death in 1632. He spent a total of eleven years in two terms there, during which he left his mark on the history, if not on the actual landscape, of the valley. Unlike the monumental biography of 'Abdur-Rahim by Nihavandi, Zafar Khan's biographical account was written not by a contemporary of his, but almost a century after his death by a Mughal nobleman. The eighteenth-century biographer Shahnavaz Khan Samsam al-daula includes an entry of a few pages on Zafar Khan. Although he would not have known his subject personally, as Nihavandi had done with his, given that both families had connections with Lahore would have meant that Zafar Khan and his family still had some local renown. Shahnavaz Khan writes, "Zafar Khan would give gold to the people from Iran, he showed special generosity towards poets. Talented poets left their homeland and arrived at his court with great hopes where their desires would be fulfilled."[28] There is no record of Zafar Khan's knowledge of or any engagement with poetry in any languages other than Persian, whether in Kashmiri or any variety of Hindi, but he did compose some fine poetry in Persian. He left a *divan* of *ghazals* and three *masnavis* on Kashmir-related themes. A trope that all the poets writing on Kashmir had in common was an account of the difficult journey to the province, the valley's magnificent architecture, gardens, and pristine countryside. Beyond that the more creative poets tried to do something a little bit different that would distinguish their poems. Given his personal connection to the province,

Zafar Khan's *masnavi*s on Kashmir are strikingly innovative and unique in this regard.

In his eighteenth regnal year, on May 14, 1645, the Mughal emperor Shah Jahan returned to the province of Kashmir, where he was graciously received by the governor, Zafar Khan, in his residence garden.[29] In recognition for his positive contribution to life in the valley, the emperor honored him by increasing his rank by 1,000 horse. Shahnavaz Khan records that Zafar Khan had made an autograph album with a selection of the poems of every poet connected with him, along with their portraits.[30] This book, if it ever existed, is probably lost, but we are fortunate that a lavishly produced manuscript of Zafar Khan's Kashmir poems did survive, which includes several paintings depicting his life in Kashmir, one of which we have seen already (Figure 1).

The manuscript with the *masnaviyat* of Zafar Khan (Persian 310) was housed in the Royal Asiatic Society in London in the nineteenth century and recently moved to the University of Cambridge.[31] It is in fact an autograph manuscript that includes five double-paged paintings and two others that were also originally next to each other but were separated at some point. We learn from an inscription in the manuscript that they were done by the Mughal painter Bishandas.[32]

Scholars have concentrated on these paintings and remarked on the slim connection between them and the text, such as Ralph Pinder-Wilson's comment: "The Zafar Khan manuscript is a personal record of the life of a cultured amir in the reign of Shah Jahan. There is the slenderest connection between miniature and verse."[33] But the manuscript taken as a whole allows us to explore several important issues connected to seventeenth-century Mughal culture, centering on Zafar Khan's relationship to the province he governed and how certain historical circumstances led to its production. The manuscript includes three loosely connected *masnavi*s by Zafar Khan, each one describing a different aspect of his life in Kashmir. These poems may have been written at different periods of his residence there and compiled as a single manuscript over an extended period of time. In a short introduction to the first poem, Zafar Khan states that it was written when Shah Jahan was in residence in Kashmir in the twelfth year of his accession, (i.e., in 1640), and he had invited his poets to write poems about Kashmir. Zafar Khan naturally employed the same poetic language that the court poets of the time did, but the overall structure of his poems reveals a more complex relationship to the place.

The first poem, *Jalva-yi naz* (Display of airs),[34] begins with the conventional preliminary sections that are found in long poems, praise of God, the Prophet Muhammad and his night journey (*mi'raj*), Hazrat 'Ali, which marks Zafar Khan as Shia, followed by a panegyric to Shah Jahan's just rule. The first painting is found in this section of the poem. It shows Shah Jahan and his sons on the terrace of a building on the banks of the Jumna in discussion with some nobles, including Zafar Khan. The background landscape shows that the poet-governor is still in the plains, which gives him an opportunity to praise Hindustan and Shah Jahan's capital, Akbarabad, though Zafar Khan states that he welcomes the imminent journey because the flowers on the wall of the palace there remind him of Kashmir.

Drawing on the tradition of describing the positive qualities, *faza'il*, of India and Delhi, the poet praises the virtues of Hindustan, including the monsoon season, which is really the local spring. As the poet takes us through the streets of Agra, he pauses to gaze at the young men from certain professional and social groups: *bazzaz* (cloth seller), *tanboli* (pan seller), *baqqal* (grocer), *'attar* (perfume seller), Brahman, Afghan, Rajput, and *shaikhzada*. This collocation of people is remarkably similar to the one in Kalim's Agra poem, which Zafar Khan would have read and admired, and also perhaps 'Abdur-Rahim's *Nagar-shobha* poem on women of the city. As he goes on to describe an assembly that includes song and dance performances, Zafar Khan is taken by the dusky beauties (*gandumgun sabzan*) who outrank the fair creatures of Iran and China, and the enchanting setting: "The aged world has not seen anything like India where *one* of its gardens is the orchard of Kashmir" (*chu Hindustan nadida 'alam-i pir / ki yak baghash buvad bustan-i Kashmir*), his point being that as enchanting as Kashmir may be, it is only one of the wonderful places to be found in the empire.

Zafar Khan then moves into the requisite ethnographic mode and provides several lists that especially represent the diversity of India, as Babur had done over a century before, to dazzle audiences across the Persianate world with the richness of Indian life. In the description of the music and poetry session mentioned earlier, various instruments such as the *rubab, tanbur, bansuri, kamancha,* and *pakhavaj* are named; among the luscious fruits found here are *ananas, kamrak, narangi, limu, falsa, anba, amritphal, kela,* and *naishikar;* the flowers of the land include *champa, maulsri, keora, juhi, jahi, kachnar, ja'fari, karhal;* among the birds are the *tuti, maina, koyal,* and of course, the diva of the Persian garden, the *bulbul* (nightingale).

The next stop in Lahore, whose atmosphere is reminiscent of Khurasan and 'Iraq, takes us directly on to the difficult road to Kashmir. The second painting, a double-page production, shows preparations for the journey to be in full swing (see Figure 6). The mountains and boats indicate that the huge party is getting close to its destination. Zafar Khan does not wax long on the difficulties of the path to the valley, and we find ourselves in the valley rather suddenly. Here the scene presents itself to the reader in all its beauty. The geography of the sites around Srignar are familiar to readers of these poems: Dal Lake, with its lotuses and the various gardens, is described briefly. The Farahbakhsh garden is where we are made to stop and admire the orchard and the architecture. The garden depicted in a painting in this section of the manuscript may be the renowned Nishat Bagh. A catalogue of fruits highlights the tempting offerings of Kashmir's orchards: *shah-alu, alubalu, sib, amrud, nashpati, shaftalu, anar, pista,* and *badam.* Not only are these in contrast to the fruits that were seen in the plains, but they are closer to what would be found in the Iranian world. Also mentioned here is the Nasim Bagh, which then makes Zafar Khan think in a nostalgic vein of the lovely Jahanara and Afzalabad gardens in Kabul.

After viewing all the Mughal sites of imperial grandeur, we arrive at Zafar Khan's garden-palace, Zafarabad, which he constructed in a relatively short time.[35] Paintings of flowers adorn the walls, birds warble in the garden, fish sport in the pond, and his drinking companion and a favorite companion is a young barber (*hajjam*). The poet assures the reader that this is a purely Platonic relationship (*havas ra nist ba man ashna'i*). So lovely is this arboreal abode that he declares: "Our Zafarabad is no less than paradise—there is no such bounteous garden in the world" (*Zafarabad-i ma kam az jinan nist/chunin pur-faiz baghi dar jahan nist*). The setting for the next painting, which is a representation of one of his assemblies (see Figure 1), would seem to be the interior of this residence. During his governorship the best of the literati of the time flocked there; these are names that have been encountered already: the poet laureate Kalim, Qudsi, Salim, Bihishti, Salik, and Munir, as well as two local poets, Fani and Ghani Kashmiri, the last two being more firmly enshrined in the local memory.[36] Zafar Khan was said to have been fond of *musha'ira*s and the richly arrayed courtly assembly with the poets seated before him, along with other courtiers, musicians, and the veteran artist Bishandas himself is a testimony to the lively atmosphere he created there. The ethnomusicologist Bonnie Wade has described this painting as "extremely important for several musical historical reasons, including the depiction of a remarkably Persianate ensemble in the period of Shah Jahan."[37] Various musical instruments such as the *na'i, ghichak* (long-necked lute), *da'ira,* and *qanun* are found together. Through a window we also get a glimpse into the pristine Kashmiri landscape outside.

The following section is reserved for the praise of spring, and the painting in this section shows Zafar Khan in a natural setting in contrast to the indoor *majlis*. The occasion is an outdoor picnic livened up by musicians and, no doubt, poets. Men kneading dough and stirring food in a pot add an intimate tone to this scene. The rest of the poem takes on a more pastoral tone as Zafar Khan leads the reader on a tour of the sights outside Srinagar: the lake at Safapur, saffron fields of Avantipura, followed by the description of a natural waterfall that comes down from the mountains with superhuman force. The next painting accompanies the section in praise of the saffron season and various gardens.[38] The garden in the painting is Verinag, recognizable by its distinctive architecture, where both natural and man-made elements come together harmoniously (see Figure 7). The scene captures an elite gathering of the emperor Shah Jahan with

FIGURE 6 Preparations for a trip to Kashmir (above and opposite)

the crown prince Dara Shikoh and Zafar Khan in a garden setting. The artist wants the viewer to recognize the place and appreciate the uniqueness of this garden, rather than conjure up a generic ideal scene. This scene is similar to others that show Shah Jahan in urban settings, but here the backdrop is the natural world. The pond with its source in a natural spring connects the man-made structure to the landscape beyond. A school of goldfish sport in the water. The natural spring here was a sacred spot for local Hindus, and Verinag, the last stop in the valley, connects the Mughals to the most ancient layer of Kashmiri culture. At the end of the poem the scene suddenly shifts to Kabul and its lovely gardens, Shahrara and Jahanara, which recall one of the original homelands of the Mughals. The jump in Zafar Khan's itinerary is a fitting reminder of the connectedness of parts of the empire, which together form a mosaic of his life. The haunts in Kashmir may have been a brief part of his illustrious life but they were significant nonetheless.

The remainder of the manuscript has no paintings, nor was the decoration of all the folios completed. The second poem in the trilogy, *Maikhana-yi raz* (Tavern of secrets), is introspective in tone and less about the physical world around the poet.[39] Zafar Khan repeatedly addresses the metaphoric *saqi* as his interlocutor. Railing against ascetics of hypocritical bent, he celebrates the culture of drinking wine. After a short general description of the beauty of the Kashmiri landscape, he ruminates on the change of seasons, the sadness of autumn, and the harshness of winter. But it is sitting around with friends drinking wine at night that makes life pleasurable. Then he can say: "Kashmir is a paradise and I am its gatekeeper; I am the poet of every rose, like the nightingale" (*bihisht ast Kashmir u rizvan manam / bihar gul chu bulbul ghazal-khvan manam*). In the summer he goes to the *hammam*, where the luminous body of his young *hajjam* friend puts the mirror to shame and even makes the water drunk. Nearing the end of the poem, Zafar Khan reflects on the virtues of contentment and expresses a desire to visit the holy stone Kaba in Mecca. In conclusion, he discusses the art of poetry, confesses how he struggled to write this poem for six months and was inspired by the master Persian poet of the Deccan, Zuhuri, who was the first early modern Indo-Persian poet to write a poem on a topographical theme.

The third *masnavi* in Zafar Khan's work, *Haft manzil* (Seven stages), is a guide to seven stops on the way back to the Pir Panjal pass, a poetic but also practical description of the arduous and picturesque Mughal Road.[40] But before leaving the valley, there is another round of the sites that visitors will remember so fondly once they quit this Shangri-La. The gardens are mentioned again as Zafar Khan returns to the Dal Lake and its boats, the Shalimar Bagh, a dozen other gardens, including one called Sadiqabad, better known as Hazrat Bal today. Then he begins the return journey south, from the saffron fields of Pampore, Avantipora, Islamabad (also known as Anantnag), Machbavan, Sahibabad, Aurangabad, Verinag, right up to Hirapur, before crossing over back to the plains.[41]

The colophon in this manuscript states that the work was completed on 26 Zu'l-Hija 1073 (August 1, 1663) at the capital Lahore, by Ahsanullah Zafar Khan, son of Abu'l-Hasan. By this time, years after his governorship of Kashmir, the world of the Mughals had changed: the emperor Shah Jahan was incarcerated by his son the new emperor, Aurangzeb, who ruled as 'Alamgir. Zafar Khan had actually sided with the loser in the bloody war of succession, the crown prince Dara Shikoh, but managed to survive in retirement. Another inscription, by Zafar Khan's son, 'Inayat Khan "Ashna," the superintendent (*darogha*) of the library and author of one of the prose chronicles of Shah Jahan's reign, the *Shahjahannama*, is dated four years later: "Poems by my late father in his hand, on 14th Zu'l-Hija 1077 [June 6, 1667] in the pleasure house (*'ishratkada*) of Kashmir, illustrated by my father's servant Bishandas." A third inscription reveals that the manuscript was sold by his heirs in 1089 [1679], about eight years after his son's death. Were the heirs in such reduced circumstances that they allowed such a precious manuscript to leave their possession? Nothing is known of the intervening history of this object until 1834 when it appeared in the collection of the Royal Asiatic Society in London.

In contrast with some of the other court poets who also wrote poems on Kashmir to display their virtuosity, it is clear that Zafar Khan's poems are not a mere performance for a literary readership, rather they are heartfelt paeans to a place that he was deeply attached to and that was also linked with other parts of the empire that he

FIGURE 7 Verinag Garden (above and opposite)

knew. His poetry marks a departure from the way that Kashmir was represented in court poetry, from a distinctly ceremonial mode to a personal one. Zafar Khan's Kashmir book is thus a somewhat unique object that is both an individual's attachment to a place but also his loyalty to the success of an empire and literary culture. Zafar Khan enshrined the Kashmir that he administered and loved in the text and images of this richly illustrated manuscript, bringing words and paintings in dialogue with each other.

A generation earlier 'Abdur-Rahim Khankhanan did not produce anything similar to this manuscript. His contribution to the arts was evident in his Hindi verses that live on in an oral context of the vernacular sphere and in the works of the poets and artists who benefited from his patronage. As a patron, unlike Zafar Khan who created a salubrious colony for Persian poets in the Kashmir valley, 'Abdur-Rahim built his own mini-empire with an extensive network of people on a transregional level, creating a vibrant multilingual literary culture in an important part of the Persianate world. The lives of these two men are a contrast in how the first generation of émigrés became Mughals in the grandest sense and actively shaped the way that literature was produced and performed in their respective cultural spheres. Mostly living in the Persianate environment of Kashmir, Kabul and Lahore, Zafar Khan's literary engagement seemed to be exclusively Persian, while in 'Abdur-Rahim Khankhanan's milieu, Hindi, Dakhni, and other literary traditions were strong as well. What the two men had in common was a strong attachment to the places they administered, leaving behind traces of their cultural legacy in works of architecture, poetry, and painting.

Further exploration into the personalities and literary activities of other Mughal administrators in the provinces—and there were others—will lead to a deeper understanding of the cultural history of the period, though not many will be able to match up to men such as 'Abdur-Rahim and Zafar Khan in the range of their works and patronage. In his three poems, Zafar Khan dealt with all the main motifs found in the various Kashmir poems of this period: the preparations and journey, arrival in the valley, description of the *faza'il* of different places; the pastoral theme with an excursus on both nature and his relaxed lifestyle; and the stations on the Mughal Road. In these *masnavi*s we get the fullest experience of what Kashmir had become for many people in the reign of Shah Jahan. In this sense, the Persian literary texts of this period were unique creations.

FROM KASHMIR TO BENGAL

Poets of ethnic Indian background under Shah Jahan wrote about Kashmir using the same literary devices as their more esteemed colleagues of Iranian stock, but like Zafar Khan they brought a personal element into an imperial narrative. We encountered the young poet Munir Lahauri earlier, who wrote candidly about being marginalized as an Indian in the literary circles of his time. Munir's short career took him to Kashmir, among other places in the empire. In 1635 he entered the service of Mirza Safi Saif Khan, governor of Agra and brother-in-law of Empress Mumtaz Mahal. After his patron's death in 1639, Munir joined the court of I'tiqad Khan Shapur Mirza, the governor of Jaunpur, who was the brother of the dowager empress, Nur Jahan and uncle of Mumtaz Mahal. Munir soon returned to Agra where he died in 1644 at the age of thirty-four. It is not entirely clear when Munir was in Kashmir, but it is clear that a visit there had left a deep impression on him. If the dark-skinned poet in the painting of Zafar Khan's assembly really was Munir, then he would have been in the valley during his governorship. Having found the atmosphere at court and society in general oppressive for poets of non-Iranian origin, the extended time away from the imperial centers would have been liberating for the poet from Lahore.

Munir's Kashmir poem, called *Masnavi-yi bahar-i javid* (Poem of eternal spring),[42] is a long work comprising 1,337 lines. It shows clear influences of the poems by Kalim and Qudsi, as well as a familiarity with other Kashmir poets. The title of his work is the same phrase that both Abu'l-Fazl and Jahangir used to describe the land of Kashmir: "eternal spring." *Bahar-i javid* is dedicated to I'tiqad Khan, who had served as governor of the province at the end of Jahangir's and beginning of Shah Jahan's reigns. In the prefatory section, where he describes the reason for the composition of this work, Munir uses a poetic convention to explain that once in the season of spring he was sitting despondently in his home when an ethereal creature (*dil-ruba, parizad*) visited him. After expressing appreciation for his talents as a poet, she urged him to write a poem following the examples of Qudsi, Kalim, Ilahi, and Salim. Munir agreed and became the one to fashion a bouquet of verses on Kashmir (*guldasta-band-i vasf-i Kashmir*). He also states early on that in the poem he has described the gardens, mountains, and city (*numudam husn-i bagh u shahr-i ura / sutudam dasht u kuh u bahr-i ura*), bringing all these places together under his poetic gaze.

Beginning with praises for the paradise-like quality of Kashmir, Munir describes the city of Kashmir (i.e., Srinagar) as the envy of the great Persianate cities Isfahan, Shiraz, Kabul, and Constantinople. The poet notes that every street of this city is filled with beautiful people (*bi-har kucha-yi nigar-parvar / ki bi-shikasta kalla az naz bar sar*). In order to show this, as Kalim had done before him in his Agra poem, he goes on to list a series of professionals engaged in different occupations who represent the best qualities of the city. But his eye takes in a different group of people from that of Kalim or Zafar Khan: here we find a *bazdar* (falconer), *kamangar* (archer), *najjar* (carpenter), *bazzaz* (cloth-seller), *sarban* (camel driver), *murdashuy* (washer of corpses), and *saqqa* (water-carrier). Although none of these professions are exclusive to Kashmir, it appears that Munir deliberately did not repeat any of the types found in earlier poems.

Munir launches into the natural beauty of the province, its cold but invigorating climate and charming wooden houses, even playing with an extended pun about various musical instruments in harmony with the bodies of water. In terms of the geographical topography of the province, the impressive Pir Panjal range is next on his list, followed by specific mountains such as Koh-i Maran, also known as Hari Parbat, which in their loftiness are reminiscent of a city rather than a village (*ki shahri hast nabuvad rustay*). Kashmir is proud of this bounty and the world is exalted next to it. After the mountains, Munir describes the flowers and lakes of the valley. The endless beds of unnamed flowers on land and water are likened to army troops. The water lily or lotus (*kaval*) is his particular favorite, and the riot of color on the surface of the lake makes him think that it has chewed *pan,* the betel leaf that stains the mouth. The boats on the lake are described next and compared to waterfowl, who are in a precarious state because they must bear the weight of the handsome boatmen. Even as Munir's gaze wanders around, he focuses back to the courtly aspects of the topography.

The chief imperial gardens feature on Munir's list of Mughal courtly locales in and around Srinagar. His first choice is not surprisingly the Shalimar garden, then Farahbakhsh with its flowers, Nishat with its fruits, Bahrara with its chinar trees, followed by a description of 'Aishabad. The avenues in the gardens make him think of streets (*khiyaban*) in a city, and he also uses the bazaar metaphor for the thick foliage. Munir generally does not describe the buildings in these gardens, only picking out natural formations to bestow praise on. This is in contrast to a poet such as Kalim who never failed to mention a city's architectural features. A saffron field and the Shalimar *shah-nahr* canal, along with some verses on a fountain and waterfall complete the picturesque features of the landscape. The Takht-i Sulaiman hill in the southeast of Srinagar also draws praise from him. Sindh Brari—the Sindh Valley in the north of Srinagar that leads to the Zojila pass en route to Central Asia and where the renowned Sonamarg (Golden meadow) is located—is the last item on his list of features. In the end, Munir compares his verses to a cypress in a garden and the lines in his notebook to an avenue. He exclaims in ecstasy, "There are a hundred tulip beds in the garden of poetry; it is spring, it is spring, it is spring" (*bi-gulzar-i sukhan sad lalazar ast / bahar ast u bahar ast u bahar ast*), being reminiscent of the oft-quoted line about paradise being here and now. Whereas Kalim had ended his poem with the Pir Panjal mountain range, Munir takes us to the northernmost limits of the empire where he also seems to realize the limits of his own talent. In his Kashmir poem, Munir strives to distinguish himself from the other, more venerable, poets, and his excitement in his experience of the valley comes through even as he remains within the parameters of the courtly poetic form.

Munir had to travel much further away from the imperial centers to compose an entirely original topographical poem. His poem on the province of Bengal, located on the eastern boundary of the empire, was actually completed before the Kashmir one. This is his best remembered work and is known by the title *Mazhar-i gul* (Manifestation of the rose) or *Masnavi dar sifat-i Bangala* (Poem on the description of Bengal).[43] Munir informs us that it was composed in a fortnight in 1639 and was dedicated to his patron Saif Khan, who died soon after. It is in effect a travelogue of an exciting and at times perilous trip down the river Ganges, from Patna into Bengal. He praises the dark-skinned boatman who skillfully steers the craft. Annoyances such as mosquitoes out on the open boat only add a realistic touch to the narrative. When they finally arrive in Bengal, Munir feels he has entered a different world:

bihishti didam az gulha nigarin / gulash chu chihra-yi huran baharin . . .
bi-nau'i pur zi sabza in diyar ast / ki shahr-i sabz az vay sharmsar ast

I saw a paradise of lovely flowers; spring flowers like the faces of
   houris.
This land is filled with foliage so that the Green City is ashamed
   before it.

The Green City could refer to Kish, where Timur was born and thus revered by the Mughals, or to any place that never sees autumn.

In his most poetic sections, the flora of Bengal is more that of the classical Persian garden, but later Munir lists the local flora, fauna, and climate in exuberant but more ethnographic tones, in the same way that Babur, Zafar Khan, and others had done for India or Kashmir. He is struck by the geography of the landscape around him, "What do I say about that bounteous land? It has put the water there to shame" (*chi guyam zan zamin-i faiz-gustar / ki ab az sharm-i khak-i u shud tar*), and is completely taken by the lush greenery both on land and water (*chunan bar ab sabza ashkara ast / ki darya dar haqiqat sabzazar ast*). In fact, as much of the landscape is described from the vantage point of the river, his extensive description of the waters is liberating for him coming from the confines of the landmass. Munir's catalogues and praise of around thirty-five kinds of flowers, eleven varieties of fruits (*nariyal, naishikar, anba, kela, ananas, falsa,* among others), and several species of animals and birds (*fil, kargadan, tuti, gav-mish, maina*) is a kaleidoscopic display of poetic ethnography.

From the flora and fauna, Munir turns to the climate of the region, describing the force of the monsoon season, the winds, the extreme heat—the only three things that his patron informs him are found here (*ab u atish u bad*). Munir sums up his appreciation for the Bengal landscape by declaring, "Everywhere you look there is lush greenery; there is spring, there is spring, there is spring" (*har janib ki bini sabzazar ast / bahar ast u bahar ast u bahar ast*), employing the thrice repeated phrase that we read in his Kashmir poem. Whereas Kashmir was physically more similar to the ideal Persian garden, and Bengal represented nature in its pristine state despite its inclement climate, both places are characterized by an abundance of water and vegetation. Ultimately, for the peripatetic poet, both these regions are in contrast to the life experienced in the imperial capitals, which despite its pomp and magnificence is beset with court intrigues and petty rivalries between poets.

SUFI KASHMIR

Kashmir was not just celebrated by court poets who, with their various relationships to the land, had the expectation of a monetary reward for their efforts. Due to the long history of Sufism in the valley and because of the presence of living mystics, it also found a place in the Sufi literature of the Shah Jahan period. The emperor's two eldest children, Princess Jahanara and Prince Dara Shikoh, followed his example and were committed patrons of the arts and learning. In their young years, both had authored works on Sufi topics themselves and were deeply immersed in the cause of various mystical orders. Dara Shikoh, who met a tragic death in the war of succession against his brothers, was a complicated person. According to the historian Munis Faruqui, he "enjoyed a sense of his own omnipotence, a certain spiritual exaltedness, and an entitlement to the Mughal throne ordained by God himself."[44] He is, not without reason, sometimes compared to his great-grandfather Akbar because of his interest in

Hinduism and attempts to use translation as a mechanism to bring the Indian and Perso-Islamic thought and learning into a sustained dialogue.[45] However, Dara Shikoh's life experience was very different from that of Akbar's, and the Mughal Empire was not the same in the mid-seventeenth century as it had been a century earlier when Akbar began his lifelong project of forging a Mughal cultural ethos. The art historian Linda Leach wrote, "Dara was a brittle, over-refined, somewhat unimaginative patron who valued superficial prettiness far too highly. As emperor his patronage might have broadened and matured with the increase in prestige as Jahangir's had done, but indications are that his personality was far less vivid and robust than his grandfather's."[46] This is contrary to the common "what if" view of South Asian history in some parts of Indian society. As it may have been, fate did deal him a cruel blow with an undignified death for him and his entire family. In his short life, the prince managed to create a congenial intellectual and literary community of men of letters around him. There were also two important women in his life: his wife Nadira Begum and his sister Jahanara, who were his companions in various literary and mystical pursuits.

Dara and Jahanara showed a greater zeal toward mysticism than was the practice for members of the imperial family. The Chishti order had a historical connection with the Mughal family members, who made frequent visits to the holy shrines at Ajmer, Delhi, and Fatehpur Sikri. In addition to continuing this profound devotion to the Chishtis, the siblings came in contact with the Qadiri order in Lahore, and due to that connection they became passionate followers of a mystic called Mulla Shah, who was also popularly known as Akhund Mulla. It was he who initiated them into the Qadiri order. This Sufi order was headed by Mian Mir until his death in 1635. Mian Mir was by all accounts a charismatic individual and his tomb in Lahore is a venerated spot in the city to this day. Mian Mir inhabited an area outside Lahore at a time when "suburban gardens were becoming spiritual centers, a dramatic departure from their almost exclusively dynastic functions up to that point."[47]

Dara, like most male members of the imperial Mughal family, also tried his hand at poetry. He wrote *ghazal*s in a simple style using the pen name Qadiri signifying his affiliation with the Sufi order. In the following verses he links the figure of Mian Mir with Lahore and Hindustan, microcosm and macrocosm for both a temporal and spiritual empire:

dil u janam fida-yi Miyan Mir / didan-i haqq liqa-yi Miyan Mir
dar rah-i faqr auliya-yi zaman / sharmsar-i ghina-yi Miyan Mir
digaran dar riza-yi haqq bashand / haqq buvad dar riza-yi Miyan Mir
bihtarin-i bilad Hindustan / shahr-i Lahaur ja-yi Miyan Mir[48]

My heart and life are sacrificed to Mian Mir, seeing the divine visage of Mian Mir.
The saints of the age in their poverty are ashamed of the wealth of Mian Mir.
Others seeks God's acceptance—the real is in the acceptance of Mian Mir.
Hindustan is the best land and Lahore is the abode of Mian Mir.

The refrain "Mian Mir" becomes a chant in this poem, inspiring the reader or reciter to experience a heightened emotion of pious devotion. Sufis were usually connected to a specific place, and here India and Lahore are attached to Mian Mir's name.

In another *ghazal* Dara declares: "Since the pir is my lord and master, Hazrat-i Kashmir is my Kaba" (*chun khuda u sahib-i man pir hast / ka'ba-yi man hazrat-i Kashmir ast*).[49] As the favorite son of Shah Jahan, Dara was given free rein to explore his spiritual interests. After his rather dismal military record—he led Mughal troops in a long drawn-out campaign to regain the fortress of Qandahar—Dara seems to have turned even more toward esoteric interests in the area of comparative religion. His dealings with yogis and Hindu scriptures date from the last few years of his life, including completing the Persian translation of the Sanskrit text, the *Upanashids*, the version through which Europe learned about this Hindu philosophical work.

Known by the respectful title of Begum Sahib, Jahanara participated in her brother's early spiritual quest to the fullest extent that she could as a princess with her own funds to spend on charity and building projects. After Gulbadan Begum, the sister of her great-great-grandfather Humayun, Jahanara was the second Mughal princess to have written something in Persian that has come down to us, although her works had a more modest circulation than those of her predecessor.[50] Jahanara authored two prose texts about her involvement with Sufi orders: *Munis al-arvah* (Confidant of spirits), the better known of the two, is a hagiographical history of the Chishti order, while the other work, which was less known and did not circulate widely, is a short account of her relationship to Mulla Shah with a biographical sketch.[51] Both works reveal facets about her personality that enable us to view her as a sensitive but strong person. Her second work, the *Risala-yi Sahibiya* (Begum Sahib's treatise), was completed at the end of 1641, and describes her first personal and touching encounter with Mulla Shah:

> My esteemed father set out for Kashmir, the peerless and charming place that does not need any praise or description. I reached Kashmir with him on the 31 March 1640 of the same year. Since I had no knowledge of the truth of the felicitous lives of the saints there, at the beginning of my entry there I heard from the tongues of many that the land of Kashmir today is adorned by the grace of the happy existence of that refuge of sainthood and guide on the path, Hazrat Maulana Shah. From the auspiciousness of his blessed feet this place has become heaven's partner, but rather it makes a higher claim than that. In the great and exalted Qadiri order from the magnificence of companions and most virtuous disciples, Hazrat Mian Mir is the possessor of saintly virtues, first in the list of great *shaikh*s, leader of renowned saints, informed of the esoteric and exoteric, leader of the small and big. My successful brother, of lofty nature and exalted rank, who is a knower of God and my master in truth and guidance, is also devoted to Hazrat Mian-jiv. From his sincere tongue I heard such praise of the virtues of that guide that in my heart and soul I became devoted to him out of perfect sincerity and belief. I became successful in my search and goal by the meaning of the prophetic hadith "Whoever seeks something will find." Audaciously I wrote

two or three petitions full of extreme sincerity and expression of total
belief in his service:

> If that sun-like visage becomes accessible to me
> I will make a claim of lordship, not just of kingship.

Knowing that sending gifts was a breach of form, the first time I
sent *nan* and *sag* cooked with my own hands along with a note
through my chamberlain Gharib. At first for about a month he did
not respond and showed great detachment. But he read the notes and
said what do I have to do with worldly people and kings. But I did not
desist from sending notes and expressing my sincerity and servitude.
My exalted brother who was in his service continuously spoke about
my sincerity and belief. Later by his discovery and inner light he
found me to be sincere in my search and need and knew that my true
intention was nothing but searching for the path of God. Out of
kindness he answered my notes bit by bit and the scent of perfect
hope that he would guide me reached the olfactory part of my soul.

In an appendix to her other work, *Munis al-arvah,* which was completed in 1640, Jahanara describes another pilgrimage, this time to the
Chishti shrine of the Sufi Mu'inuddin *gharib-navaz* (Blandisher of the
indigent) in Ajmer in 1643 where she was accompanied by her father.[52]
She was a woman who would have written a lot more, or perhaps did,
if circumstances had been more favorable to such endeavors.

Originally from the Badakhshan region in Central Asia, Shah Muhammad who came to be known as Mulla Shah represented a different kind of Persophone émigré in Mughal India than the ones we
encountered earlier: one who provided spiritual guidance rather than
linguistic authority to the Mughals. But like many of his compatriots
he could not stand the heat in the plains and preferred to live in
Kashmir. In 1649 the imperial family built a mosque for his use
with living quarters for him and his attendants in a modest-sized
compound.[53] On June 23, 1651, Shah Jahan's visit to Mulla Shah's
mosque is described in an official chronicle: "Constructed in an exquisite artistic style, the mosque cost 40,000 rupees, with the re-
quested funds having been provided by Princess Jahanara Begam. It
was surrounded by large buildings serving as habitations for the

poor."[54] This is a desolate place today, almost in ruins, but it was described as a felicitous space in a poem by Mulla Shah himself. It is surprising to find a *masnavi* on Kashmir in the works of this Sufi master, given that his life was totally removed from courtly affairs and was spent in meditative seclusion and prayers. It is probable that he was in regular touch with not just the members of the imperial family but also other courtiers, including court poets, who spent time there. He seemed to be aware of the fashion for writing poems on Kashmir and as a resident of the place contributed his own point of view. Since his tour of Kashmir begins with his own house and not at the court, he dispenses with praising the king or other patrons. In this respect, his work is quite different from Zafar Khan's poems.

Mulla Shah's poem is a description of the houses, gardens, and places of charming Kashmir (*ta'rifat-i khanaha va baghha va manazil-i Kashmir-i dilpazir*). In the few lines of a prose preface he indicates that his is a different kind of poem, stating that it is not possible to imagine the greatness of God without the manifestation of his beauty in external forms. With love and longing one can see it all revealed. In describing his house with an attached *hammam* and the chinar and fruit trees in the garden, he comes to the realization that one's own home is as close to paradise as one can get. Mulla Shah's poetic tour of the sites in and around Srinagar is more comprehensive than provided by any poet before or after him. There is also a variety in the range of places he lists: from the city's congregational mosque, Dal Lake and the mountains around it, to a dozen or so gardens. His list of gardens includes Nishat, Shalimar with both the Farahbakhsh and Faizbakhsh, Nasim, Jahanara, Nurafza, the dwellings of the emperor and Dara Shikoh, the saffron fields, Zafarabad and praise for Zafar Khan, Achval, Verinag, and Sind Brari. The last section of his poem is a paean to the bucolic and enchanting land:

> *divlakh ast digar dar Kashmir / khar-i anjast gul-i daman-gir*
> *khar ra nist dar anja jay / shikufad gul-i hama naqsh-i pay*
> *gah yak gul bi-hazaran rang ast / gah hazaran nahr az ahang ast*
> *gah hazaran gul u ba ham yakrang / man u bulbul ham azin ham-ahang*
> *ab-i u daru-yi har dard-i dil / nush u ba madar kun shir bihil*[55]

There is another spot in Kashmir where the thorns are roses to be
   gathered.
There is no room for thorns there; every footprint blossoms into a
   flower.
Here is a flower with a thousand colors, there a thousand singing
   streams.
A thousand flowers and together one hue; the nightingale and I are in
   tune about this. . . .
Its water is the cure for every heart's pain; drink it and forgive your
   mother's milk.

With the word *divlakh,* which means a secluded spot abounding with
demons (*div*), Mulla Shah could also have had another magical
building in mind, the Pari Mahal (Abode of fairies), located high on
the Zabarwan mountain with stunning views of Srinagar. Although
there is no clear evidence about its use, this romantic group of buildings with six terraces is believed to have been set up by Dara Shikoh
as some sort of retreat or school for learned men. Mulla Shah concludes on a pious note, stating that his work is an offering to the
divine:

> *dustan-i harf-i man-i divana / bud chand az gul u bagh u khana*
> *chand harfi ki zadam az Kashmir / bud dar vahdat-i an zat nafir*

The friends of the words of this madman
were a few roses, gardens, and homes.
The few words that I uttered about Kashmir
were trumpeting the oneness of that essence.

The congregation of buildings and spaces that made up his Kashmir
was in this way put to a different use in Persian poetry and enshrined
in the Mughal imagination.
   As in Zafar Khan's case, Mulla Shah's poems on Kashmir did not
circulate as widely as those by professional poets such as Kalim and
Qudsi, which were produced for the widest possible audience. It is
more likely that Mulla Shah's words were for a smaller group of his

devotees, including the royal siblings, who shared his idea to ensure that the land would be enshrined as a mystical place as well, not just a courtly retreat. Even if the gardens and buildings were lovingly built by the Mughals, and Mulla Shah was certainly appreciative of their efforts, for him it was not enough to merely invoke the divine at the beginning of a poem but rather to constantly remind oneself that the natural landscape is a manifestation of a higher reality.[56] The mystical is also a warning about the superficiality of the material world and its snares. Mughal Arcadia was, of course, largely a literary and to some extent ideological construction, even though the actual landscape of Kashmir supported this view. But the political history of the empire reveals its many negative aspects as well, which also play into the way places were described by the literati of the time. The inspiring encounter between poets, places, and empire was about to come to an end.

Conclusion
Paradise Lost

⌣∵ *Clausus est paradisus* ∵⌣
Paradise has closed

The war of succession between Shah Jahan's four sons in 1558–1559 is a dramatic story that has been recounted numerous times by both academic scholars and popular historians. The violence and rancor that marked this dramatic episode in Mughal history resulted in the death of three brothers, the house arrest of Emperor Shah Jahan, who would die in captivity eight years later, and the Mughal throne being claimed by his second son Aurangzeb, who took the title 'Alamgir (World-seizer). Different factions put forward their own versions of the events in historical and poetic texts. The poet Bihishti Shirazi, whose name ironically means paradisiacal, composed a poem, *Ashub-i Hindustan* (Upheaval in India), which was a widely read work judging by the number of extant manuscripts and printed editions from the nineteenth century. As tutor to Prince Murad-bakhsh, who had sided with Aurangzeb and to whom the work was dedicated, Bihishti attempted to provide an unbiased account of the struggle for power among the brothers. For Bihishti the garden that had been Mughal India was now ravaged by autumn, a place where law and order had broken down:

chunan mulk-i Hindustan shud kharab / ki daryash darad mizaj-i sharab
darin khak-i tira sara'i namanad / bijuz khana-yi jughd ja'i namanad[1]

> The kingdom of India was ruined in such a way
> that its seas have the quality of wine.
> In this dark land, no building remains,
> except for a house of bats.

Bihishti's lament on Hindustan, and Delhi in particular, would become the model for the poetic genre of the city in decline (*shahrashob*) in eighteenth-century Urdu literature.

The rather austere Emperor Aurangzeb was schooled in the literary arts and was fond of classical Persian poetry, but over time was not keen on supporting professional poets at his court. Musta'id Khan, an official at his court, in a history composed after the emperor's death, describes the latter as "possessing great skill in prose composition and letter-writing, and was well-versed in prose and poetry (literature). But holding firmly to the precept of the holy verse: 'It is the erring who follow the poets,' (*Quran,* 26:224), he did not incline to the hearing of useless poetry. How then could he be expected to listen to adulatory verses?? But poems breathing moral advice (he liked).

> In order to please God the High and Splendid, I have not
> Turned my eyes on any *ghazaal* (fawn-like beauty)
> nor my ears on any *ghazal* (erotic ode)."[2]

Literary life in and outside court did continue, of course, since poetry was one of the mainstays of courtly communities, but gone were the days of Akbar's reign, when poets by the dozen were presented to the emperor, or the early Shah Jahan years, when poetry was imbued with a glamour and was a staged performance for a translocal audience. After Aurangzeb left Delhi for the subjugation of the Deccan in 1681, never to return, there was a discernable shift in the nature of the literary culture in the north that is part of the story of the long eighteenth century.[3]

Already by the early 1650s the literary atmosphere at Shah Jahan's court had changed considerably. Many if not most of the senior poets of his early reign had died or retired and a new crop of poets and historians had come to the fore. The tumultuous decade also witnessed a shift in the power dynamics among court poets as fewer men of letters from Iran came looking for patronage at the imperial level. No longer assured of a lucrative career in India, and with the improvement in the economic conditions in late Safavid Iran, the tide of migrants from Iran was greatly reduced. Although Shah Jahan's illness and the dramatic events around the war of succession between his sons provided ample material for poets and historians, the way court poetry had been produced through the patronage of a strict network of administrators and rulers, and even the choice of genres and topics, underwent a transformation. It is significant that there was no poet laureate after the venerable Kalim, who had died in Kashmir in 1651, and Persian poetry in the following decades was increasingly composed under the sponsorship of princes, administrators, and others outside courtly circles. The early twentieth-century magisterial scholar of Persian poetry, Shibli Nu'mani, declared that with Kalim a chapter in the history of Persian poetry had ended.[4] The decades after Kalim are an understudied period in Indo-Persian literary history, but this was a vibrant time for literati nonetheless, with Persian becoming more or less equal in status with a number of local languages, thus facilitating a more equal process of borrowing and influence. The story of the fate of Persian in the decades and centuries to come is too complicated to go into here, but there were some key developments regarding the fading out of Mughal Arcadia.

By the last years of Shah Jahan's reign, Kashmir had fallen off the imperial circuit for the imperial family and was left to be ruled by a succession of governors. Yet even as court poets began to lose interest in writing about the province with the waning of Shah Jahan's authority, the popularity of this poetic genre continued to some extent among local poets, either those who had a sentimental attachment to the valley or were native Kashmiris. In addition to glorifying the bucolic aspects of the region as Shah Jahan's poets had done in the early years of his reign, in its last phase the genre also allowed one poet who had served in the Mughal administration to explore the darker aspects of Mughal rule during the last years of the emperor's reign. This was Muhammad Muhsin Fani Kashmiri, not a professional poet but one who held a distinguished record of imperial service. Fani had worked in Allahabad as a judge (*sadr*) but was forced into retirement after a disgraceful scandal that ensued when it was found out that he had written a praise poem (*qasida*) dedicated to Nazr Muhammad Khan, the Uzbek ruler of Balkh and Shah Jahan's enemy in his campaign of 1646–1647 to annex the Mughal ancestral lands in Central Asia.[5] The life of a professional court poet had its negative side.

Fani's poem on Kashmir, entitled *Maikhana* (Winehouse), was composed in 1655 and dedicated to his Sufi master Shaikh Muhibullah Ilahabadi of the Chishti order. This poem cleverly combined features of two popular genres of the time: the Kashmir poem and the *saqinama*. A long *masnavi* that was an address to the mystical figure of the young wine server, the *saqinama* in the early modern period was a popular poetic genre among Mughal, Safavid, and Ottoman poets.[6] In his study of such poems Paul Losensky notes that "the quest for self-identity enacted in the *saqi-nama* also opened the genre to more personal concerns and further modes of symbolic immortality."[7] Fani's poem is explicitly localized in the topography of Kashmir and in addition to its mystical content has some striking pastoral imagery. It is clear that he was familiar with the output of Shah Jahan's court poets, but his poem is longer and with more original features. Fani mentions some of the same gardens of Kashmir that the other poets had referenced, while also bringing in a new element by declaring that a comparison of the garden of the king, Bagh-i Shah, the Chashmashahi bagh in Srinagar, to the more prominent gardens is like comparing a house to a Sufi lodge (*azin bagh-ha bih buvad bagh-i shah / ki farqast az khana ta khanaqah*).[8] Since he and Prince Dara Shikoh were both attached to Shaikh Muhibullah, Fani explicitly mentions him in connection with this garden.

Beginning with an extended description of a symphony of various musical instruments, Fani goes on to narrate how the different seasons affect the vegetation and nature of the land. He declares that he is going to praise Shah Jahan's Hindustan, but then surprisingly picks a humble bullock cart, the mainstay of rural life in India, as the symbol of what is great about this land. The bullocks are like the cow that holds up the world in Muslim cosmology (*magar gav-i bahlast gav-i zamin/ki bar sar kashad bar-i 'alam chunin*). He also praises the cart driver (*bahlban*). Charmed by the latter's curls, Fani suggests to him that they drink some wine together and go to an idol temple to offer prayers (*namaz*), in a subversive gesture that is in keeping with the antinomian posturing of the poet in a *saqinama* as well as of a lover in *ghazal* poetry. Fani sees the driver as an empathetic person who takes him away in his cart on a mystical quest. Moving on from there, he encounters a lovely *pan* seller:

> *furushad bi-jan bira-yi pan-furush/chu u hichkas nist arzan-furush*
> *dukan ra chunan basta a'in zi pan/ki chun asmanast sabz an dukan . . .*
> *chu tiflan girifta bi-dast an javan/kitab-i Gulistan zi-auraq-i pan*

> The *pan* seller sells leaves for the price of a life—and no one sells so cheaply!
> He has set up his shop in such a way with *pan*s that the green is like the sky.
> The young seller holds the *pan*s like children holding the *Gulistan.*

He goes on to praise the fine qualities of *pan* in the *faza'il* mode. The youthful pan seller is the familiar beloved of Persian lyric poetry, but like the bullock cart driver also represents the simple and sincere folk of the countryside. The reference to Sa'di's *Gulistan* (Rose garden), the primary text in the spread of Persian learning that he references several times, anchors the allusion in a deeply classical tradition, besides being an attractive image.

These verses are followed by praise for sugarcane, and then, in a somewhat abrupt shift of locales, the poet nostalgically ruminates about two cities, Kalpi and Payag (Prayag or Allahabad), where he had spent some years in imperial service. This thought brings tears like the spring of Verinag to his eyes. He imagines the confluence of the two sacred rivers, Ganga and Yamuna in Payag, which seem to him like two whales facing each other, with the city floating over the waters. Its gardens compare well to those of Kashmir. He remembers the neighborhood of Khuldabad in Allahabad as the best place and a veritable *gulzar-i jannat* (rose-garden of paradise). Every year people gather in this town like deer in a plain for a fair, referring to a Hindu festival, the mini-Kumbh *mela*:

hama ahl-i an shahr darya-dil and / bi-laya-yi ma'ni chu ma vasil and
zi faiz-i du darya-yi 'ilm u 'amal / hama yafta abru az azal

> The people of that city are generous and connected to subtle mean-
> ings like us.
> From the bounty of the sea of knowledge and deeds, they have all
> obtained honor from pre-eternity.

As he did with the country folk, Fani feels an empathy with the people of the city, irrespective of their religious or ethnic affiliation.

Then follows praise for his Sufi master and an autobiographical discourse on his growth as a mystically oriented poet. At the end of the poem, in another shift, Fani lapses into a mystical reverie and begins to exhort his readers about the importance of morally correct conduct in these times. He paints a horrific picture of a dystopia, where virtue is absent and vice reigns supreme. In such a place in-stead of doing their respective tasks, as people do in a well-governed city, everyone is busy with something else. The king with his crown resembles a rooster, the *shaikh* robs the innocent like Satan, the *qazi* who is supposed to uphold the law takes bribes, the people are oc-cupied in drunkenness and debauchery.[9] Religion is the only refuge for good men. Fani's somber tone is in contrast to the earlier exuber-ance of the poem, but it seems to signify that as someone who is no longer part of the Mughal imperial machinery, he can choose to not leave the reader in a paradise-like Kashmiri garden but remind them of loftier spiritual and religious truths. Fani's poem displays a con-cern about the moral welfare of the world, and given his association with the Mughals, its political subtext and critique of the later years of Shah Jahan's rule cannot be ignored.

The literary representation of India in confusion is also found in the poetry of Muhammad Sa'id "Ashraf" of Mazandaran, an Iranian émigré poet who arrived in India just when Aurangzeb began his rule. Ashraf was appointed tutor to the emperor's daughter, Princess Zebunnisa.[10] By this time Iranian poets at the Mughal court were in a minority and the new emperor was not the generous patron of poetry that his predecessors had been. Like many a poet coming from Iran before him, on his way to India over the land route, Ashraf made a stop at the Shia holy shrine of Imam 'Ali Riza in Mashhad, where he began to regret his decision to leave the garden of his homeland (*gulzar-i vatan*) for liver-eating India (*Hind-i jigarkhvar*). Later, when he was domiciled in India, in his poems in the *masnavi* form addressed to his wife Maryam and son Muhammad Amin, he expresses the emotional turmoil that he was going through as an expatriate separated from his loved ones and homeland: "How can you compare India to Iran? The copy does not match up to the original" (*ba mulk-i Hind, nisbat-i Iran chi mikuni / chun i'tibar-i asl nadarad savad ra*).[11] Although this sentiment could have been expressed by a poet half a century earlier at the height of the attraction of India, this verse has a more sincere ring to it.

Ashraf's poem (*masnavi*) to his wife, Maryam, was apparently written in response to a letter he had just received from her. He informs his dear spouse that her letter arrived when he was feeling particularly downcast about being far away in India (*dil az Hind-i jigarkhvar-am zabun bud*) and exhorts her to defeat melancholy and the sorrow of parting by reading the Koran and being patient. Being the poet, Ashraf sees himself as the ancient Iranian king Khusrau Parviz who temporarily left his beloved Shirin for another wife, Maryam. If Maryam stands for India, then he is the suffering Farhad who loved and died for Shirin, who is Iran. His upside-down fate (*bakht-i varun*) taught him a bitter lesson in life. Consolation comes from literary pursuits and writing, and he likens the act of receiving a letter to an experience of religious revelation (*zi maktubat chunan khurram shavad dil / ki pindaram kitabi gashta nazil*). It is all too clear that Ashraf had arrived when the glamor of Mughal Arcadia was quickly fading:

darin Hind-i jigarkhvaram-i zamin-duz / fisharam bar jigar dandan shab u ruz
nashud dar bagh-i Hindam dilgusha'i / khuda kesav u parmesar duha'i.

In this liver-eating crushing India, I grit my teeth day and night.
I did not succeed in the garden of India, by the Hindu gods.

The last hemistich is actually in Hindi, presumably not a language his wife Maryam would have understood, but it serves to highlight the strangeness of his life.

Ashraf also composed a short satirical *masnavi* in which he describes the riotous Indian spring festival of Holi as a carnivalesque event that unsettles the Persianate social order and subverts the rules of *adab*.[12] This is in contrast to Sa'ib's lyrical poem on the Indian spring *basant* written almost half a century earlier. In his poem, Ashraf mocks the revelry and merrymaking of the natives as the dazzling array of colors of Holi contrasts with the Bacchanalian spirit of the celebration. He watches the wild spectacle with a fascinated revulsion, afraid of being swallowed by the chaos. In the beginning of the poem, despite his feelings Ashraf exhorts the wine server to lift the veil of modesty that preserves order in the world: "O Saqi, pull aside the veil of beautiful modesty" (*saqiya parda-yi hijab bikash / vaz jamal-i haya naqab bikash*). He warns the reader that:

baz sauda-yi Hind tughyan kard / rasm-i divanagi numayan kard
fitna-yi khufta dar khurush amad / dig-i Hindustan bi-jush amad

Once again the blackness of India is in surge, as has the custom of madness.
Slumbering sedition has started to roar as the pot of India begins to boil over.

It seems to Ashraf that the Day of Resurrection has arrived in full force. The sewer (*manjalab*) of the world is permeated with a stench (*gand*) and society is devoid of honor (*azarm*), shame (*sharm*), and dignity (*abru*). As he sees the black-faced peopled thronging the streets, the binaries of man-woman, son-daughter, ugly-beautiful, good-evil have completely collapsed into a chaotic singleness. Everyone is equal as all hierarchies and social rules are suspended (*hama dar bi-hamyati yaksan*) as the lowly Indian becomes the same as a lady from Iran (*paji-i Hind u baji-yi Iran*). Woe to the wretches and women, more literally "ranis" and "fuckers," of India (*dad az raniyan-i Hindustan / chut-maraniyan-i Hindustan*). The image of the topsy-turvy world that he had used in the letter to his wife makes complete sense in this context since India's affairs are always upside down (*bazhguna ast Hindiyan ra kar*), like an unfortunate constellation (*bazhguna chu tali'-i varun*). After feeling the full impact of the carnivalesque scene before him, Ashraf concludes that this is not reality but an artistic representation, using both the image of puppets (*hama chun lu'batan-i shab-bazi*) and a display of *siyah-qalam*, a style of drawing that obscures the true subject of a picture.

For Ashraf, this wanton (*bu'l-fuzuli*) occasion is the cause for long established metaphors and binaries to collapse. He comes up with a new hybrid where the rose and thorn are mixed up (*gul u khari biham bar anduzam*), and in opposition to the classical trope of Hindus being the dark slaves, they are now the Turkish plunderers (*turktaziyan-i Hindiyan*). This is reflected in the confusion of literary genres, as he weighs the possibility of satire versus panegyric for his poem, a choice akin to a bee sipping nectar or stinging (*nuskha-yi zamm u madh pisham hast/hamchu zanbur nush u nisham hast*). Ashraf's use of quotidian Hindi words in his poem such as *juti, rani,* and *chutmaran* indicates the pollution of the Persian language in the Babel that is India. Previously, court poets had mostly employed the native names of flora in their poems, preserving the purity of Persian, but now things have changed. Ashraf's inner turmoil about his displaced state is projected in the confusion and disregard for the conventions of Persian *adab* as he describes the riotous festival of Holi.[13]

The term "carnivalesque" as used by the Russian literary critic Mikhail Bakhtin seems appropriate when reading Ashraf's description of Holi. Bakhtin wrote, "Carnival celebrated temporary liberation from the prevailing truth and from the established order; it marked the suspension of all hierarchical rank, privileges, norms, and prohibitions. . . . People were, so to speak, reborn for new, purely human relations. These truly human relations were not only a fruit of imagination or abstract thought; they were experienced. The utopian ideal and the realistic merged in this carnival experience, unique of its kind."[14] Although there is liberation from social and linguistic restrictions, for Ashraf there is also the disregard of proper conduct during the festival. There are several paintings of Mughal emperors celebrating Holi, mostly from the eighteenth century, but one from the seventeenth century attributed to the artist Govardhan depicts Emperor Jahangir enjoying the festival with the womenfolk of his household. As the only male figure in the painting, a tipsy Jahangir seems to be supported by two women. The face of one of them is upside down, as a sign of revelry. But while this was a joyful occasion, by the time Ashraf wrote he could only see the darker side of the picture. His encounter with India challenged Ashraf's ideas about ownership of culture, power, and language.

A few years before Ashraf arrived, a historical shift in the Mughal court's relationship with Iran and Iranians had begun. The Safavid capture of the frontier fort of Qandahar in 1649 resulted in a cooling off period between the two powers. When Aurangzeb came to the throne, an embassy led by Budaq Khan had arrived from Iran in 1661 and was received graciously by the Mughals. Aurangzeb made sure there would be a regular supply of *pan* for Shah 'Abbas II who, it would seem, had developed a taste for betel-leaf.[15] Following this, in 1664 a Mughal embassy under Tarbiyat Khan reached Iran, where due to mysterious and conflicting reasons given by historical sources, the Indian ambassador was not treated well. After this visit, relations between the two courts soured. The conclusion, in the view of a prominent historian, is that although Aurangzeb was not the primary cause for the breaking of ties with Iran, he did nothing to repair the damage.[16] By the end of his reign, the Mughals did not maintain diplomatic relations with either the Safavids or the Ottomans.

THE LAST TRIP TO KASHMIR

As we saw, Kashmir with its cypresses and beauties had lent itself perfectly to being the ideal garden of Persian poetry, a Persianate Arcadia for the Mughals. At one level, the neatly laid out and serene gardens of Kashmir represented the taming of nature and the countryside, on another level the province served as a synecdoche for the empire. For Fani it actually came to represent the refuge from the corrupt heart of the empire. Although many of the poems on the praise of the province, starting from the poems of Faizi and 'Urfi on Kashmir at Akbar's court and all the way to those by poets at Shah Jahan's court, were composed under courtly patronage to celebrate the expansion of the empire, the personal investment and attachment of individual poets to certain places would redefine the literary geography of Indo-Persian literature. The poet Munir was from Lahore and took great pride in the early Indian poets of his city and those of Delhi; he found similarities between the wild vegetation of Bengal and the idyllic gardens of Kashmir, indicating that there was a more personal investment and individual program of representation in his poems. Fani was originally from Kashmir but fondly recalled his time in Allahabad, meditating on his checkered career in the Mughal administration. Nature was liberating for these poets, whether in a courtly or a mystical setting, but for Munir it opened up his world and provided a freedom that allowed him to celebrate the flowering of Persian culture in India in its Persianate manifestation, while for Fani it was an escape from the wickedness of the material world. The equivalent of the simple but idealized life of the shepherd or farmer found in Western pastoral poetry is that of simple country folk in Fani's poem, and praise is reserved for his Sufi master rather than for the emperor.

Whatever particular stakes poets had in a place, their literary works marked a sophisticated development in a literary tradition that was nurtured by certain ritual journeys of the Mughal court on which we, as armchair travelers, are guided by the poet—from the frequent trips to Kashmir to travelling down the Ganga or Jumna by boat—and the complex patronage and administrative system that facilitated this mobility. Especially in the case of Kashmir, in the post-Shah Jahan period when it lost its importance for the court, it nevertheless came to be inscribed in the artistic imagination in a romantic mode.

In the last years of Shah Jahan's reign, at about the same time Fani wrote his poem, a peripatetic poet named Mulla Tughra also expressed dissatisfaction about Kashmir where he had settled.[17] Tughra was from Mashhad in Iran, but not part of Shah Jahan's inner circle of poets. He served as a *munshi* to Prince Murad-bakhsh and excelled in both prose and poetry. Tughra's complaint about Kashmir, all expressed in general tones without specifying the cause of his dis-satisfaction, is found in a *qasida* form whose rhyme word is "Kashmir."[18] His writings suggest that Tughra wanted to be more original in writing about Kashmir, the *masnavi* form having become overused in recent decades. He also wrote in an elegant mixed prose and po-etry, using the *insha* form. Tughra's *Ti'dad al-navadir* (Enumeration of novelties) is a rhapsodic guidebook listing the eight stations on the Mughal road to Kashmir, each one described in flowery prose and a few lines of verse: Chokhati, Naushahra, Changez Hatli, Rajaur, Thana, Bairam Kala, Poshana, then the Pir Panjal pass.[19] Some of these places have slightly varying names today. In addition, he wrote two other short essays in this mixed form on Kashmir.[20] In the tradition of Nihavandi's descriptions of 'Abdur-Rahim Khankhanan's building and renovation projects from several decades earlier, the vogue for writing about topographical subjects in rhetorical prose continued in the last years of Shah Jahan's rule, probably also because of so many chronicler-*munshi*s becoming prominent in this period. The histo-rian Muhammad Salih Kambo's *Bahar-i sukhan* (Spring of poetry) contains descriptions of the architectural wonders and gardens of the four great Mughal cities: Shahjahanabad, Lahore, Akbarabad, and Kashmir (Srinagar).[21] In times of political uncertainty it was even more urgent to be reminded of the glorious achievements of the empire.

Although the imperial circuit no longer included the valley of Kashmir as a requisite destination in these years, Aurangzeb under-took his only official trip to the province along with his court in 1663, which incidentally was also the last trip of a Mughal ruler to the valley. The journey was planned at the insistence of his sister, Princess Raushanara, who was probably eager to imitate the ritual journeys to the valley of their unfortunate siblings, Dara Shikoh and Jahanara, for whom the valley had been sacred land. The trip did not start off well. In a tragic accident, several elephants carrying women from the harem fell off the mountain path in the Pirpanjal range. With such a bad omen, the emperor would have been conscious that Kashmir was not familiar territory for him. He was more at home in the central and southern regions of the subcontinent, and the mountainous province would have seemed remote, especially in the initial anxious years of his rule. Fortunately for posterity, an observant European traveler accompanied the court on this journey and left a·detailed record of his impressions of the valley and the court's activities there.

The French scholar-physician, François Bernier, after traveling through Syria and Egypt, arrived in India in 1658 during the war of succession. He had initially met Dara Shikoh whom he genuinely liked, but then finally ended up in the service of the Mughal courtier Danishmand Khan. Like the many Europeans traveling in the gunpowder empires, Bernier picked up some Persian and was able to adapt himself to Mughal culture. As a traveler to Kashmir with the court, his narrative of the whole trip in nine letters to a friend he addresses as Monsieur de Merveilles is a remarkably lively narrative, mixing wonder and ethnographic observation.[22] Coming from the hot plains Bernier was struck by the resemblance of the climate and flora of Kashmir to that of Europe. More interestingly, Bernier was one of the few Europeans in Mughal India who left a firsthand account of a courtly poetic assembly.

Present at a literary *majlis* in Srinagar during Aurangzeb's stay there, Bernier noted the way that hyperbole in Persian poetry was used by poets to great effect in describing Kashmir:

> I was quite prepared to witness the emulous contest between the Kashmiri and the Mogol poets. We were no sooner arrived than Aurangzeb received from the bards of both nations poems in praise of this favored land, which he accepted and rewarded with kindness. They were written in a strain of extravagant hyperbole. One of them, I remember, speaking of the surrounding mountains, observed that their extraordinary height had caused the skies to retire into the vaulted form which we see; that Nature had exhausted all her skill in the creation of this country, and rendered it inaccessible to the attack of hostile force; because being the mistress of the kingdoms of the earth, it was wise to preserve her in perfect peace and security, that she might exercise universal dominion without the possibility of ever being subject to any. The poet went on to say that the summits of the

higher and more distant mountains were clothed resplendently in white, and the minor and more contiguous preserved in perpetual verdure and embellished with stately trees, because it was meet that the mistress of the kingdoms of the earth should be crowned with a diadem whose top and rays were diamonds issuing from a basework of emeralds.

Bernier then, somewhat tongue in cheek, feels that the poets could have gone even further in their hyperbolic flights of imagination:

"The poet" (I remarked to my Navab Danishmand Khan, who wished me to relish these productions) "might easily have amplified his subject. He could, with a pardonable license, have included the neighboring mountainous regions within the kingdom of Kashmir, since it is pretended that they were once tributary to it. I mean Little Tibet, the states of Raja Jammu, Kashgar, and Srinagar [Garhwal]. He might then have gone on to say that the Ganges, the Indus, the Chenab, and the Jamna issue from the kingdom of Kashmir, rivers which cannot yield in beauty and importance to the Pison, the Gihon, or the two other rivers spoken of in Genesis; and that it may therefore be reasonably concluded that the Garden of Eden was planted in Kashmir, and not, according to the received opinion, in Armenia."[23]

It is likely that Bernier would have understood the poems in their original and seems to be eager to display his own knowledge of the geography of the Himalayan region and the northern plains. Remarkably, he also understood the aesthetics of the poetry on Kashmir and suggests bringing in the geography of the Abrahamic traditions into the Indo-Iranian mix. The Kashmiri poets mentioned by him were probably Binish and Juya, the last to write poems in the genre. Even as the Mughal perception of Kashmir became mythologized and frozen as a poetic image, for Europeans such as Bernier and those who would follow him in the colonial period, this was the beginning of a larger ethnographic project to record the topography and cultures of the region.[24] Bernier's map of Kashmir, which appeared in the early printed editions of his work, was vital to the European understanding of the topography of this region (see Figure 8).

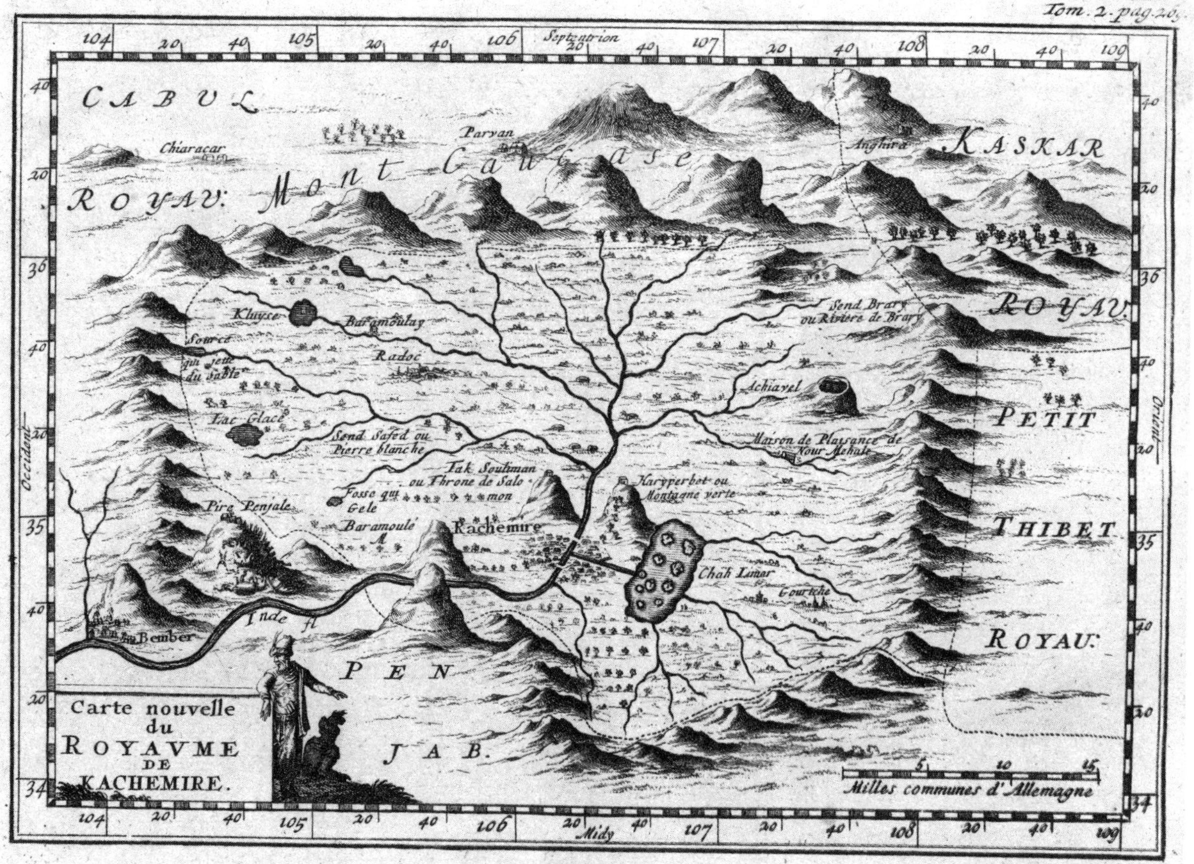

FIGURE 8 Bernier's Map of Kashmir

Although many Mughal literary manuscripts have still not been studied or published, it is safe to deduce from a survey of catalogues of major library collections and available textual evidence that other provinces or cities had not been the subject of so many poems in the seventeenth century, not even Delhi or Lahore. Kashmir, and occasionally Panjab because it was adjacent to it and the road to Kashmir passed through it, continued to be the enchanted garden of the empire in the literature of the last years of Shah Jahan and early years of Aurangzeb's reign. The Aurangzeb period poets who continued the tradition of composing poems on Kashmir in the *masnavi* form are not so well known. In their poems, the region is viewed more on its own terms than as an integral part of the Mughal Empire, and sometimes even connected to Iran in its Persianate orientation. Of these poets, two were Kashmiris of Iranian ancestry: Isma'il "Binish" and Mirza Darab Beg "Juya," while Nasir 'Ali was from Sirhind, Punjab. Although Binish wrote poems about Lahore, Delhi, and even cities in Iran, it is not clear whether he ever left the valley. Rather he would have read the output of the poets of Shah Jahan's age and synthesized them with concerns of his own society. His *masnavi, Gul-dasta* (Bouquet of flowers), is in a distinctly mystical vein, which is not surprising since mysticism offered a refuge from the vicissitudes of the world. It is unusual however that it was rarely so intimately linked to the topography of a particular place and its natural landscape.[25] The poet Juya was Shia and found a patron in the Mughal governor Ibrahim Khan, under whose rule the valley witnessed strife between its various communities—Sunnis, Shias, and Hindus.[26] The poet from Punjab Nasir 'Ali also found a patron in a governor, Saif Khan Faqirullah, who was stationed in the poet's native Sirhind and then in Kashmir. Faqirullah gained fame for authoring a treatise on music, *Rag darpan*.[27] When Nasir 'Ali writes about Kashmir, "Describing this garden has made me a poet since it reminds me of Isfahan and Shiraz" (*bi-vasf-i in chaman gardam sukhansaz/dihad chun yad az Isfahan u Shiraz*),[28] he seems to be somewhat jaded in his use of the trope of Kashmir.

Mughal rule in Kashmir endured until the advent of Durrani rule in 1753 that commenced as a result of the raids of the Afghan warlord

Ahmad Shah 'Abdali, regarded as the founder of the modern nation of Afghanistan. Ironically, in this period of shift of power, which was a dark period in the history of the region marred by incompetent administrators and communal and sectarian conflicts, the region came to be inscribed in the imagination of the subcontinent as a romantic paradise.[29] Over time Kashmir turned into an abstract metaphor without any reference to a place that was visited and experienced firsthand. This was one of the legacies of the Persian century of Mughal court literature on the bucolic features of the valley. The visualization of this romantic image of Kashmir can be seen in a painting called "Village Life in Kashmir," by the eighteenth-century artist in Lucknow, Mir Kalan Khan, whose work shows distinct European influences in the depiction of everyday life in the valley (see Figure 9). The rural and handsome inhabitants of a village go about their work against the backdrop of a gentle landscape that combines nature and man-made buildings. An inscription on the painting bears the title *Majlis-i Kashmir* (Assembly of Kashmir), the word *majlis* evoking images of courtly gatherings of princes and poets.

The Mughal active engagement with Kashmir lasted less than a century, from Akbar's conquest of the province in 1586 to Aurangzeb's last trip to the valley in 1663. Whereas the encounter began with Persianate courtiers and Iranian poets discovering the valley as a familiar place, a little Iran, due to its topography and climate, where the pantheon of mythical figures from classical Persian literature, such as Khizr, Iskandar, Sulaiman, Bilqis, 'Isa, Majnun, Laila, Shirin, Farhad and Isfandiyar, could be relocated, for Persian poets of Kashmir and Panjab it was briefly a source of local pride. In the long run, Indo-Persian and Urdu poets of the next century would include abstract allusions to the garden of Kashmir as they did with other fabulous places such as Shiraz and Bukhara. The idea of Kashmir as a pristine Arcadia persisted in the South Asian imagination, even though a history of oppressive rulers and botched politics all the way to the partition of India in 1947 and beyond has left a legacy of violence and turmoil in the valley.

FIGURE 9 Village Life in Kashmir by Mir Kalan

IMAGINING INDIA IN ISFAHAN

The story of Mughal Arcadia could end here with the passing of the Kashmir literary phenomenon and steep decline in the number of émigré poets from Iran at court. But there is a corollary to the larger narrative of Mughal Persian literary culture for which we must view things from the Safavid point of view. As we saw earlier, from the very beginning of the early modern Iran-India cultural encounter, émigrés displayed a wide spectrum of emotions with respect to Mughal India that ranged from hyperbolic enthusiasm to antipathy. Other than the received images of India as the land of wonders, place of refuge, and paradise, the negative one of the country as hell was relevant to the experience of many who were alienated or in exile. During the course of the seventeenth century, another trope associated with India took hold in the Persianate imagination, especially in Iran: this was the figure of the Hindu or Indian woman. The Hindu woman symbolized the love-hate relationship of the Safavids with India: for an extended period of time she was the faithful beloved, then oftentimes she showed a more alluring and dangerous side. An underlying anxiety on the part of the Safavids about the porous frontiers of Persian's linguistic and cultural realms that allowed unregulated modes of influence was increasingly equated with the Indian woman. The literary representations of the range of things she signified is worthy of investigation.

In the early modern period visitors or migrants from Iran and Central Asia observed all kinds of women in India at close range. An example of this fascination with Hindu women is the Central Asian visitor Mahmud, son of Amir Vali, who traveled in North India in the years 1624–1631. Richard Foltz has written about Mahmud's "personal fascination with Indian women" and "wet-sari voyeurism." When Mahmud describes the ritual bathing in the Jumna at Raja Man Singh's temple in Mathura, he admires the devotees, both men and women, and states, "Really, it is not surprising that in this nice landscape with so many beautiful women, the feet of Muslims slip and their purity is broken by the stones of their beauty." He experiences the same thing again in Benares on the bank of the Ganges.[30] Observing and sexualizing the body of real women was not unconnected to an exoticized view of her in poetic texts.

Many Muslims and European writers in the premodern period displayed an obsession with the practice of *sati,* or suttee, but for the most part this was connected to the marvels of India. A poem that depicted the Hindu woman in the most positive terms and one that played a surprisingly symbolic role in the representation of power was the verse romance *Suz u gudaz* (Burning and melting), composed around 1604 by the émigré poet Muhammad Riza Nau'i Khabushani for Akbar's son Prince Daniyal.[31] This *masnavi* features the tragic story of two unnamed lovers who are about to get married. When the expected happy union of the lovers ends in the death of the male, his female beloved, who is the true heroine of this work, chooses to be cremated with him as a *sati*. In the prefatory section of the work, Nau'i had explained that classical love stories such as that of Farhad and Shirin and the images of the moth and nightingale were now clichéd and called for a new literary ethos for the age. This was a common device whenever a poet wanted to introduce a new subject. In the classical Indo-Persian tradition, Amir Khusrau had versified the actual love story of Prince Khizr Khan for the Hindu princess Devaldei (*'Ishqiya* or *'Ashiqa*), which also ended tragically. Mughal court poets also looked to Indic tales as a source for new romances, the chief sources being the Sanskrit epics *Ramayana* and *Mahabharata*. The fact that an émigré poet such as Nau'i chose an Indian theme for his poem held an extra significance because the story he told was supposed to be taken from reality rather than history or mythology. Thus, there is an imagined ethnographic element in his narration. The traditional view of representing India as an exotic and wondrous place was paramount in his work, and what was more suitable than the topic of *sati*.

The mystical meaning embedded in such an act of annihilation by fire, a frequent theme in Sufi Persian poetry associated with the images of the moth and candle,[32] would have been obvious to readers of this text. The Hindu heroine of Nau'i's work is like the moth that burns itself in the flame out of its devotion and love. Perhaps not surprisingly, *Suz u gudaz* enjoyed great popularity among Persian audiences, especially in Safavid Iran. The Iranian poet Sa'ib who visited Mughal India enshrines the Hindu woman as a stock image in poetry, just as the dark Hindu slave had been for centuries: "The fire of love rises high from the ashes of India; in this land of sparks, a woman burns herself with her husband" (*atash-i 'ishq zi khakistar-i Hindustan buland/zan darin shu'lastan bar sar-i shauhar suzad*).[33] Amir Khusrau was one of the first poets to utilize this particular image, if not the first.

There appears to be only one Mughal illustrated manuscript of Nau'i's poem, probably the very one commissioned by Prince Daniyal for presentation to his father, with simple images that graphically show the act of *sati*.[34] While the Mughals made use of this text to create a new and more inclusive canon of Persian literature where the subject matter was drawn from the local landscape, the Safavids read it with great interest for different reasons. Many more Safavid illustrated manuscripts of Nau'i's *Suz u gudaz* survive, attesting to the fact that it enjoyed great popularity throughout the seventeenth century. The various paintings of the *sati* scene depict the woman in different ways, either about to enter the funeral pyre of her husband or already in the fire in her dead lover's embrace.[35] In the Harvard Art Museums, there is a painting of this scene, not from a copy of the poem but probably from an album page, suggesting that the iconography was recognizable and did not require a text around it to orient the viewer.[36] At the bottom left of the painting there is a half-verse that the woman utters, "I will seize the kingdoms of the West and East" (*mulk-i 'Arab u 'Ajam misitanam*). This line, actually not from the romance but a hemistich from a *ghazal* by the classical poet Sa'di, had a deeper meaning in the context of the subject of Iran-India cultural relations.

Apart from the subject of the poem that still held a fascination for audiences in Iran, the figure of the tragic Hindu *sati* was connected to the prolonged struggle between the two polities over Qandahar. The art historian Sussan Babaie has convincingly argued that one of the mural paintings found in the Chihil Sutun palace in Isfahan is the *sati* scene from Nau'i's poem.[37] The painting in the Safavid pavilion is of an agitated woman who is being restrained by several people before a large fire in the background. This is sometimes thought to represent a celebration of some sort. The scene indirectly commemorates the capture of the Mughal fort of Qandahar by the Safavids in 1649, with the *sati* being the Indian power that is about to be crushed. The mural painting was produced almost half a century after Nau'i composed his poem, but it apparently still resonated in a meaningful way with Safavid audiences.

The question is, why did this fight over Qandahar matter so much to the Safavids when it is hardly mentioned in Mughal sources? The frontier city of Qandahar was an ongoing and ultimately decisive factor in the balance of power and prestige between the Mughals and Safavids. It was a constant and the only major cause of conflict between the two polities. The Mughals successfully defended the fortress in 1638, and in a major gain for them, the Safavid Kurdish

governor, 'Ali Mardan Khan, defected to the Mughal side. But a decade later, when Qandahar was lost to the Safavids once and for all,
it was a major blow to the Mughals. On the Safavid side, this event
resulted in a number of victory poems by court poets. The multiple
ways of commemorating the Qandahar event—in poetry, painting,
and chronicles—should not surprise us, as Babaie explains: "The role
the conflict with Ottoman adversaries played in state propaganda in
the sixteenth century was played by the encounter with and the final
defeat of the Mughals in Qandahar in the seventeenth."[38] The Safavid
relationship with India, however, was more complicated due to the
brain drain from Iran that allowed the Mughals to appropriate the role
of custodians of the Persian language. The new centers of Persian literary production had been in India for almost a century by this time.

None other than the Safavid poet laureate Sa'ib, who had established
friendships with various individuals during his time in India, composed at least three major poems in commemoration of the victory: a
panegyric *qasida* to Shah 'Abbas II, one on the defeat of Dara Shikoh,
and a three-hundred-line mini heroic epic.[39] In the panegyric, Sa'ib
boasts about the victory:

> *khali fuzud bar rukh-i Iran zi ru-yi Hind / tigh-i jahangusha-yi shahanshah-i*
>   *namdar*
> *butkhana-yi nikhvat-dara-yi hind ra / bar yak digar shikast bi-taufiq-i*
>   *kirdagar*
> *shakh-i ghurur-i vali-i Hindustan shikast / bikh-i nifaq kanda shud az bagh-i*
>   *ruzgar*
> *dar Hind gasht khutba-yi isna' ashara buland / shud kamil al-'iyar zar az*
>   *nam-i hasht o char*[40]

A mole has been added to Iran's face due to India; the victorious
  sword of the renowned king.
The mighty idol temples of India fell upon each other by God's favor.
The branch of pride of India's ruler has been broken; the root of
  discord from the world's garden has been uprooted.
The *khutba* of Ithna asharis has been proclaimed; gold has become of
  perfect standard with the name of the eight plus four.

This type of rhetorical bravado is not unusual in such poems, but here the victory of twelver Shiism is particularly significant in the Safavid context. Other Safavid poets and historians narrated the events around the triumphant victory in clever ways in a range of genres.

Muhammad Tahir Vahid was secretary-poet-chronicler under the Safavid monarchs Shah 'Abbas II, Shah Sulaiman I, and Shah Husain for almost half a century in the seventeenth century.[41] He became the grand vizier during the last decade of his life with the title " 'Imad al-daula" (Pillar of the state). He had never been to India but it was a strong part of his literary imagination. Vahid's chronicle of Shah 'Abbas II's reign, 'Abbasnama, is a mine of information on Safavid foreign relations and the construction of various gardens and buildings under royal patronage. His voluminous divan and his collection of letters (insha), some of them to the Mughals, have not been published to this day, though it is evident that his role in the intellectual and literary life of seventeenth-century Persianate circles was not at all insignificant. Vahid described the Qandahar events in his chronicle and composed a ghazal that in his own words gained some popularity among his contemporaries.[42]

The opening line of Vahid's poem is a celebration of the military victory. He mentions Qandahar explicitly rather than employing a subtle allusion, as would be more appropriate for the ghazal form: "Few people acquired the spoils of war in this way, [the way] that Qandahar and joyful fortune were acquired" (kasi ra shahid-i fathi bi-dinsan kam bi-dast amad / ki mulk-i Qandahar u daulat-i khurram bi-dast amad). The word shahid refers to a beloved or beautiful person, and here Qandahar is the beauty that was taken as the booty of war. This establishes the power relationship between lover and beloved. In the next line, the poet celebrates this victory in a physical display of his happiness: "I dance triumphantly with joy in the manner of tipplers, for the wine cup that does not cause intoxication came into my hands from a carefree heart" (zi shadi hamchu rang-i mai-kashan dar pust miraqsam / ki jam-i bi-khumaram az dil-i bigham bi-dast amad). The images are unusual and complex here, in keeping with the fashionable "fresh style" of Vahid's age. The rare idiomatic expression dar pust miraqsam (literally, "I dance in my skin") would seem to be derived from *dar pust khandidan* (to sneer) to mean gloating at the expense of a victim. The wine cup that does not intoxicate the drinker is due to the dispelling of sorrow; in a subversive twist to the traditional poetics of the *ghazal*, the poet does not valorize the state of drunkenness as a mystical state, in fact the opposite holds true here where sobriety is the cause of joy.

The next line is a familiar, albeit somewhat hackneyed, interaction of the poet-lover with his beloved: "By the command of a glance the coquetry of beauties became dark-hued; the impudent reins of that robber of men came into our grasp" (*bi-farman-i nigah shud 'ishva-yi sabzan gandumgun / 'inan-i shukhi-i an rahzan-i adam bi-dast amad*). The dusky beauties possess all the characteristics of the beloved: they are coquettish, cheeky, and stealers of hearts, but here instead of succumbing to their alluring ways, the poet-lover is able to tame them and gain the upper hand. In the next line, Vahid links the generic characteristics of the beloved to India, returning to the more specific topic of the Qandahar victory: "If India was ever unruly, like the curly hair of beauties, praise be to God—those disheveled curls came into our grasp" (*chu zulf-i shahidan Hind ar numudi sarkashi gahi / bihamdulilah sar-i an turra-yi dar ham bi-dast amad*). The dark hair of the beauties suggests a semiotic association with India, black and Hindu being synonyms in poetry, and the identification of the beloved with that land is clearly spelled out here. The dark disheveled curls are by extension the Mughal troops who have been subjugated.

The next line again moves to a general level, describing the celebratory mood of the victors: "After this no one will rail against fate. Joy became so widespread that [we] gained the world's heart" (*shikayat nist kas ra ba'd azin az gardish-i gardun / ki az bas 'am shud shadi dil-i 'alam bi-dast amad*). This celebration has a magical dimension, as well as the sanction of Islamic tradition, with a reference to the prophet Sulaiman or Solomon and his magical seal-ring: "The ancient celestial sphere's fortune became available for enjoyment. The world's Solomon captured the demon with the ring" (*sipihr-i pir ra sarmaya-yi 'ishrat muhayya shud / sulaiman-i jahan ra div ba khatam bi-dast amad*). The demon does Sulaiman's bidding and the ring brings success—the demon is the Mughal and the ring is Qandahar.

In the closing line (*maqta'*) of the *ghazal*, Vahid hints that the hard times when one was deprived of the good things in life have come to an end. The word *jins* denotes material goods that have finally come to them, a likely reference to Qandahar's role in the trade routes. The word *khurram* is repeated again, after first appearing in the first line: "Vahid, at last I plucked the rose of luxury from the garden of joy; these plentiful goods also came into our hands" (*gul-i 'aishi 'Vahid' akhir az bagh-i khurrami chidam/faravan shud zi bas in jins ma ra ham bi-dast amad*).[43] The poem thus ends on a triumphant note, celebrating material gain and the ultimate prize for a lover: union with the beloved. The polysemic nature of this *ghazal* is not atypical and the images are fairly easy to unpack, but there is a delicate balance between conventional and fresh, forcing the reader to acknowledge that this poem must be appreciated in its appropriate context. Vahid also wrote other poems on this subject such as one called *Masnavi-yi alat-i jang* (On the implements of war) that describes the various kinds of weapons used by the Safavids in this battle.

In a chronicle entitled *Qisas al-khaqani* (Kingly stories), composed in 1664–1674, the Safavid historian Vali Quli Shamlu narrated the supposedly true story of the wife of a certain Mathuradas, Mughal commander during the Qandahar siege, whose wife immolated herself in an act of *sati* when her slain husband was cremated. Shamlu included his own short *masnavi* on this real event in his history. In the poem within the chronicle, just before the wife of Mathuradas dies, the people at Qandahar ask her whether Mughal forces would arrive from India to save them. She prophecies that in forty days the Shah would be victorious and in twelve years Hindustan would be torn by strife.[44] Actual events like this on the Indo-Persian border and the popularity of the romance *Suz u gudaz* rendered the Hindu woman a distinctive literary trope and metaphor for the declining power of the Mughals. Among men of letters, the triumphant mood in late Safavid Iran had much to do with the reclamation of Persian to its supposedly rightful home, a sentiment that was exploited even further.

Vahid completed a short romantic *masnavi* of around 660 lines with the title *Gulzar-i 'Abbasi* (Rose garden of 'Abbas) in 1671 and dedicated it to Shah 'Abbas II.[45] None of the characters are given personal names in this story, as in Nau'i's *Suz u gudaz*. The plot of this romance involves the king of Iran, a handsome, wise, generous, and just ruler with an equally fine young son. The prince spends his time in debauchery, drinking parties, and chasing beautiful girls, something that is of great concern for his father. On the advice of a respected counselor, the king finds a famous beauty to marry his son, and she happens to be the daughter of the king of India. The king woos her hand with camel-loads of lavish gifts (*gasht ta mulk-i Hind az Iran / bahr az mauj-i gardan-i shuturan*). The prince, however, is not happy with the arranged marriage and refuses to see his wife. Being very clever and resourceful, the Indian princess holds a festive party of women that takes place in a garden near the prince's abode, to which he is naturally drawn since his nature is inclined toward pleasure. All the beauties are dressed in white and the prince is attracted to his own wife, though he does not know her identity. She tells him that she and her two sisters are the daughters of the King of Europe (Farang) who have come upon hard times. The prince has a good time partying with them, bewitched by their flirtatious behavior and dancing, until she suggests that he go and make himself ready to spend a few days with her. But when he returns he finds that there is no sign of anyone, the whole place is desolate. The prince is terribly upset and does everything to find her, but without success. His wife then arranges another similar setting, this time acting as the second sister, and this time all the women are dressed in yellow-gold. The same scenario is repeated again and in the end the prince finds himself all alone. This happens a third time, with the wife playing the part of the third sister with all her companions dressed in red, only for the paradisiacal scene to vanish without a trace once again.[46] Frustrated and dejected, the prince decides to leave his native land and become an exile. Hearing this news his wife sends him a farewell present. He is reluctant to accept anything from a woman he has not acknowledged as his spouse, but when he does take it he sees his own belt that he had left with the first woman in white in the garden. In an instant he understands everything and is happily united with his wife, the woman he has fallen in love with without knowing who she really was. Finally, all is right with the world and the lovers:

'alami gasht khurram u khandan / dahr shud naubahar-i pir u javan
gasht shahzada kamyab az yar / gulshan-i 'ishratash namud bahar

The world became joyful and smiling;
   it was a new spring for the old and young.
The prince was successful in love;
   a rose garden of luxury blossomed into spring.

The lovers lived happily ever after in Iran.

A deeper meaning could be read into the plot of this seemingly simple story at this particular juncture in the history of Iran-India cultural relations. With the narrative of the Iranian prince and his Indian bride, Vahid the poet and historian of Shah 'Abbas II's court tips the balance of power on the Safavid side. The Indian woman in Vahid's romance is virtuous and devoted, like the admirable *sati* of literature and life, but she used her feminine wiles, as India had done to draw scores of talented Iranians to her for a century, to bring her husband into her power. In the classical romances of Nizami and Amir Khusrau on the romantic exploits of the Iranian ruler Bahram Gur, the king wed seven women to assert a symbolic claim over the seven climes of the world. This Iranian prince in Vahid's romance is depicted as a monogamous lover attached to his Indian wife after having resisted her for some time. After a century-long phenomenon of the brain drain from Safavid Iran, partly motivated by the wealth and glamour of Mughal India, it is the Indian woman who comes to Iran and makes the land her home, settling there within the institution of a respectable marriage. The image of the alluring Indian woman, with negative connotations as well, was alive in the Safavid artistic imagination toward the end of the seventeenth century. She is often depicted as a force that threatened to overwhelm the traditional values and morals of Iran. An oil painting that was made in Iran around this period is one of several others of Indian women, in which the female is depicted as a courtesan attempting to seduce an Iranian prince with wine and her beauty (see Figure 10).[47] The heroine of Vahid's romance is also an unnamed generic character who puts on the mask of a temptress but is actually a virtuous wife.

FIGURE 10 Courtier refusing wine from Indian courtesans

Late in his long life, Vahid wrote another romantic poem, *Masnavi-yi 'ashiq u ma'shuq,* which simply translates as "Story of the Lover and Beloved," also dedicated to Shah Sulaiman. This was an allegorical tale about yet another unnamed pair of lovers, an Indian prince and princess who overcome the obstacles to their love in India and travel to Isfahan where they admire the beautiful city.[48] Their elopement involves the hero's friend taking the heroine's place dressed in drag in a wedding ceremony that she was being forced to go through. This tale of Vahid implies that the direction of the caravan's movement has once again changed, with Indians now being drawn to visit Iran and its impressive capital city. The poem is more about showcasing the splendors of late Safavid Isfahan, whose buildings, gardens, and the bazaar with its many handsome shopkeepers are described in the familiar genre of *shahrashub.* An early eighteenth-century manuscript in the Bibliothèque Nationale in Paris provides a clue about the reading culture of the time.[49] It is in the form of an anthology of poems of various lengths that juxtaposes Nau'i's *Suz u gudaz* with Vahid's romances, showing their relationship with each other. They were read together, it seems, and were connected in terms of the shared character of the Indian woman and her Indian or Iranian lovers.

In Vahid's lifetime, the view in Iran about India had undergone a transformation. The ambivalence about leaving home for a place no longer known for its rich patrons was markedly different from the feelings of émigrés in previous decades. A persistent idea among scholars of literary studies has been that the decline of the Safavids started after the reign of Shah 'Abbas II, which ended in 1666, and literature was a victim of the political situation. This tends to lead to the teleological argument that "the time was yet to come when, by turning to the literature of the earlier centuries, hopes for a revival of Persian letters were to materialize."[50] But new studies on the late Safavids does not view the entire seventeenth century as a cultural void. The historian Rudi Matthee is of the opinion that well until after the middle of that century Isfahan was at the "peak of its economic energy and cultural vitality."[51] Sources on the literary production and arts of the late seventeenth century also reveal the existence of a vibrant culture with a new orientation.[52]

In the next century in Iran, when there was an awareness of the disconnectedness of the Persophone domains, it would eventually lead to the rejection of the fresh style that was connected to India and a "return" (*bazgasht*) to a purer, more pristine form of poetic expression. The utopian ideal of Mughal India as Arcadia and El Dorado lasted just over a century, leaving a legacy of Persianate cosmopolitanism for posterity that people in South Asia grapple to embrace or reject. In fact, in contrast to the seventeenth-century attempts to recreate Iran in India, especially in Kashmir, the subcontinent was to become "an imperfect imitation of Iran," as seen in the early nineteenth-century travel narrative of the Iranian religious scholar Aqa Ahmad Bihbihani.[53]

The historian of Persian literature, Azar Begdili, writing in post-Safavid Isfahan expressed a feeling of otherness with both the physical space and culture of India.[54] In his monumental work of literary history and biography, *Atashkada,* dating from 1760, in which he accords a few pages to poets outside Iran, he describes India as: "That vast expanse of earth comprises many countries and countless cities. Its climate is generally hot. The customs and laws there are mostly opposite of those of the people of Iran, even Turan. Their strange fruits cannot be found in this land. Because of its great distance, people of Iran have no complete information about the circumstances of this land."[55] In a twist of fate or historical circumstance, things returned to the way they were in the medieval period, with a fantastic image of India as a distant and strange land, despite the accumulated knowledge of half a millennium available to poets and scholars and a century of intense interaction during the Safavid period. Azar's work that privileged Iran as the center of poetic production is rightly considered a milestone in the history of the fragmentation of the Persophone world into local and unconnected domains, although literary history informs us that this process began earlier.[56] Azar praised Kashmir, as one would expect, for by his time "places like Kashmir were understood to be paradisiacal, whether or not an author had been there, and whether or not the place was within the larger land with which the author was affiliated."[57] While Azar's *bazgasht* movement signified a return to the classics for Iranians, it also meant a return to the pre-early modern view of India as a place of wonders. While in India, at around this time, heated debates over the usage and ownership of Persian livened up literary salons even as Indo-Persian literature continued to flourish in new circles and genres.[58]

Poets who wrote in Persian in India from the second half of the seventeenth century to the early twentieth century continued to feel connected to Iran in multiple ways. Many did not feel the otherness toward other Persianate societies because of the shared classical tradition. The children and descendants of Persophone émigrés from the early Mughal period were enthusiastic proponents of the vernacular languages, whether Braj-bhasha Hindi or Urdu, in the seventeenth and eighteenth centuries. We already saw the case of the Hindi poet Rahim or 'Abdur-Rahim Khankhanan, whose father the general Bairam Khan was of Turkman stock from Iran and came to India with Babur. Fa'iz Dihlavi, a poet of the early Urdu register called *rekhta*, was descended from an ethnic Kurd, the Safavid general 'Ali Mardan Khan, who had defected to the Mughals in Shah Jahan's time. There were many other people like these whose individual and collective stories remain to be narrated.

Delhi had a Persian literary renaissance in the first half of the nineteenth century in which the poet Asadullah Khan, "Ghalib," who wrote in Persian and Urdu, was a major authority on poetics, and in many ways the last one in the so-called twilight of Mughal culture. Although Ghalib never visited Iran, he declared in a verse: "If you have the requisite passion, it is only half a step from Kashi (Banaras or Varanasi in India) to Kashan (Iran)" (*jununat gar bi-nafas-i khud tamam ast/zi Kashi ta bi-Kashan nim-gam ast*).[59] To Kashi and Kashan, one can add Kashmir since it was the ideal locale for a coming together of Iranian and Indian cultural worlds. This leap from one place to the other in the imagination sustained Ghalib, but those after him felt a nostalgia for the past along with a great deal of cultural amnesia, without the connection to the living language. Nature imagery in an idealized form had been prominent in classical Persian literature, and despite the overuse of the epithet "paradisiacal" in early modern Persian literature, the natural world of Kashmir and other spaces came to be forever celebrated as the pristine paradise of which the urban world was a pale reflection.

A painful irony in the story of Mughal Arcadia is that the people who actually inhabit the fabled valley of Kashmir, still advertised as a paradise on Earth for tourists, pilgrims, and honeymooners in India, have been repeatedly disillusioned by successive rulers and occupiers. In the era of modernization and nationalism, there is a stronger sense of belonging to a nation, whether Iran, India, Afghanistan, Pakistan, or Bangladesh, and some Muslims find links to various Sunni or Shia communities of the Islamic world, rather than to the idea of a Persianate cultural area. The Mughals, though, are present everywhere in South Asia, from the silent presence of the monumental architecture that people live and work around to Bombay films such as *Mughal-e-Azam* (1960) and *Jodhaa-Akbar* (2008), in which characters speak modern Urdu and Hindi, as well as in the cultures of food, clothes, and the arts. The early Mughal era has either been romanticized as a golden age or portrayed as a dark age of conquest and violence. On both sides of the nationalist view, the story of the dominant role of the Persian language and the presence and contributions of scores of Persians at and outside court in the sixteenth and seventeenth centuries is largely ignored or forgotten. The literary works and poetic imagery in a variety of languages still remain our guide to understand how Mughals such as Faizi and 'Urfi, Munir and Kalim, 'Abdur-Rahim Khanan and Zafar Khan viewed the world around them and were viewed by people as far away as Istanbul and Isfahan.

Notes

Introduction: *Lingua Persica*

1. Iqbal, "Payam-i mashriq," *Ash'ar-i Farsi-yi Iqbal Lahauri,* ed. Mahmud 'Ilmi (Tehran: Javidan, 1991), 214.

2. The case of classical Chinese is discussed by Benjamin A. Elman in the introduction to *Rethinking East Asian Languages, Vernaculars, and Literacies, 1000–1919* (Leiden: Brill, 2014), 1–28; for Latin, see A. H. Morton, "The Transmission of Persian Texts Compared to the Case of Classical Latin," in *Literacy in the Persianate World: Writing and the Social Order,* ed. Brian Spooner and William H. Hanaway (Philadelphia: University of Pennsylvania Museum of Archaeology and Anthropology, 2012), 143–158. Richard M. Eaton and Phillip B. Wagoner explain the idea of the Persian cosmopolis in its historical intersections with the Sanskrit cosmopolis as put forward by Sheldon Pollock, in *Power, Memory, Architecture: Contested Sites on India's Deccan Plateau, 1300–1600* (New Delhi: Oxford University Press, 2014), 18–27.

3. *The Travels of Pietro Della Valle in India: From the Old English Translation of 1664* (London: Hakluyt Society, 1892), 1: 96–97.

4. The widespread social phenomenon of composing poetry in this period in Iran and Central Asia is discussed by Paul Losensky in *Welcoming Fighani: Imitation and Poetic Individuality in the Safavid-Mughal Ghazal* (Costa Mesa: Mazda, 1998), 138–141.

5. There are strong parallels between the role of Persian and English as languages of administration and empire in South Asia. The British colonial machinery continued many Mughal practices of protocol and administration, except the important role accorded to poetry. For a brief discussion of these cosmopolitan languages, see Sheldon I. Pollock, "Introduction," in *Literary Cultures in History: Reconstructions from South Asia* (Berkeley: University of California Press, 2003), 33.

6. For comparative purposes, an insightful study on classical Arabic and Persian literary cultures and the socioeconomic, religious, and ethnic identities of poets is found in Jocelyn Sharlet, "The Socially Mobile Professional Poet," chap. 9 in *Patronage and Poetry in the Islamic World: Social Mobility and Poetry in the Islamic World* (London: I. B. Tauris, 2011), 204–235.

7. The surveys in English of Mughal Persian literature are: Annemarie Schimmel, "Languages and Literature," in *The Empire of the Great Mughals: History, Art and Culture,* trans. Corinne Attwood, ed. Burzine K. Waghmar (London: Reaktion Books, 2004), 229–261; Wheeler M. Thackston, "Persian Literature," in *The Magnificent Mughals,* ed. Zeenut Ziad (Oxford: Oxford University Press, 2002), 84–111; Muzaffar Alam, "The Pursuit of Persian: Language in Mughal Politics," *Modern Asian Studies* 32 (1998): 317–349; Annemarie Schimmel, *Islamic Literatures* (Wiesbaden: O. Harrassowitz, 1973); Hadi Hasan, *Mughal Poetry, Its Cultural and Historical Value* (Madras: Islamic Literature Society, 1952); Abdul Ghani, *A History of Persian Language and Literature at the Mughal Court* (Allahabad: Indian Press, 1929).

8. E. G. Browne, *A Literary History of Persia* (Cambridge: Cambridge University Press, 1959), 4: 24. Browne's work is a history of Persian literature in Iran but he does include some major Safavid poets who visited India; also see Jan Rypka, *History of Iranian Literature* (Dordrecht: D. Reidel, 1968), 292.

9. Losensky, *Welcoming Fighani,* 3.

10. Marshall Hodgson, *Venture of Islam: The Gunpowder Empires and Modern Times* (Chicago: University of Chicago Press, 1974), 2: 293; also see Audrey Truschke, *Culture of Encounters: Sanskrit at the Mughal Court* (New York: Columbia University Press, 2016), 8.

11. Waris Kirmani, *Dreams Forgotten: An Anthology of Indo-Persian Poetry* (Aligarh: Aligarh Muslim University, 1984), xiii.

12. This has been a flourishing topic of investigation among Persian literati since the seventeenth century; for modern scholarship see Losensky, *Welcoming Fighani,* and Rajeev Kinra, "Making Indo-Persian Literature Fresh: Chandar Bhan's Poetic World," chap. 5 in *Writing Self, Writing Empire: Chandar Bhan Brahman and the Cultural World of the*

Indo-Persian State Secretary (Oakland: University of California Press, 2015), 201–239.

13. Kinra rightly reminds us in his discussion of the *sabk-i hindi* or *taza-gu'i* debate that quibbling about the connection of this style with India "distracts us from the actual social, cultural, and historical dynamics that animated the Indo-Persian literati of the early modern period, nearly all of whom were far more interested in questions of newness and literary ingenuity than in 'Indianness' as such," *Writing Self, Writing Empire*, 205.

14. Truschke, *Culture of Encounters*, 233–234, 239.

15. Busch, *Poetry of Kings: The Classical Hindi Literature of Mughal India* (New York: Oxford University Press, 2011); Kinra, *Writing Self, Writing Empire*.

16. Michael A. Elliott and Claudia Stokes, eds., *American Literary Studies: A Methodological Reader* (New York: New York University Press, 2003), 8.

17. Losensky, *Welcoming Fighani*, 142.

18. One of the criticisms leveled against the New Historicism is an ahistorical privileging of the synchronic over the diachronic, as discussed in Neema Parvini, *Shakespeare's History Plays: Rethinking Historicism* (Edinburgh: Edinburgh University Press, 2012), 72–73. This is true to some degree in the scholarship of early modern Persian literature and more awareness is required of the great degree of intertextuality and *imitatio* in texts.

19. Salma Khadra Jayyusi, "Andalusi Poetry: The Golden Period," in *The Legacy of Muslim Spain*, ed. Salma Khadra Jayyusi (Leiden: Brill, 1992), 318.

20. Recent comparative studies, such as Stephen F. Dale's *The Muslim Empires of the Ottomans, Safavids, and Mughals* (Cambridge, UK: Cambridge University Press, 2010) and Douglas E. Streusand's *Islamic Gunpowder Empires: Ottomans, Safavids, and Mughals* (Philadelphia: Westview Press, 2011), both devote sections to literature and the arts.

21. Muzaffar Alam and Sanjay Subrahmanyam, *Indo-Persian Travels in the Age of Discoveries, 1400–1800* (Cambridge, UK: Cambridge University Press, 2007), 15; also see, Kathryn Babayan, "The Topography of Travel in Early Modern Persianate Landscapes," *Harvard Library Bulletin* 23 (2012): 25–34; and Kinra, *Writing Self, Writing Empire*, 201–202.

1: Mughal Persian Literary Culture

1. The modern biographical dictionary-cum-anthology of poets who emigrated from Persophone regions to India in the sixteenth and seventeenth

centuries (Ahmad Gulchin-Ma'ani, ed., *Karvan-i Hind* [Mashhad: Astan-i Quds-i Razavi, 1990], vi), includes the names of 742 poets. The most were in Akbar's reign (259), followed by Jahangir (173), Shah Jahan (114), and Aurangzeb (66). These were only the most prominent men, and individuals in other fields whose lives were not recorded are not included.

2. The career of one such individual, Fath Allah Shirazi, who was an émigré at the Mughal court, is studied in detail by Ali Anooshahr in "Shirazi Scholars and the Political Culture of the Sixteenth-Century Indo-Persian World," *The Indian Social and Economic History Review* 51 (2014): 331–352.

3. This work has been largely neglected by literary scholars, as have most of Amir Khusrau's so-called historical poems. An English translation of middling quality by I. H. Ansari and Hameed Afaq Siddiqui has appeared recently: *Khusrau's Qiran us Sa'dain, Conjunction of Two Lucky Planets* (Delhi: Idarah-i Adabiyat-i Delli, 2012).

4. Amir Khusrau, *Qiran al-sa'dain*, ed. Muhammad Isma'il Sahib (Aligarh: Aligarh College Press, 1918).

5. Amir Khusrau, *Nuh sipihr*, ed. Mohammad Wahid Mirza (London: Oxford University Press, 1950).

6. Adam is followed by a host of mythical figures from the Persian epic tradition (Hushang, Jamshid, Zahhak, Garshasp, Isfandiyar, Bahman), one from the Abrahamic tradition (Ham), then various people such as Mani the painter, Alexander the conqueror, the pre-Islamic Iranian king Bahram Gur along with his minister Burzuya, and then Muslim rulers (Muhammad Qasim to Humayun). Abu'l-Fazl, *The A'in-i Akbari*, trans. H. S. Jarrett (Delhi: Taj, 1989) 2: 359–387.

7. Muzaffar Alam explains the literary situation in the Delhi area just before the Mughals: "There is hardly a notable Persian writer to be found in the fifteenth and sixteenth centuries," even as there was more prevalence of Hindi (or Hindavi) at the time. Alam, *The Languages of Political Islam in India, c. 1200–1800* (Delhi: Permanent Black, 2004), 123–124.

8. The proportion of Uzbeks and Chaghatais to Iranians remained pretty consistent from the time of Humayun's return from Iran to the Shah Jahan period, although the latter were increasingly appointed to the highest posts; see Richard C. Foltz, *Mughal India and Central Asia* (Karachi, PK: Oxford University Press, 2001), 36–37. The larger historical phenomenon of the Iranian migration to South and Southeast Asia, especially in terms of the context of trade and politics, is studied in de-

tail by Sanjay Subrahmanyam in "Iranians Abroad: Intra-Asian Elite Migration and Early Modern State Formation," *The Journal of Asian Studies* 51 (1992): 340–363.

9. Masahi Haneda deals with the complex question of the backgrounds of the Iranians in this phenomenon, "Emigration of Iranian Elites to India during the 16th–18th Centuries," *Cahiers d'Asie Centrale* 3/4 (1997): 129–143.

10. Juan R. I. Cole, "The Imagined Embrace: Gender, Identity, and Iranian Ethnicity in Jahangiri Painting," in *Safavid Iran and Her Neighbors*, ed. Michel Mazzaoui (Salt Lake City: The University of Utah Press, 2003), 50–51.

11. Compared to the Deccan courts, where there was a violent history of tensions between the "foreigners" and "indigenous" people, as well as Shia-Sunni conflicts, the situation at the Mughal court was much more cordial; see Jamal Malik, *Islam in South Asia: A Short History* (Leiden: Brill, 2008), 135–140.

12. The subject of Shah Tahmasp's "spiritual rebirth" is discussed by Colin Mitchell in "Tahmasp I," *Encyclopaedia Iranica Online* (2009).

13. Iskandar Beg Munshi, *History of Shah 'Abbas the Great*, trans. Roger M. Savory (Boulder, CO: Westview, 1978–1986), 274.

14. Abu'l-Fazl, *The A'in-i Akbari*, 617–618; also quoted in C. M. Naim, "Mughal and English Patronage of Urdu Poetry: A Comparison," *Urdu Texts and Contexts: The Selected Essays of C. M. Naim* (Delhi: Permanent Black, 2004), 156–157.

15. Aziz Ahmad, "Safavid Poets and India," *Iran* 14 (1976), 118; Ghani, *Persian Language and Literature*, 1: 168–171; Fazli Beg, a historian of the Safavid court, openly admits that it was greed (*ziyada-talabi*) that drew him to India, in *A Chronicle of the Reign of Shah 'Abbas*, ed. Kioumars Ghereghlou (Cambridge, UK: Gibb Memorial Trust, 2015), 1: xxvii.

16. Quoted in Muzaffar Alam, "The Pursuit of Persian," 320–322; for the entire document, see Riazul Islam, *Calendar of Documents on Indo-Persian Relations, 1500–1750* (Tehran: Iranian Culture Foundation, 1979), 1: 101.

17. Islam, *Calendar of Documents*, 1: 117–118.

18. Colin Mitchell, *The Practice of Politics in Safavid Iran: Power, Religion and Rhetoric* (London: Tauris, 2009), 110.

19. Jean Chardin, *Travels in Persia, 1673–77* (New York: Dover, 1988), 130. The other two reasons given by Chardin are the Persian predilection for pederasty and "immoderate luxury."

20. Losensky, *Welcoming Fighani*, 141.

21. In the late Mughal period poets gave themselves this title to conjure up the grandeur of the court in earlier times; Naim, "Mughal and English Patronage of Urdu Poetry," 158–159.

22. Michael Axworthy, *A History of Iran: Empire of the Mind* (London: Hurst, 2007), 134.

23. 'Abdun-Nabi Fakhruz-Zamani Qazvini, *Tazkira-yi Maikhana*, ed. Ahmad Gulchin-Ma'ani (Tehran: Iqbal, 1961), 809; for a discussion of the ethical (*akhlaq*) and philosophical background that informed the Mughal concept of justice and toleration, see Alam, *The Language of Political Islam in India*, 61–76.

24. Rajeev Kinra, "Handling Diversity with Absolute Civility: The Global Historical Legacy of Mughal *Sulh-i Kull,*" *The Medieval History Journal* 16 (2013), 253; in this regard, also see the discussion of Abu'l-Fazl's renowned inscription in a Kashmir temple, which inspired Alfred Tennyson's poem "Akbar's Dream," Wendy Doniger, *On Hinduism* (Oxford: Oxford University Press, 2014), 132–134.

25. 'Abdus-Sattar Lahauri, *Majalis-i Jahangiri*, ed. 'Arif Naushahi and Mu'in Nizami (Tehran: Miras-i Maktub, 2006), 45.

26. F. Lehmann, "Akbar I," *Encyclopaedia Iranica Online* (2011).

27. Jahangir, *The Jahangirnama*, trans. Wheeler M. Thackston (New York: Oxford University Press, 1999), 40.

28. Quoted in Ebba Koch, "The Influence of the Jesuit Missions on Symbolic Representations of the Mughal Emperors," *Mughal Art and Imperial Ideology: Collected Essays* (New Delhi: Oxford University Press, 2001), 1.

29. This phenomenon was particularly centered on the Islamic millennium that fell at the end of the sixteenth century. One such "radical Sufi" group from Iran, the Nuqtavis, were driven out of Iran and sought refuge in Akbar's India, see A. Azfar Moin, *The Millennial Sovereign: Sacred Kingship and Sainthood in Islam* (New York: Columbia University Press, 2012), 162–166.

30. Aditya Behl, "Pages from the Book of Religions: Encountering Difference in Mughal India," in *Forms of Knowledge in Early Modern Asia: Explorations in the Intellectual History of India and Tibet, 1500–1800* (Durham, NC: Duke University Press, 2011), 210–239; also useful are M. Athar Ali, "Pursuing an Elusive Seeker of Universal Truth: The Identity and Environment of the Author of the *Dabistan-i Mazahib,*" in *Mughal India: Studies in Polity, Ideas, Society, and Culture* (New Delhi: Oxford University Press, 2006), 216–228, and Daniel Sheffield, "The Language of Paradise in Safavid Iran: Speech and Cosmology in the Thought of Azar Kayvan

and His Followers," in *There's No Tapping around Philology*, ed. Alireza Korangy and Daniel Sheffield (Wiesbaden: Otto Harrassowitz, 2014), 161–183.

31. Behl, "Pages from the Book of Religions," 233.

32. Fakhruz-Zamani Qazvini, *Tazkira-yi Maikhana*, 631.

33. I learned about these individuals from Theodore Beers who works on Safavid literary culture. The poets' biographies are cited in Taqi Auhadi's biographical dictionary, *Tazkira-yi 'Arafat al-'ashiqin va 'arasat al-'arifin*, ed. Muhsin Naji Nasrabadi (Tehran: Asatir, 2009), 3073–3074, 3102–3104.

34. The only general study of the literature under Shah Jahan is the second half of M. L. Rahman's *Persian Literature in India during the Time of Jahangir and Shah Jahan* (Baroda: Department of Persian and Urdu, M. S. University of Baroda, 1970). No separate biographical dictionary (*tazkira*) of poets was compiled in Shah Jahan's reign; instead, several imperial historians appended a list and short biographies of contemporary poets to their works.

35. Walter Andrews and Mehmet Kalpaklı, *The Age of Beloveds* (Durham: Duke University Press, 2005), 30; the historian Cornell H. Fleischer discusses the phenomenon of "Iranian-preferment" during Sultan Murad III's reign in the late sixteenth century, *Bureaucrat and Intellectual in the Ottoman Empire: The Historian Mustafa Ali (1541–1600)* (Princeton: Princeton University Press, 1986), 154–155.

36. This verse was quoted by the poet Lami'i. A fruitful discussion on this topic with Gülru Necipoğlu resulted in my learning of this quotation and the similar situation at the Ottoman court; see her "Visual Cosmopolitanism and Creative Translation: Artistic Conversations with Renaissance Italy in Mehmed II's Constantinople," *Muqarnas* 29 (2012), 15.

37. Alam and Subrahmanyam, *Indo-Persian Travels*, 217.

38. Valih Daghistani, *Tazkira-yi riyaz al-shu'ara*, ed. Muhsin Naji Nasrabadi (Tehran: Asatir, 2005), 1: 634. Hazin's relationship with India is also discussed at length in Alam and Subrahmanyam, *Indo-Persian Travels*, 229–239.

39. On the subject of native speakers of Persian at the Mughal court, see Alam, "The Pursuit of Persian," 341. Jean Calmard discusses the "unidirectional flow" of such professionals at this time; Indian traders and moneylenders did settle in Iran, "Safavid Persia in Indo-Persian Sources and in Timurid-Mughal Perception," in *The Making of Indo-Persian Culture: Indian and French Studies*, ed. Muzaffar Alam, Françoise "Nalini" Delvoye, and Marc Gaborieau (New Delhi: Manohar, 2000), 355.

40. Chandarbhan Brahman, *Chahar Chaman*, ed. Muhammad Yunus Jaffrey (New Delhi: Markaz-i Tahqiqat-i Farsi-yi Rayzani-yi Farhangi-yi Jumhuri-yi Islami-yi Iran, 2007), 176. I have condensed this section of the letter to avoid references to specific texts. On this author see Kinra, *Writing Self, Writing Empire*.

41. Hindu poets of Persian were increasingly mentioned in biographical dictionaries of the late Mughal period; see Stefano Pellò, *Tutiyan-i hind: Specchi identitari e proiezioni cosmopolite indo-persiane (1680–1856)* (Firenze: Società Editrice Fiorentina, 2012).

42. Ruby Lal studies the Mughal harem in the context of broader issues in *Domesticity and Power in the Early Mughal World* (Cambridge: Cambridge University Press, 2005). The subject of women poets is discussed in Sunil Sharma, "From 'Aesha to Nur Jahan: The Shaping of a Classical Persian Poetic Canon of Women." *Journal of Persianate Studies* 2 (2009): 147–164.

43. The details of 'Urfi's life have been gathered together from various biographical dictionaries and chronicles, Gulchin-Ma'ani, *Karvan-i Hind*, 872–884.

44. 'Urfi, *Kulliyat-i 'Urfi Shirazi*, ed. Javahiri Vajdi (Tehran: Kitabkhana-yi Sana'i, 1990), 152.

45. The history of how the image of the black Hindu came to be a synecdoche for black India has only been spottily traced in poetry, but it certainly predates the Mughal period. See Schimmel, "Turk and Hindu, a Poetical Image and its Application to Historical Fact," in *Islam and Cultural Change in the Middle Ages*, ed. Speros Vryonis, Jr. (Wiesbaden: Harrassowitz, 1975), 107–126. Jamali, a pre-Mughal poet of Delhi, wrote, "If Khorasan has a whiteness full of light / well, prosperous India's blackness has no equals" (*khurasan gar bayazi dasht pur-nur / savad-i a'zam amad Hind-i ma'mur*), quoted in Stefano Pellò, "Local Lexis? Provincializing Persian in Fifteenth-Century North India," in *After Timur Left: Culture and Circulation in Fifteenth-Century India*, ed. Francesca Orsini and Samira Sheikh (New Delhi: Oxford University Press, 2014), 166. The earlier poet Amir Khusrau had also put Khurasan and Hindustan in binary opposition, always in favor of the latter.

46. This aspect of 'Urfi's life is discussed in Sunil Sharma, "Forbidden Love, Persianate Style: Re-reading Tales of Iranian Poets and Mughal Patrons," *Iranian Studies* 42 (2009): 765–779.

47. Badauni, *Muntakhab al-tavarikh*, ed. Mawlavi Ahmad 'Ali Sahib and Taufiq Subhani (Tehran: Anjuman-i Asar va Mafakhir-i Farhangi, 2000), 3: 195.

48. Munibur Rahman, "Fayzi, Abu'l-Fayz," *Encyclopaedia Iranica Online* (2012).

49. Abu'l-Fazl, *The History of Akbar,* trans. Wheeler M. Thackston (Cambridge, MA: Harvard University Press), 4: 329–331.

50. The transregional phenomenon of Bedil is studied by Kevin L. Schwartz, "The Local Lives of a Transregional Poet: 'Abd al-Qader Bidel and the Writing of Persianate Literary History," *Journal of Persianate Studies* 9 (2016): 83–106.

51. Faizi, *Divan-i Faizi,* ed. A. D. Arshad (Tehran: Furughi, 1983), ii–iii.

52. Paul Losensky, "Taleb Amoli," *Encyclopaedia Iranica Online* (2004).

53. Munir, *Karnama-yi Abu Barakat Munir Lahauri va Siraj-i munir-i Siraj al-Din 'Ali Khan-i Arzu,* ed. S. M. A. Ikram (Islamabad: Markaz-i Tahqiqat-i Farsi-yi Iran va Pakistan, 1977), 27; for a close reading of this work by Munir, especially on the *taza-gu'i* style, see Kinra, *Writing Self, Writing Empire,* 233–234.

54. Quoted in Gulchin-Ma'ani, *Karvan-i Hind,* 439–440; also in Browne, *A Literary History of Persia,* 4: 166–168.

55. Abu'l-Fazl, *The A'in-i Akbari,* 1: 654.

56. Badauni, *Muntakhab al-tavarikh,* 3: 139–140.

57. Ibid., 246.

58. Ibid., 184–185.

59. Ibid., 235.

60. Nizamuddin Ahmad, *The Tabaqat-i-Akbari of Khwaja Nizamuddin Ahmad,* trans. Brajendranath De (Delhi: Low Price Publications, 1992), 3: 714–753.

61. There has been little comparative work done between Safavid and Mughal chronicles; pioneering studies are by Sholeh A. Quinn, "Through the Looking Glass: Kingly Virtues in Safavid and Mughal Historiography," *Journal of Persianate Studies* 3, no. 2 (2010): 143–155.

62. Iskandar Beg Munshi, *History of Shah 'Abbas the Great,* 279.

63. Truschke, *Cultures of Encounters,* 233–234.

64. Kalim, *Divan-i Abu Talib Kalim Hamadani,* ed. Muhammad Qahraman (Mashhad: Astan-i Quds-i Razavi, 1990), 22.

65. Babur, *The Baburnama: Memoirs of Babur, Prince and Emperor,* trans. Wheeler M. Thackston (New York: The Modern Library, 2002), 156.

66. Iqtidar Alam Khan, "The Mughal Empire and the Iranian Diaspora of the Sixteenth Century," *A Shared Heritage: The Growth of Civilization in India and Iran,* ed. Irfan Habib (New Delhi: Tulika, 2002), 102.

67. Quoted from Jadunath Sarkar, "Adab-i 'Alamgiri," in *Studies in Aurangzib's Reign* (Calcutta: M. C. Sarkar & Sons, 1933), 40, 42–43; for the

education of Mughal princes, see chapter 3 in Munis D. Faruqui, *The Princes of the Mughal Empire, 1504–1719* (Cambridge: Cambridge University Press, 2012), 66–133.

68. Shamsur Rahman Faruqi, "The Strange Case of Persian and Urdu in the Nineteenth Century," *Annual of Urdu Studies* 13 (1998): 3–30.

69. An overview of the rise and fall of Persian is offered by Muhammad Aslam Syed, "How Could Urdu Be the Envy of Persian (*rashk-i-Farsi*)! The Role of Persian in South Asian Culture and Literature," in *Literacy in the Persianate World: Writing and the Social Order,* ed. Brian Spooner and William H. Hanaway (Philadelphia: University of Pennsylvania Museum of Archaeology and Anthropology, 2012), 298.

70. Busch, *Poetry of Kings,* 3–22.

71. The normative text on advice to a Mughal nobleman emphasizes knowledge of Arabic, Persian, Hindi, and Turkish, M. Hidayat Husain, "The Mirza Namah (The Book of the Perfect Gentleman) of Mirza Kamran with an English Translation," *Journal of the Asiatic Society of Bengal* 9 (1913), 4; also, Aziz Ahmad, "The British Museum Mirzanama and the Seventeenth Century Mirza in India," *Iran* 13 (1975): 99–110.

72. Corinne Lefèvre, "The Court of 'Abd-ur-Rahim Khan-i Khanan as a Bridge between Iranian and Indian Cultural Traditions," in *Culture and Circulation: Literature in Motion in Early Modern India,* ed. Thomas de Bruijn and Allison Busch (Leiden: Brill, 2014), 104.

73. Audrey Truschke, "Setting the Record Wrong: A Sanskrit Vision of Mughal Conquests," *South Asian History and Culture* 3 (2012): 373–396.

74. For a recent study that connects various premodern and modern literary traditions in a specific space, see Francesca Orsini, "The Multilingual Local in World Literature," *Comparative Literature* 67 (2015): 345–374.

75. Ebba Koch, "The Taj Mahal: Architecture, Symbolism, and Urban Significance," *Muqarnas* 22 (2005), 147; also see Truschke, *Culture of Encounters,* 1–2.

76. Nihavandi, *The Ma'asir-i-Rahimi,* ed. Hidayat Husain (Calcutta: Asiatic Society of Bengal, 1925), 2: 590–592.

77. Chhotubhai Ranchhodji Naik, *'Abdu'r-Rahim Khan-i-Khanan and His Literary Circle* (Ahmedabad: Gujarat University, 1966), 258.

78. For 'Abdur-Rahim's role as a guide, see C. M. Naim, "Mughal and English Patronage of Urdu Poetry," 158.

79. Stuart McGregor, *Hindi Literature from Its Beginnings to the Nineteenth Century* (Wiesbaden: Harrassowitz, 1984), 121.

80. John Seyller, *Workshop and Patron in Mughal India: The Freer Ramayana and Other Illustrated Manuscripts of 'Abd al-Rahim* (Zurich: Artibus Asiae, 1999), 251.

81. Translated by Busch, *Poetry of Kings,* 92.

82. Ibid., 93.

83. *The Jahangirnama,* 93; also discussed in Christopher Shackle, "Settings of Panegyric: The Secular Qasida in Mughal and British India," in *Qasida Poetry in Islamic Asia and Africa,* ed. Stefan Sperl and Christopher Shackle (Leiden: Brill, 1996), 1: 213. Shackle makes some comparative observations on the Persian *qasida* and Sanskrit and Hindi *prashasti* (p. 214).

84. 'Inayat Khan, *The Shah Jahan Nama of 'Inayat Khan,* trans. A. R. Fuller, ed. W.E. Begley and Z. A. Desai (Delhi: Oxford University Press, 1990), 33.

85. Kinra, *Writing Self, Writing Empire,* 3–5; the case of a functionary from Shah Jahan's court is illustrative: "Chandar Bhan himself was quite aware that there was something relatively "new"—modern, even—about his own family's place in Indian society and that it was specifically their literacy and expertise in the domain of the secretarial arts that made it possible for them to take advantage of the possibilities afforded by the Mughal cultural and political world to move beyond a more "traditional" Brahmanical role," 163.

86. A novel style of literature combining linguistic registers of early modern Hindi and Urdu appeared in a Rajput cultural context, for which see Heidi Rika Maria Pauwels, *Cultural Exchange in Eighteenth-Century India: Poetry and Paintings from Kishangarh* (Berlin: EB-Verlag, 2015).

87. Sukumar Ray, *Humayun in Persia* (Calcutta: The Asiatic Society, 1948), especially chapter 4.

88. Ghazali, *Divan-i Ghazali Mashhadi (asar al-shabab),* ed. Husain Qurbanipur Arani (Tehran: Intisharat-i 'Ilmi va Farhangi, 2008), 334.

89. Ahmed, "Safavid Poets and India," 125.

90. Badauni, *Muntakhab al-tavarikh,* 3: 133.

91. See John Seyller, *The Adventures of Hamza: Painting and Storytelling in Mughal India* (Washington, DC: Smithsonian Institution, 2002), for a history of and reconstruction of the Mughal manuscript of this work.

92. The world of professional storytelling in the early modern world is discussed in Pasha Khan, "A Handbook for Storytellers: The *Tiraz al-akhbar* and the *Qissa* Genre," *Tellings and Texts: Music, Literature and Performance in North India* (Cambridge, UK: Open Book Publishers, 2015), 185–207.

93. Nihavandi, *Ma'asir-i Rahimi,* 590–591.

94. 'Abdus-Sattar Lahauri, *Majalis-i Jahangiri, ,* 258–260.

95. Ibid., 256.

96. On orality and performance of poetry at the early Mughal court, see Sunil Sharma, "Reading the Acts and Lives of Performers in Mughal Persian Texts," in *Tellings and Texts: Music, Literature and Performance in North India,* ed. Francesca Orsini and Katherine Butler Schofield (Cambridge, UK: Open Book Publishers, 2015), 283–302.

97. Mutribi Samarqandi, *Khatirat-i Mutribi,* ed. 'Abd al-Ghani Mirzayif (Karachi: Mu'assasa-yi Tahqiqat-i Asiya-yi Miyana va Gharbi, Danishgah-i Karachi, 1977), 70.

98. Ibid., 88.

99. Losensky, *Welcoming Fighani,* 145; a fine study of the Mughal arts of the book in the context of the larger Indian tradition is found in Jeremiah Losty, *The Art of the Book in India* (London: The British Library, 1982).

100. Some of these points are discussed in Sunil Sharma, "The Production of Mughal *Shahnama*s: Imperial, Sub-Imperial, and Provincial Manuscripts," in *Ferdowsi's* Shahnama: *Millennial Perspectives,* ed. Olga M. Davidson and Marianna Shreve Simpson (Boston: Ilex, 2013), 86–107; reprinted in *Firdawsii Millennium Indicum: Proceedings of the Shahnama Millenary Seminar,* ed. Sunil Sharma and Burzine Waghmar (Mumbai: K. R. Cama Oriental Institute, 2016), 122–134.

101. David J. Roxburgh explains the motivation behind the creation of albums: "The album compiler composed the preface and album in the hope that the end result would satisfy, delight, and perhaps even surprise the recipient as he became reacquainted with his collected materials enhanced through techniques of decoration and processes of recontextualization," *Prefacing the Image: The Writing of Art History in Sixteenth-Century Iran* (Leiden: Brill, 2001), 53.

102. On the Dara Shikoh album, see J. P. Losty and Malini Roy, *Mughal India: Art, Culture and Empire* (London: The British Library, 2012), 124–137.

103. Emine Fetvaci's study of book culture in the Ottoman imperial household provides useful comparative insight, *Picturing History at the Ottoman Court* (Bloomington: Indiana University Press, 2013), 25–57.

104. Milo Cleveland Beach and Ebba Koch, *King of the World: The Padshahnama, An Imperial Mughal Manuscript from the Royal Library, Windsor Castle* (Washington, DC: Sackler Gallery, 1997). There has been little attempt to match poems composed by court poets to the paintings in the text.

105. Seyller, *Workshop and Patron in Mughal India,* 23.

106. Walter Feldman, "Imitatio in Ottoman Poetry: Three Ghazals of the Mid-Seventeenth Century," *The Turkish Studies Association Bulletin* 21, no. 2 (1997): 45–46.

107. These tales have been studied in detail by some scholars; see Muzaffar Alam and Sanjay Subrahmanyam, "Faizi's *Nal-Daman* and Its Long Afterlife," in *Writing the Mughal World: Studies in Political Culture* (Ranikhet: Permanent Black, 2011), 204–248; Supriya Gandhi, "Retelling the Rama Story in Persian Verse: Masihi Panipati's *Masnavi-i Ram va Sita,* in *There's No Tapping around Philology,* ed. Alireza Korangy and Daniel Sheffield (Wiesbaden: Otto Harrassowitz, 2014), 309–324.

2: The Mughal Discovery of India

1. Travis Zadeh explains that "Anecdotes of marvels and monsters offer a means of engaging with the foreign and liminal spaces of the frontier," *Mapping Frontiers across Medieval Islam: Geography, Translation, and the 'Abbasid Empire* (London: I. B. Tauris, 2011), 34; an engaging popular account of the long history of the way India was imagined, experienced, and written about through the centuries is Sam Miller, *A Strange Kind of Paradise: India through Foreign Eyes* (New Delhi: Penguin Books, 2014).

2. C. E. Dubler, " 'Adja'ib," in *Encyclopedia of Islam,* 2nd ed., ed. P. Bearman, Th. Bianquis, C. E. Bosworth, E. van Donzel, and W. P. Heinrichs (Brill Online, 2015), accessed on April 3, 2017, http://dx.doi.org.ezp-prod1.hul.harvard.edu/10.1163/1573-3912_islam_SIM_0319; also see Persis Berlekamp, *Wonder, Image, and Cosmos in Medieval Islam* (New Haven: Yale University Press, 2011), especially the pages on medieval Eurasia, 169–174.

3. Buzurg ibn Shahryar, *The Book of the Wonders of India, Mainland, Sea and Islands,* ed. and trans. G. S. P. Freeman-Grenville (London: East-West Publications, 1981).

4. Alberuni, *Alberuni's India,* trans. Edward C. Sachau, ed. Ainslie T. Embree (New York: Norton, 1971), 17. In such works, information about India was often inseparable from that of the religious practices of the inhabitants. The religion of Indians was viewed as the single category of Hinduism in the eyes of Muslims for the most part. The interaction between Islam and Hindusim in the early modern period is discussed in several essays in the edited volume, *Religious Interactions in Mughal India,* ed. Vasudha Dalmia and Munis D. Faruqui (New Delhi: Oxford University Press, 2014).

5. The travelogue portion of this large historical work was translated by Wheeler M. Thackston, *A Century of Princes: Sources on Timurid History and Art* (Cambridge, MA: The Aga Khan Program for Islamic Architecture, 1989), 299–321; both the Persian text and translation are found

in Wheeler M. Thackston's *Album Prefaces and Other Documents on the History of Calligraphers and Painters* (Leiden: Brill, 2001), 68–87.

6. See http://www.bbc.com/news/world-asia-india-20038986. Two comparative studies are Sanjay Subrahmanyam, "Monsters, Miracles and the World of *'Ajaib-o-gharaib:* Intersections between the Early Modern Iberian and Indo-Persian Worlds," in *Naturalia, mirabilia & monstrosa en los imperios Ibéricos (siglos XV–XIX),* ed. Eddy Stols, Werner Thomas, and Johan Verberckmoes (Leuven: Leuven University Press, 2006), 274–306; Jorge Flores, "Distant Wonders: The Strange and the Marvelous between Mughal India and Habsburg Iberia in the Early Seventeenth Century," *Comparative Studies in Society and History* 49 (2007): 533–581.

7. Giancarlo Casale, *The Ottoman Age of Exploration* (Oxford: Oxford University Press, 2010), 6; the section on "European Cartography and Arabic Geography: The Background of Discovery," 15–22, is also of interest here. Also see Naimur Rahman Farooqi, *Mughal-Ottoman Relations: A Study of Political and Diplomatic Relations between Mughal India and the Ottoman Empire, 1556–1748* (Delhi: Idarah-i Adabiyat-i Delli, 1989).

8. The transmission of Ptolemaic ideas from his *Geography* to and further elaboration by Muslim geographers such as Ibn Khurradadhbih in his *Kitab al-masalik wa'l-mamalik* (Book of routes and realms) and then into Persian is discussed by Zadeh in *Mapping Frontiers across Medieval Islam,* 23–24. The globe was known to the Mughals; in a study of the iconography of the globe in Mughal paintings, mainly from Emperor Jahangir's court, Sumathi Ramaswamy proposes that the object was used consciously to assert their own agendas rather than just inserted as an exotic prop, "Conceit of the Globe in Mughal Visual Practice," *Comparative Studies in Society and History* 49 (2007): 751–782.

9. Zadeh, *Mapping Frontiers,* 85.

10. *The Baburnama,* 332.

11. Irfan Habib, "Cartography in Mughal India," *The Indian Archives* 28 (1979): 90–95.

12. This phenomenon is described in a text from 1741, Dargah Quli Khan's *Muraqqa'-i Dihli,* edited with an Urdu translation by Nuru'l-Hasan Ansari (Delhi: Department of Urdu, University of Delhi, 1982); an English translation was done by Chander Shekhar and Shama Mitra Chenoy, *Muraqqa'-e-Delhi: The Mughal Capital in Muhammad Shah's Time* (Delhi: Deputy Publication, 1989).

13. *The Baburnama,* 329.

14. Ibid., 171.

15. Ibid., 332.
16. Ibid., 358; also see Stephen F. Dale, *The Garden of the Eight Paradises: Babur and the Culture of Empire in Central Asia, Afghanistan and India (1483–1530)* (Leiden: Brill, 2004), 90.
17. *The Baburnama*, 164.
18. Ibid., 399.
19. Ibid., 352.
20. Ibid., 335.
21. Ibid., 407; a useful edition for comparative purposes is the three-volume trilingual edition of this text prepared by Wheeler M. Thackston, *Baburnama, Chaghatay Turkish Text with Abdul-Rahim Khankhanan's Persian Translation* (Cambridge, MA: Department of Near Eastern Languages and Civilizations, Harvard University, 1993).
22. *The Baburnama*, 417.
23. Susan Stronge, *Painting for the Mughal Emperor: The Art of the Book, 1560–1660* (London: V&A, 2002), 88; also Ebba Koch, "My Garden is Hindustan: The Mughal Emperor's Realization of a Political Metaphor," in *Middle East Garden Traditions: Unity and Diversity, Questions, Methods and Resources in a Multicultural Perspective* (Washington, DC: Dumbarton Oaks Research Library and Collection 2007), 159–175.
24. Geographical descriptions of Kashmir before Mirza Dughlat, including those of India, are found in the Mongol history in Persian by Rashiduddin Fazlullah Hamadani, *Jami' al-tavarikh: Tarikh-i Hind va Sind va Kashmir*, ed. Muhammad Raushan (Tehran: Miras-i Maktub, 2005), and the Timurid history by Sharafuddin 'Ali Yazdi, *Zafarnama*, ed. Sa'id Mir Muhammad Sadiq and 'Abdu'l-Husain Navvabi (Tehran: Kitabkhana-yi Muzih va Markaz-i Asnad-i Majlis-i Shura-yi Islami, 2008).
25. Haidar Dughlat, *Mirza Haydar Dughlat's* Tarikh-i Rashidi: *A History of the Khans of Moghulistan*, trans. Wheeler M. Thackston (Cambridge, MA: Harvard University, Department of Near Eastern Languages and Civilizations, 1996), 258–261.
26. Abu'l-Fazl, *The A'in-i Akbari*, 352.
27. Ibid., 355.
28. The practice of describing local provinces continued in a chronicle completed in the Deccan a few years later by Farishta. Known by the title *Gulshan-i Ibrahimi* (Abraham's rose-garden) or *Tarikh-i Farishta*, this work provides histories of the Muslim polities in India. Farishta's section on Kashmir also offers details about its climate and local crafts. He writes in a romantic vein about the buildings, both royal edifices and others, especially its temples, some of which would have been in

ruins, *Tarikh-i Farishta,* ed. Muhammad Riza Nasiri (Tehran: Anjuman-i Asar va Mafakhir-i Farhangi, 2016), 4: 443–453.

29. Abu'l-Fazl, *The History of Akbar,* forthcoming volume.

30. The entire poem is found in *Divan-i Faizi,* 42–47. These lines are quoted by Razi in his description of Kashmir, *Tazkira-yi haft iqlim,* ed. Sayyid Muhammad Riza Tahiri "Hasrat" (Tehran: Surush, 1999), 2: 618.

31. 'Urfi, *Kulliyat-i 'Urfi Shirazi,* 31–32.

32. Kalhana, *Kings of Kashmira, being a translation of the Sanskrita work Rajataranggini of Kalhana Pandita by Jogesh Chunder Dutt* (Calcutta: I. C. Bose, 1879), 3; the transition from Sanskrit chronicles on Kashmir to Persian is discussed by Satoshi Ogura, "Transmission Lines of Historical Information on Kasmir: From *Rajataranginis* to the Persian Chronicles in the Early Mugal Period," *Journal of Indological Studies* 22–23 (2010–2011): 23–59.

33. Ronald Inden, "Kashmir as Paradise on Earth," in *The Valley of Kashmir: The Making and Unmaking of a Composite Culture?* ed. Aparna Rao (New Delhi: Manohar, 2008), 542, 546; for the use of this metaphor by the sultans of the Deccan, also see his essay "Paradise on Earth: The Deccan Sultanates," in *Garden and Landscape Practices in Precolonial India: Histories from the Deccan,* ed. Daud Ali and Emma Flatt (New Delhi: Routledge, 2011), 74–97.

34. Ebba Koch, "My Garden is Hindustan," 165. Jahangir has also been compared to Rudolf II of Vienna and Prague (1583–1612) by Asok Kumar Das, *Wonders of Nature: Ustad Mansur at the Mughal Court* (Mumbai: Marg, 2012), 20.

35. A detailed discussion of these images and their significance is found in Ebba Koch, "The Mughal Emperor as Solomon, Majnun, and Orpheus, or the Album as a Think Tank for Allegory," *Muqarnas* 27 (2010), 302.

36. *The Jahangirnama,* 133.

37. Das, *Wonders of Nature,* 23. Another Mughal artist, Abu'l-Hasan, had a similar appellation: *nadir al-zaman.*

38. *The Jahangirnama,* 264. I have added italics to the Persian words.

39. *Gazetteer of the Bombay Presidency,* vol. 4, *Ahmedabad* (Bombay: Government Central Press, 1879), 253–254.

40. *The Jahangirnama,* 306–307.

41. Ellison Banks Findly, *Nur Jahan: Empress of Mughal India* (New Delhi: Oxford University Press, 1993), 245.

42. Ellison Banks Findly, "Nur Jahan and the Idea of Kashmir," unpublished paper, 5. I am grateful to the author for sharing this paper with me.

43. Findly, *Nur Jahan*, 245.

44. *The Jahangirnama*, 335.

45. Ibid., 332.

46. Losensky, "Taleb Amoli," *Encyclopaedia Iranica Online*; also see Nabi Hadi, *Talib-i-Amuli (The Poet-Laureate of Jahangir): His Life and Times* (Aligarh: Muslim University, 1962), 80–83.

47. Talib, *Kulliyat-i ash'ar-i malik al-shu'ara Talib Amuli*, ed. Tahiri Shihab (Tehran: Sana'i, 1967), 1000–1004.

48. Ibid., 1005.

3: Celebrating Imperial Cities

1. Paul Losensky, "The Palace of Praise and the Melons of Time: Descriptive Patterns in 'Abdi Širazi's *Garden of Eden*," *Eurasian Studies* 2 (2003), 5.

2. The classical background of this poetic genre is discussed in J. T. P. de Bruijn, "Shahrangiz, 1. In Persian," *Encyclopaedia of Islam*, 2nd ed. Its early modern form is less studied, see Sunil Sharma, "The City of Beauties in the Indo-Persian Poetic Landscape," *Comparative Studies of South Asia, Africa and the Middle East* 24 (2004): 73–81.

3. See Andrews and Kalpaklı, *The Age of Beloveds*, 27.

4. Shirine Hamadeh, *The City's Pleasures: Istanbul in the Eighteenth Century* (Seattle: University of Washington Press, 2008), 153.

5. Iskandar Beg Munshi, *History of Shah 'Abbas the Great*, 537.

6. Islam, *Calendar of Documents on Indo-Persian Relations*, 1: 164.

7. Sussan Babaie, *Isfahan and Its Palaces: Statecraft, Shi'ism and the Architecture of Conviviality in Early Modern Iran* (Edinburgh: Edinburgh University Press, 2008), 252.

8. Sellheim, R., "Fadila," *Encyclopaedia of Islam*, 2nd ed., ed. P. Bearman, Th. Bianquis, C. E. Bosworth, E. van Donzel, and W. P. Heinrichs accessed January 10, 2017. http://dx.doi.org/10.1163/1573-3912_islam_COM_0204

9. A recent study on such a text is by Arezou Azad, *Sacred Landscape in Medieval Afghanistan: Revisiting the Fada'il-i Balkh* (Oxford: Oxford University Press, 2013).

10. *Al-Farabi on the Perfect State: Abu Nasr al-Farabi's Mabadi' ara' ahl al-madina al-fadila, a Revised Text with Introduction, Translation and Commentary*, trans. and ed. Richard Walzer (Oxford: Clarendon Press, 1985), 231. I have discussed this idea more fully in "Representation of Social Types in Mughal Art and Literature: Ethnography or Trope?" *Indo-Muslim*

Cultures in Transition, ed. Alka Patel and Karen Leonard (Leiden: Brill, 2011), 17–36.

11. *Al-Farabi on the Perfect State,* 235.

12. For a contextualization of Zuhuri's poem, see Sunil Sharma, "The Nizamshahi Persianate Garden in Zuhuri's *Saqinama,*" in *Garden and Landscape Practices in Precolonial India: Histories from the Deccan,* ed. Daud Ali and Emma Flatt (New Delhi: Routledge, 2011), 159–171.

13. Losensky, "The Palace of Praise and the Melons of Time," 1–29. The five poems in the quintet are: *Rauzat al-sifat* (Garden of descriptions), *Dauhat al-azhar* (Great tree in bloom), *Jannat al-asmar* (Garden of fruits), *Zinat al-auraq* (Adornment of leaves), *and Sahifat al-ikhlas* (Page of dedication). The seasonal division of the poems is a feature also found in Amir Khusrau's *Qiran al-sa'dain.*

14. Ibid., 3.

15. For Persian literary production in the Deccan, the most comprehensive study is T. N. Devare, *A Short History of Persian Literature at the Bahmani, the Adilshahi and the Qutbshahi Courts—Deccan* (Poona: S. Devare, 1961).

16. A detailed account of his career is in Paul Losensky, "Sa'eb Tabrizi," *Encyclopaedia Iranica Online* (2003). Losensky's forthcoming monograph on Sa'ib will further our understanding of this poet's role in both Safavid and Mughal literature.

17. Sa'ib, *Divan-i Sa'ib Tabrizi,* ed. Muhammad Qahraman (Tehran: Intisharat-i 'Ilmi va Farhangi, 1995), 3626–3627.

18. Ibid., 3623.

19. Quoted by the eighteenth-century author Shahnavaz Khan, *The Ma'asir al-umara,* ed. Maulvi Mirza Ashraf 'Ali (Calcutta: Asiatic Society of Bengal, 1890), 2: 761.

20. Paul Losensky, " 'The Equal of Heaven's Vault': The Design, Ceremony, and Poetry of the Hasanabad Bridge," in *Writers and Rulers: Perspectives on Their Relationship from Abbasid to Safavid Times,* ed. Beatrice Gruendler and Louise Marlow (Wiesbaden: Reichert, 2004), 195–216.

21. Lefèvre, "The Court of 'Abd-ur-Rahim Khan-i Khanan," 76.

22. Allison Busch, "Poetry in Motion: Literary Circulation in Mughal India," in *Culture and Circulation: Literature in Motion in Early Modern India,* ed. Thomas de Bruijn and Allison Busch (Leiden: Brill, 2014), 196–197; also McGregor, *Hindi Literature from Its Beginnings to the Nineteenth Century,* 172; Sandhya Sharma, *Literature, Culture and History in Mughal North India, 1550–1800* (New Delhi: Primus Books, 2011), 147–148, 164.

23. *Rahim Granthavali,* ed. V. Mishra and G. Rajnish (New Delhi: Vani Prakashan, 1994), 112. Professor Françoise "Nalini" Delvoye was a great resource for different editions of Rahim's Hindi works.

24. Gulchin-Ma'ani, *Shahrashub dar shi'r-i Farsi,* 2nd ed. (Tehran: Rivayat, 2001), 36.

25. Many such poems, not found in the older manuscripts of Amir Khusrau's work, are attributed to him, but could date from the eighteenth century when they and other literary works were produced in his name to derive prestige from his reputation. If this poem was composed in the eighteenth century, it is also possible that it was in turn influenced by Rahim's oeuvre.

26. *The Travels of Pietro della Valle in India,* 2: 97.

27. Paul Losensky, "Naziri," *Encyclopaedia Iranica Online* (2004).

28. In her study of architectural poetry, Julie Meisami draws attention to Azraqi Haravi, an eleventh-century Seljuq poet in the employ of Malikshah's governor of Khurasan Tughanshah, "who is both a continuator of the earlier Ghaznavid tradition and something of an innovator," see "Palaces and Paradises: Palace Description in Medieval Persian Poetry," in *Islamic Art and Literature,* ed. Oleg Grabar and Cynthia Robinson (Princeton, NJ: Markus Wiener, 2001), 30. Fath Bari is also described by Jahangir in his memoirs, *The Jahangirnama,* 246, 249, and 270.

29. Salik, *Divan-i Salik Qazvini,* ed. 'Abdus-Samad Haqiqat and Ahmad Karimi (Tehran: Ma, 1994), 563.

30. William Foster, ed., *Early Travels in India, 1583–1619* (London: H. Milford, 1921), 138.

31. Irfan Habib, "Notes on the Economic and Social Aspects of Mughal Gardens," in *Mughal Gardens: Sources, Places, Representations, and Prospects,* ed. James L. Wescoat and Joachim Wolschke-Bulmahn (Washington, DC: Dumbarton Oaks Research Library and Collection, 1996), 127–138.

32. Foster, *Early Travels in India,* 138–139.

33. Koch, *The Complete Taj Mahal and the Riverfront Gardens of Agra* (London: Thames & Hudson, 2006), 19. There has been a great effort by scholars in several parts of the world in the last three decades to publish Persian historical and literary texts in modern editions or translations, but we are still nowhere near having all of them available in print.

34. I am grateful to Dr. Saqib Baburi for his insight into this subject. Anecdotal evidence exists of Shah Jahan having composed a verse or two. It is also recorded that he composed the text of several letters and *farmans.* There is no denying that he was a great patron of literary works.

35. 'Inayat Khan, *The Shah Jahan Nama of 'Inayat Khan,* 570.

36. Ibid., 573.

37. W. E. Begley and Z. A. Desai, *Taj Mahal, The Illumined Tomb: An Anthology of Seventeenth-Century Mughal and European Documentary Sources* (Cambridge, MA: The Aga Khan Program for Islamic Architecture, 1989), xxii.

38. A succinct overview of Kalim's life and career is found in Daniela Meneghini's entry in the *Encyclopaedia Iranica Online* (2012). Wheeler M. Thackston's unpublished dissertation on the poet, *The Poetry of Abu-Talib Kalim, Persian Poet-Laureate of Shah Jahan, Mughal Emperor of India* (PhD diss., Harvard University, 1974), is a valuable resource as well.

39. Mir Jumla Shahristani is not to be confused with Mir Jumla II, of Ardestan, who was a hugely successful diamond merchant with a maritime commercial empire, and was also in Mughal service.

40. A detailed study of the wide range of Kalim's topographical poetry is provided in Paul Losensky, "'Square like a Bubble': Architecture, Power, and Poetics in Two Inscriptions by Kalim Kashani," *Journal of Persianate Studies* 8 (2015): 42–70. Kalim's poems on the book arts are discussed in Sunil Sharma, "Celebrating Writing and Books in Safavid and Mughal Court Poetry," in *Écrit et culture en Asie centrale et dans le monde turco-iranien, XIVe-XIXe siècles (Writing and Culture in Central Asia and the Turko-Iranian World, 14th–19th centuries),* ed. Francis Richard and Maria Szuppe (Paris: Association pour l'Avancement des Etudes Iraniennes, 2009), 231–250.

41. Kalim, *Divan-i Abu Talib Kalim Hamadani,* 491.

42. Paul Losensky, "Qodsi Mashhadi," *Encyclopaedia Iranica Online* (2006).

43. Qudsi, *Divan-i Hajji Muhammad Jan Qudsi Mashhadi,* ed. Muhammad Qahraman (Mashhad: Danishgah-i Firdausi, 1996), 948.

44. Quoted from the *Tarikh-i Akbari,* in Michael Brand and Glenn Lowry, eds., *Fatehpur-Sikri: A Sourcebook,* (Cambridge, MA: The Aga Khan Program for Islamic Architecture at Harvard University and the Massachusetts Institute of Technology, 1985), 292.

45. Abu'l Fazl, *The A'in-i Akbari,* 3: 190–191.

46. Kalim, *Divan-i Abu Talib Kalim Hamadani,* 142.

47. Bernier, *Travels in the Mogul Empire, A.D. 1656–1658,* 2nd ed., (London: Oxford University Press, 1916), 285.

48. Quoted in Koch, *The Complete Taj Mahal,* 32.

49. Ibid., 23; also see Ebba Koch, "Mughal Agra: A Riverfront Garden City," in *The City in the Islamic World,* ed. Salma K. Jayyusi (Leiden: Brill, 2008), 555–588.

50. Abu'l Fazl, *The History of Akbar*, 4: 135.

51. Foster, *Early Travels in India, 1583–1619*, 17–18. The city is also described in Sanskrit poetry. Truschke, *Culture of Encounters*, 76–77.

52. On Fatehpur Sikri, see Rajinder S. Jutla, "Fatehpur Sikri: A Utopian Approach to Urban Planning and Design," unpublished manuscript, available at http://www.etsav.upc.es/personals/iphs2004/pdf/098_p.pdf

53. Jahangir, *The Jahangirnama*, 22–24.

54. Qudsi, *Divan-i Hajji Muhammad Jan Qudsi Mashhadi*, 895.

55. Ibid., 801–804; for a detailed history and use of this garden, see Koch, *The Complete Taj Mahal*, 41–42.

56. These lines are found in the manuscript *Kulliyat-i Qudsi*, Khuda Bakhsh Library, Patna, no. 308, f. 77b.

57. Begley and Desai, *Taj Mahal, The Illumined Tomb*, 298; for other seventeenth-century European accounts, 291–300; on later writings on the tomb, Koch, *The Complete Taj Mahal*, 231–254.

58. Vikramsinh Rathod, ed., *Rajasthani gajal sangrah* (Jodhpur: Rajasthan Shodh Sansthan, 1995), 13–21. I am grateful to Dipti Khera for sharing this poem and the one on Lahore, and discussing them in the context of our interests in topographical themes in painting and literature.

59. Razi, *Tazkira-yi haft iqlim*, 1: 384.

60. Ibid.

61. Quoted in Koch, "The Influence of the Jesuit Missions on Symbolic Representations of the Mughal Emperors," in *Mughal Art and Imperial Ideology: Collected Essays* (New Delhi: Oxford University Press, 2001), 11. One of the Mughal historians who records this event does not mention the details of this incident but merely writes that, "To the various poets assembled at the foot of the throne, who had composed verses and chronograms in honor of that occasion, robes of honor and handsome sums of money were bestowed," 'Inayat Khan, *Shah Jahan Nama*, 408.

62. An engaging Persianate history of the city is by Arthur Dudney, *Delhi: Pages from a Forgotten History* (New Delhi: Hay House India, 2015).

63. William Glover, *Making Lahore Modern* (Minneapolis: University of Minnesota Press, 2008), 8; also see Mehreen Chida-Razvi, "Where is 'the greatest city in the East'? The Mughal City of Lahore in European Travel Accounts (1556–1648)," in *The City in the Muslim World: Depictions by Western Travel Writers*, ed. Mohammad Gharipour and Nilay Özlü (London: Routledge, 2015), 79–100.

64. Talib, *Kulliyat-i ash'ar,* 40–41; Talib also has a short poem on Kabul, 1064–1065.

65. Shibli Nu'mani made the identification of this person to the Qadiri Sufi Shah Abu'l-Ma'ali. *Shi'r al-'ajam* (Azamgarh: Dar al-Musannifin, Shibli Academy, 1991), 3: 137.

66. Munir, *Surudahha va navishtaha-yi Munir Lahauri,* ed. Farid Akram (Tehran: Bunyad-i Mauqufat-i Duktur Mahmud Afshar Yazdi, 2009), 105–113.

67. The building activities of Vazir Khan are discussed in James Wescoat, "Gardens, Urbanization, and Urbanism in Mughal Lahore: 1526–1657," in *Mughal Gardens: Sources, Places, Representations, and Prospects,* ed. James L. Wescoat and Joachim Wolschke-Bulmahn, 159–160.

68. Ibid., 168.

69. Muni Kanti Sagar, ed., *Nagarvarnatmak Hindi padya sangrah* (Surat, 1948), 1–6.

70. Wescoat, "Gardens, Urbanization, and Urbanism in Mughal Lahore," 168.

4: Mughal Arcadia

1. The various versions of this story are given in Ahmad Gulchin-Ma'ani, *Karvan-i Hind,* 1: 570–573.

2. Some books on Kashmir and the Wikipedia entry (https://en.wikipedia .org/wiki/Mazar-e-Shura) reproduce photographs of the cemetery, but my attempts at locating it in the summer of 2011 were unsuccessful. I gratefully acknowledge the assistance of Professor Mudasir Mufti of the University of Kashmir's Department of English as an informed expert about Srinagar and for answering my queries about Kashmir and its literature. I have also benefited from discussions with Jan Haenraets on the subject of gardens in Kashmir.

3. William L. Hanaway, Jr., "Paradise on Earth: The Terrestrial Garden in Persian Literature," in *The Islamic Garden,* ed. R. Ettinghausen (Washington, DC: Dumbarton Oaks, 1976), 46. There is an extensive body of scholarship on gardens, both historical and metaphoric, in Persianate literature and societies. Dominic P. Brookshaw discusses the uses of garden spaces for courtly gatherings, "Palaces, Pavilions and Pleasure-gardens: The Context and Setting of the Medieval *Majlis," Middle Eastern Literatures* 6, no. 2 (2003): 199–223; a recent study is Mohammad Gharipour, *Persian Gardens and Pavilions: Reflections in History, Poetry and the Arts* (London: I. B. Tauris, 2013); for the Indo-Persian and South Asian

context, see the various essays in James L. Wescoat and Joachim Wolschke-Bulmahn, eds., *Mughal Gardens: Sources, Places, Representations, and Prospects,* and Daud Ali and Emma Flatt, eds., *Garden and Landscape Practices in Precolonial India: Histories from the Deccan* (New Delhi: Routledge, 2011); also, Ali Akbar Husain, *Scent in the Islamic Garden: A Study of Literary Sources in Persian and Urdu,* 2nd ed. (Karachi: Oxford University Press, 2012).

4. Monica Juneja, "On the Margins of Utopia—One More Look at Mughal Painting," *The Medieval History Journal* 4, no. 2 (2001): 206–207. Ebba Koch discusses the shift in the way that landscapes were depicted by painters of Shah Jahan's court in Beach and Koch, *King of the World,* 134–141.

5. Tahir Vahid, *Tarikh-i jahanara-yi 'Abbasi,* ed. Sa'id Mir Muhammad Sadiq (Tehran: Pizhuhishgah-i 'Ulum-i Insani va Mutala'at-i Farhangi, 2004), 679–680.

6. Quoted in Amy S. Landau, "Man, Mode, and Myth: Muhammad Zaman ibn Haji Yusuf," *Pearls on a String: Artists, Patrons, and Poets at the Great Islamic Courts* (Baltimore: Walters Museum of Art, 2016), 173.

7. Jayyusi, "Nature Poetry in al-Andalus and the Rise of Ibn Khafaja," in *The Legacy of Muslim Spain,* ed. Salma Khadra Jayyusi (Leiden: Brill, 1992), 369.

8. Williams, *The Country and the City* (Oxford: Oxford University Press, 1973), 20.

9. A seminal study on the topic is Julie S. Meisami, "Allegorical Gardens in the Persian Poetic Tradition: Nezami, Rumi, Hafez," *International Journal of Middle Eastern Studies* 17 (1985): 229–260. The classical poet Manuchihri at the Ghaznavid court was particularly noted for his fondness for flowers and many more than the usual varieties are mentioned in his poems. But this does not extend to the wider landscape at large.

10. I have been able to count at least eighteen poets of the seventeenth century who composed poems on Kashmir, most of them from the Shah Jahan period; see Sunil Sharma, "Kashmir and the Mughal Fad of Persian Pastoral Poetry," *Eurasiatica: Quaderni di studi su Balcani, Anatolia, Iran, Caucaso e Asia Centrale* 5 (2016): 183–202. Selections of many of the poems are found in S. H. Rashidi, *Tazkira-yi shu'ara-yi Kashmir* (Karachi: Iqbal Academy, 1967–1969).

11. Valerie Ritter, *Kama's Flowers: Nature in Hindi Poetry and Criticism, 1885–1925* (Albany: State University of New York Press, 2011), 40; for an

illuminating discussion of the concept of nature and nature poetry in premodern Indic poetry, also see 38–45.

12. Following the Mughals, European visitors also took notice of the variety and beauty of flowers cultivated in the gardens, Findly, *Nur Jahan*, 247.

13. Koch, *The Complete Taj Mahal*, 224. This metaphor was particularly exploited in the ornamental decoration in the Taj Mahal since the monument was supposed to evoke the idea of paradise.

14. Kinra discusses this "minigazetteer" of empire, *Writing Self, Writing Empire*, 151–158.

15. Chandarbhan Brahman, *Chahar chaman*, 136.

16. Kalim, *Divan-i Abu Talib Kalim Hamadani*, 174–181. Kalim's other poems on Kashmir are shorter and exclusively about architectural monuments, see Losensky, "'Square Like a Bubble,'" 52.

17. Qudsi, *Divan-i Hajji Muhammad Jan Qudsi Mashhadi*, 768–801.

18. For copies of manuscripts and fragments of a third verse epic on Shah Jahan by the poet Yahya Kashi, who was the imperial librarian and panegyrized the emperor and Dara Shikoh, see C. A. Storey, *Persian Literature: A Bio-Bibliographical Survey* (London: The Royal Asiatic Society of Great Britain and Ireland, 1970), 1: 568–570, 572–573.

19. The Persian works of this genre are described in Storey, *Persian Literature*, 1: 309; a detailed discussion of Ottoman verse histories is found in Sara Nur Yildiz, "Ottoman Historical Writing in Persian, 1400–1600," in *Persian Historiography*, ed. Charles Melville (London: I. B. Tauris, 2012), 450–469.

20. Salim, *Divan-i kamil-i Muhammad Quli Salim Tihrani*, ed. Rahim Riza (Tehran: Ibn Sina, 1970), 526–549.

21. The story of how this poet was motivated to travel is discussed in Derek Mancini-Lander, "Dreaming the Elixir of Knowledge: How a Seventeenth-Century Poet from Herat Got His Name and Fame," in *Dreams and Visions in Islamic Societies*, ed. Özgen Felek and Alexander D. Knysh (Albany: University of New York Press, 2012), 77–97.

22. Bihishti Haravi, *Nur al-mashriqain, safarnama-yi manzum az 'ahd-i Safavi*, ed. Najib Ma'il Haravi (Mashhad: Astan-i Quds-i Razavi, 1998), 266.

23. Salik, *Divan-i Salik Qazvini*, 611.

24. Saidi, *Divan-i Saidi Tihrani*, ed. Muhammad Qahraman (Tehran: Ittila'at, 1985), 61–67.

25. Ibid., 21.

26. Ibid., 64–67.

27. Truschke, *Culture of Encounters*, 89–92. As the author explains, while Jagannatha "drew on Sanskrit norms to describe Kashmir, his Mughal audience would have heard resonances with their own literary tradition," 89.
28. Shahnavaz Khan, *The Ma'asir al-umara*, 2: 761.
29. 'Inayat Khan, *The Shah Jahan Nama of 'Inayat Khan*, 324.
30. Shahnavaz Khan writes, "*intikhab-i ash'ar-i shu'ara'i ki ba vay rabita-yi ikhlas dashtand bi-khatt-i har kudam navisanida bar pusht-i har varaq surat-i an ma'ani-sanj musavvar sakht*," *Ma'asir al-umara*, 761–762.
31. This is the most complete manuscript of the text. Other copies seem to be rare. The University of Kashmir library has an autograph manuscript of the *divan* of Zafar Khan.
32. According to Barbara Schmitz, Bishandas painted the faces while the Iranian émigré painter Muhammad Khan painted the bodies, interiors and gardens, "India xxi. Indian Influences on Persian Painting," *Encyclopaedia Iranica Online* (2012). The images from this manuscript were first published by Ralph Pinder-Wilson, "Three Illustrated Manuscripts of the Mughal Period," *Ars Orientalis* 2 (1957), 413–422.
33. Pinder-Wilson, "Three Illustrated Manuscripts of the Mughal Period," 421.
34. Zafar Khan, *Masnaviyat-i Zafar Khan*, ed. Muhammad Aslam Khan (Delhi: Indo-Persian Society, 1985), 15–50. His other poems, chiefly *ghazals*, have also been published, *Zafar Khan Ahsan: Tahqiq dar ahval va asar va afkar va ash'ar*, ed. Muhammad Aslam Khan (Delhi: Indo-Persian Society, 1976). This *divan* was compiled by the author himself in 1643–1644; the date of this occasion is provided in a chronogram by Kalim, 131.
35. The historian 'Abdu'l-Hamid Lahauri in the *Padshahnama* gives the location of this house and garden which do not survive: "Zafar Khan's garden is built on the banks of Jadi Bal, which is a tank near the city," quoted in W. M. Thackston, "Mughal Gardens in Persian Poetry," *Mughal Gardens: Sources, Places, Representations, and Prospects*, ed. James L. Wescoat and Joachim Wolschke-Bulmahn, 256; Zafar Khan's son 'Inayat Khan also mentions this in his chronicle, *The Shah Jahan Nama of 'Inayat Khan*, 127.
36. Ghani is one of the few Mughal period poets whose poems have been translated in our times by Mufti Mudasir Farooqi and Nusrat Bazaz, *The Captured Gazelle: The Poems of Ghani Kashmiri* (New Delhi: Penguin Books, 2013).

37. Bonnie Wade, *Imaging Sound: An Ethnomusicological Study of Music, Art, and Culture in Mughal India* (Chicago: University of Chicago Press, 1998), 151.

38. This section appears earlier in the printed edition of the text.

39. Zafar Khan, *Masnaviyat-i Zafar Khan*, 51–77.

40. Ibid., 77–111. This road was also referred to as the Royal or Imperial Route in the colonial period. For a summary of the various roads to the valley, see Brigid Keenan, *Travels in Kashmir: A Popular History of Its People, Places, and Crafts* (Delhi: Permanent Black, 2006), 46–47.

41. Apparently, "The Machh Bawan, so called because of the abundance of fish in it, is a spring that is sacred to the Hindus of Kashmir. In Mughal histories it is called Asafabad, because of its connection to the governor Asaf Khan," S. Maqbul Ahmad and Raja Bano, *A Study of Persio-Arabic Sources on the Historical Geography of Kashmir* (Srinagar: Jaykay Books, 2011), 124.

42. Munir, *Surudaha va navishtaha*, 195–247.

43. Ibid., 149–191.

44. Munis Faruqui, *The Princes of the Mughal Empire*, 177; also see Rajeev Kinra, "Infantilizing Baba Dara: The Cultural Memory of Dara Shekuh and the Mughal Public Sphere," *Journal of Persianate Studies* 2 (2009): 165–193.

45. This topic is explored in an essay by Supriya Gandhi, "The Prince and the *Muvahhid:* Dara Shikoh and Mughal Engagements with Vedanta," in *Religious Interactions in Mughal India*, ed. Vasudha Dalmia and Munis D. Faruqui (New Delhi: Oxford University Press, 2014), 65–101.

46. Linda Leach, *Mughal and Other Indian Paintings from the Chester Beatty Library* (London: Scorpion Cavendish, 1995), 1: 355.

47. Wescoat, "Gardens, Urbanization, and Urbanism in Mughal Lahore," 166.

48. Dara, *Divan-i Dara Shikoh*, ed. M. Haidariyan (Mashhad: Navid, 1985), 114–115; on Dara's *divan*, comprising *ghazal*s and quatrains, which had been lost and was rediscovered in the twentieth century, see Bikrama Jit Hasrat, *Dara Shikuh: Life and Works* (New Delhi: Munshiram Manoharlal, 1982), 129–132.

49. Dara, *Divan-i Dara Shikoh*, 67.

50. An introduction to the princess's life is found in Afshan Bokhari, "The "Light" of the Timuria: Jahan Ara Begum's Patronage, Piety, and Poetry in 17th-century Mughal India," *Marg* 60 (2008): 53–61. For a more detailed study, see Qamar Jahan Ali, *Princess Jahan Ara Begam: Her Life and Works* (Karachi: S. M. Hamid, 1991); on her predecessor, see Re-

becca Gould, "How Gulbadan Remembered: The *Book of Humayun* as an Act of Representation," *Early Modern Women: An Interdisciplinary Journal* 6 (2011): 187–193.

51. The *Sahibiya* is a short text whose authenticity is somewhat questionable. No manuscript of it exists today, but fortunately transcriptions of the Persian text were made by scholars in the twentieth century. My study and translation of it leads me to believe it is a genuine work. The original text was edited by Muhammad Aslam as "Risala-i Sahibiya," *Journal of the Research Society of Pakistan* 16, no. 4 (1979): 78–110. An Urdu translation is found in 17, no. 1 (1980): 69–107 of the same journal.

52. This excerpt has been translated by Carl Ernst, see "A Princess of Piety," in *Women of Sufism, A Hidden Treasure: Writings and Stories of Mystic Poets, Scholars & Saints,* ed. Camille Adams Helminski (Boston: Shambhala, 2003), 128–132.

53. G. M. D. Sufi, *Kashir, Being a History of Kashmir from the Earliest Times to Our Own* (Lahore: University of the Panjab, 1949), 2: 519.

54. 'Inayat Khan, *The Shah Jahan Nama of 'Inayat Khan,* 458.

55. Mulla Shah's works have not been published. The manuscript I consulted is IOL 561, ff. 51–61. I am immensely grateful to Ursula Sims-Williams, curator of the British Library's Persian collection, for her assistance in providing copies of the relevant folios.

56. These sentiments are echoed by the historian Kambo as discussed and translated in Abdul Rehman and Shama Anbrine, "Unity and Diversity of Mughal Garden Experiences," in *Mughal Gardens: Sources, Places, Representations, and Prospects,* ed. James L. Wescoat and Joachim Wolschke-Bulmahn (Washington, DC: Dumbarton Oaks), 226–228.

Conclusion: Paradise Lost

1. The Persian text has been edited by Sayyada Khurshid Fatima Hussaini, *Ashub-i Hindustan* (New Delhi: Markaz-i Tahqiqat-i Farsi-yi Rayzani-yi Farhangi-yi Jumhuri-yi Islami-yi Iran, 2009), 218.

2. *Maasir-i-'Alamgiri,* trans. Jadunath Sarkar (Calcutta: Royal Asiatic Society of Bengal, 1947), 318; for the Persian text, see *Ma'asir-i 'Alamgiri,* ed. Agha Ahmad 'Ali (Calcutta: Asiatic Society of Bengal, 1871), v. 2, 532–533.

3. The most comprehensive work on the literary culture of Aurangzeb's period is in Urdu by Nur-ul-Hasan Ansari, *Farsi adab bi-'ahd-i Aurangzeb* (Delhi: Indo-Persian Society, 1969).

4. Shibli, *Shi'r al-'ajam*, 3: 168.

5. Kirmani, *Dreams Forgotten*, 280. Fani was previously thought to be the author of the *Dabistan-i mazahib*, the valuable encyclopedia of religions of the Mughal period, but now it is believed it was authored by Mubad Shah, who was mentioned earlier; for more on Fani, see the entry by S. H. Qasemi, "Fani Kašmiri," *Encyclopaedia Iranica Online* (2012).

6. The poem is found in Fani, *Masnaviyat-i Fani Kashmiri*, ed. S. A. H. Abidi (Srinagar: Jammu and Kashmir Academy of Arts, Culture and Languages, 1964), 147–218.

7. Paul Losensky, "Vintages of the *Saqi-nama*: Fermenting and Blending the Cupbearer's Song in the Sixteenth Century," *Iranian Studies* 47 (2014), 148.

8. According to the historian 'Abdu'l-Hamid Lahauri, this garden called Shahabad was a gift to Dara Shikoh from the emperor, hence its significance as a mystical spot, Thackston, "Mughal Gardens in Persian Poetry," 255.

9. Dystopian themes were inserted in more subtle ways into Mughal paintings; Koch describes one such example, *King of the World*, 166–167.

10. A comparative study of this poet is found in Stephen F. Dale, "A Safavid Poet in the Heart of Darkness: The Indian Poems of Ashraf Mazandarani," *Iranian Studies* 36 (2003): 197–212.

11. *Divan-i ash'ar-i Ashraf Mazandarani*, ed. Muhammad Hasan Sayyidan (Tehran: Bunyad-i Mauqufat-i Duktur Mahmud Afshar, 1994), 164–170. Ashraf also has a *masnavi* in which he gives advice to a son who he has left behind with his wife.

12. Ibid., 153–158.

13. Satire became a prominent genre in the Aurangzeb period with poets such as Ni'mat Khan 'Ali and Zatalli writing major works on social and political subjects. This forms the topic of chapter 5 of Abhishek Kaicker's dissertation, "Unquiet City: Making and Unmaking Politics in Mughal Delhi, 1707–39" (PhD diss., Columbia University, 2014).

14. Mikhail Bakhtin, *Rabelais and His World*, trans. Hélène Iswolsky (Bloomington: Indiana University Press, 1984), 10.

15. Riazul Islam, *Indo-Persian Relations: A Study of the Political and Diplomatic Relations between the Mughul Empire and Iran* (Tehran: Iranian Culture Foundation), 126.

16. Ibid., 134.

17. On Mulla Tughra, see Storey, *Persian Literature: A Bio-Bibliographical Survey*, 3: 303–304.

18. *Arghavan-i shafaq: bar-guzida-yi divan-i Tughra-yi Mashhadi,* ed. Muhammad Qahraman (Tehran: Amir Kabir, 2005), 69–76.

19. The historian 'Abdu'l-Hamid Lahauri mentions four possible routes between Lahore and Kashmir, each with different stages. During Shah Jahan's 1634 trip, the court followed the same route given by Mulla Tughra, with four additional stages. Emperor Jahangir had actually died on the way between Rajaur and Changez Hatli. Mughal caravanserais in some of these places were described by the British geologist Frederic Drew in 1862, as discussed in Keenan, *Travels in Kashmir,* 47–48.

20. These are the *Firdausiya* and *Tajalliyat;* all three texts are found in the lithographed edition of his *insha, Rasa'il-i Tughra* (Kanpur: Matba'-i Mustafa'i, 1864).

21. This work has not been published yet. I consulted several manuscripts of it in the British Library. Such descriptions in a highly poeticized prose form of *insha* are separate from the historical chronicles, which also devoted space to this topic, as we have seen; Thackston compares descriptions of Kashmir gardens in two such chronicles, Lahauri's *Padshahnama* and Kambo's *'Amal-i Salih,* from Shah Jahan's court, in "Mughal Gardens in Persian Poetry," 250–257.

22. *Histoire de la derniere revolution des Etats du Grand Mogol,* which appeared in English as *Travels in the Mogul Empire.* This work "really fired European imaginations and gave Kashmir the aura of glamour that it had retained to this day," Keenan, *Travels in Kashmir,* 74.

23. *Travels in the Mogul Empire, A.D. 1656–1658,* 401–402. Personal and place names in this quotation have been modernized.

24. For instance, see the stunning illustrated manuscript in the British Library (Add. Or. Ms 1699) that depicts a broad range of craftsmen of the valley. In its structure it recalls the poetic *shahrashub* list of young men but is purely technical.

25. N. H. Ansari, "Bineš Kašmiri, Esma'il," *Encyclopaedia Iranica Online* (1989).

26. G. L. Tikku, *Persian Poetry in Kashmir, 1339–1846* (Berkeley: University of California Press, 1971), 117–24; his Kashmir poem is found in *Divan-i Juya Tabrizi,* ed. Parviz 'Abbasi Dakani (Tehran: Barg, 1999), 399–406.

27. Nabi Hadi, *Dictionary of Indo-Persian Literature* (New Delhi: Indira Gandhi National Centre for the Arts, 1995), 64.

28. *Masnaviyat-i Nasir 'Ali Sirhindi,* British Library manuscript (Or. 352, f. 2b).

29. Chitralekha Zutshi, *Kashmir's Contested Pasts: Narratives, Sacred Geographies, and the Historical Imagination* (New Delhi: Oxford University Press, 2014), especially chapter 2: "A Literary Paradise: The *Tarikh* Tradition in Seventeenth- and Eighteenth-Century Kashmir," after the political upheavals; Zutshi states that "Mughal rule allowed for a narrative turn towards asserting Kashmir's uniqueness, and hence distinctive position, within the Mughal empire," 73.

30. Richard Foltz, "Two Seventeenth-Century Central Asian Travellers to Mughal India," *Journal of the Royal Asiatic Society* 6 (1996): 367–377. This section of his travelogue is found as an appendix to a world history written for Nazr Muhammad Khān, the ruler of Balkh in Central Asia, Mahmud ibn Amir Vali, *The Bahr ul-Asrar, Travelogue of South Asia*, ed. Riazul Islam (Karachi: Institute of Central & West Asian Studies, 1980).

31. For a study of the political subtext of the poem, see Sunil Sharma, "Novelty, Tradition and Mughal Politics in Nau'i's *Suz u Gudaz*," in *The Necklace of the Pleiades: Studies in Persian Literature Presented to Heshmat Moayyad on his 80th Birthday*, ed. Franklin Lewis and Sunil Sharma (West Lafayette, IN: Purdue University Press, 2007), 251–265. The text is found in the poet's works, *Divan-i Mulla Nau'i Khabushani*, ed. Amir Husain Zakirzada (Tehran: Ma, 1995). Portions of it were translated by Mirza Y. Dawud and Ananda K. Coomaraswamy in *Burning and Melting, Being the Suz-u-Gudaz of Muhammad Riza Nau'i Khabushan* (London, 1912).

32. Annemarie Schimmel, *A Two-Colored Brocade: The Imagery of Persian Poetry* (Chapel Hill: The University of North Carolina Press, 1992), 198–199.

33. Quoted in Yunus Jaffrey, "Sati dar shi'r-i Sa'ib Tabrizi," *Armaghan-i adabi: pizhuhishha-yi adabi dar adabiyat-i farsi-i Hind* (Tehran: Mauqufat-i Duktur Mahmud Afshar, 1997), 286.

34. This is the British Library Or. 2839 manuscript.

35. Other illustrated copies are in the Walters Art Gallery, Chester Beatty Library, Israel Museum, and Bibliothèque nationale, Paris.

36. This is object 2002.50.7, Harvard Art Museums.

37. The wall painting and Shamlu's text are discussed by Sussan Babaie, "Shah 'Abbas II, the Conquest of Qandahar, the Chihil Sutun, and Its Wall Paintings," *Muqarnas* 11 (1994): 125–142.

38. Ibid., 135.

39. *Divan-i Sa'ib Tabrizi*, 3567–3571, 3602–3608.

40. Ibid., 3568.

41. On his life and career, see Kathryn Babayan, " 'Emad-al-Dawlah, Mirza Mohammad-Taher," *Encyclopaedia Iranica Online* (2011).

42. The poem appears in his *Tarikh-i Jahanara-yi 'Abbasi*, 491–492.

43. *Tarikh-i jahanara-yi 'Abbasi*, 491.

44. *Qisas al-khaqani*, ed. Hasan Sadat Nasiri (Tehran: Vizarat-i Farhang va Irshad-i Islami, 1992–1995), 1: 381. I am grateful to Yoshiaki Tokunaga, who provided helpful information regarding the historical texts of this period.

45. The text of this poem, edited by Bihruz Imani, was published in the journal *Ganjina-yi Baharistan: Adabiyat-i Farsi* 2 (2001): 643–674.

46. The vanishing pleasure garden of the night was a common trope in classical Persian literature that also found its way into the popular Arabic Thousand and One Nights cycle.

47. A similar fascination with European women in this period is discussed by Amy S. Landau, "Visibly foreign, visibly female: The eroticization of *zan-i farangi* in seventeenth-century Persian painting," in *Eros and Sexuality in Islamic Art*, ed. Francesca Leoni and Mika Natif (Farnham: Ashgate, 2013), 99–129.

48. Vahid, *Kulliyat-i Vahid*, Majlis Library, Tehran, manuscript 1161.

49. This is manuscript Suppl. pers. 788.

50. Charles-Henri de Fouchécour, "Iran viii. Persian literature (2) Classical," *Encyclopaedia Iranica Online* (2012).

51. Rudi Matthee, *Persia in Crisis: Safavid Decline and the Fall of Isfahan* (London: I. B. Tauris, 2012), xxiii.

52. The Safavid chronicle *Qisas al-khaqani* lists 101 poets of the late seventeenth century, not all of whom were at court. There has been almost no scholarship on the literature of this period.

53. Juan R. I. Cole, "Mirror of the World: Iranian 'Orientalism' and Early 19th-Century India," *Critique: Journal of Critical Studies of Iran and the Middle East* 8 (1996), 58; also see Mana Kia, "Limning the Land: Social Encounters and Historical Meaning in Early Nineteenth-Century Travelogues between Iran and India," in *On the Wonders of Land and Sea: Persianate Travel Writing*, ed. Roberta Micallef and Sunil Sharma (Boston: Ilex, 2013), 44–67.

54. See Mana Kia, "Imagining Iran Before Nationalism: Geocultural Meanings of Land in Azar's *Atashkadeh*," in *Rethinking Iranian Nationalism and Modernity*, ed. Kamran Scot Agahie and Afshin Marashi (Austin: University of Texas Press, 2014), 89–112.

55. Azar, *Atashkada-yi Azar, nima-yi duvvum*, ed. Mir Hashim Muhaddis (Tehran: Amir Kabir, 2009), 417.

56. Matthew Smith, "Literary Connections: Bahar's *Sabkshenasi* and *Bazgasht-i Adabi*," *Journal of Persianate Studies* 2 (2009): 194–209.

57. Kia, "Imagining Iran Before Nationalism," 100.

58. Arthur Dudney, "Sabk-e Hendi and the Crisis of Authority in Eighteenth-Century Indo-Persian Poetics," *Journal of Persianate Studies* 9 (2016): 60–82.

59. Ghalib, *Divan-i Ghalib Dihlavi,* ed. Muhsin Kiyani (Tehran: Rauzana, 1997), 318.

Glossary of Persian Literary Terms

adab	Proper conduct and manners, also literature
bagh	Formal garden that was the scene of courtly assemblies
divan	Collection of complete works or selections of a poet
faza'il	Praise of a city or region and its products
ghazal	Short poem chiefly about love, also see *taza-gu'i*
khamsa	Quintet of narrative poems in the *masnavi* form
mahfil, majlis	Convivial assembly or party
malik al-shu'ara	Poet laureate appointed by a king
masnavi	Narrative poem in rhymed couplets, used for romances and mystical and topographical subjects
qasida	Formal poem or ode in praise of a patron or religious figure
saqi	Wine server at courtly banquets, usually a young boy
shahrashub	Individual poem or verses on a group of handsome young boys of a city or bazaar
taza-gu'i	Novel composition, a poetic style in vogue among *ghazal* poets of the early modern period
tazkira	Anthology of poetry with biographical information on classical and contemporary poets

Bibliography

'Abdus-Sattar Lahauri. *Majalis-i Jahangiri*. Edited by 'Arif Naushahi and Mu'in Nizami. Tehran: Miras-i Maktub, 2006.

Abu'l-Fazl. *The A'in-i Akbari*. 3 vols. Translated by H. S. Jarrett. Delhi: Taj, 1989.

———. *The History of Akbar*. 4 vols. Translated by Wheeler M. Thackston. Cambridge, MA: Harvard University Press, 2015–2018.

Ahmad, Aziz. "Safavid Poets and India." *Iran* 14 (1976), 118–132.

Ahmad, S. Maqbul, and Raja Bano. *A Study of Persio-Arabic Sources on the Historical Geography of Kashmir*. Srinagar: Jaykay Books, 2011.

Alam, Muzaffar. *The Languages of Political Islam in India, c. 1200–1800*. Delhi: Permanent Black, 2004.

———. "The Pursuit of Persian: Language in Mughal Politics." *Modern Asian Studies* 32 (1998): 317–349.

Alam, Muzaffar, and Sanjay Subrahmanyam. "Faizi's *Nal-Daman* and Its Long Afterlife." In *Writing the Mughal World: Studies in Political Culture*, 204–248. Ranikhet: Permanent Black, 2011.

———. *Indo-Persian Travels in the Age of Discoveries, 1400–1800*. Cambridge, UK: Cambridge University Press, 2007.

Alberuni. *Alberuni's India*. Translated by Edward C. Sachau. Edited by Ainslie T. Embree. New York: Norton, 1971.

Ali, M. Athar. "Pursuing an Elusive Seeker of Universal Truth: The Identity and Environment of the Author of the *Dabistan-i Mazahib*." In *Mughal India: Studies in Polity, Ideas, Society, and Culture*, 216–228. New Delhi: Oxford University Press, 2006.

Ali, Qamar Jahan. *Princess Jahan Ara Begam: Her Life and Works*. Karachi: S. M. Hamid, 1991.

Amir Khusrau. *Khusrau's Qiran us Sa'dain, Conjunction of Two Lucky Planets*. Translated by I. H. Ansari and Hameed Afaq Siddiqui. Delhi: Idarah-i Adabiyat-i Delli, 2012.

———. *Nuh sipihr*. Edited by Mohammad Wahid Mirza. London: Oxford University Press, 1950.

———. *Qiran al-sa'dain*. Edited by Muhammad Isma'il Sahib. Aligarh: Aligarh College Press, 1918.

Andrews, Walter, and Mehmet Kalpaklı. *The Age of Beloveds*. Durham, NC: Duke University Press, 2005.

Anooshahr, Ali. "Shirazi Scholars and the Political Culture of the Sixteenth-Century Indo-Persian World." *The Indian Social and Economic History Review* 51 (2014): 331–352.

Ansari, Nur-ul-Hasan. *Farsi adab bi-'ahd-i Aurangzeb*. Delhi: Indo-Persian Society, 1969.

Asher, Catherine B. *Architecture of Mughal India*. Cambridge, UK: Cambridge University Press, 1992.

Ashraf. *Divan-i ash'ar-i Ashraf Mazandarani*. Edited by Muhammad Hasan Sayyidan. Tehran: Bunyad-i Mauqufat-i Duktur Mahmud Afshar, 1994.

Axworthy, Michael. *A History of Iran: Empire of the Mind*. London: Hurst, 2007.

Azad, Arezou. *Sacred Landscape in Medieval Afghanistan: Revisiting the Fada'il-i Balkh*. Oxford: Oxford University Press, 2013.

Azar. *Atashkada-yi Azar, nima-yi duvvum*. Edited by Mir Hashim Muhaddis. Tehran: Amir Kabir, 2009.

Babaie, Sussan. *Isfahan and Its Palaces: Statecraft, Shi'ism and the Architecture of Conviviality in Early Modern Iran*. Edinburgh: Edinburgh University Press, 2008.

———. "Shah 'Abbas II, the Conquest of Qandahar, the Chihil Sutun, and Its Wall Paintings." *Muqarnas* 11 (1994): 125–142.

Babayan, Kathryn. "The Topography of Travel in Early Modern Persianate Landscapes." *Harvard Library Bulletin* 23 (2012): 25–34.

Babur. *The Baburnama: Memoirs of Babur, Prince and Emperor*. Translated by Wheeler M. Thackston. New York: The Modern Library, 2002.

Badauni. *Muntakhab al-tavarikh*. 3 vols. Edited by Mawlavi Ahmad 'Ali Sahib and Taufiq Subhani. Tehran: Anjuman-i Asar va Mafakhir-i Farhangi, 2000.

———. *Muntakhabu-t-tawarikh*. 3 vols. Translated by George S. A. Ranking, W. H. Lowe, and Wolseley Haig. Delhi: Renaissance, 1986.

Bakhtin, M. *Rabelais and His World*. Translated by Hélène Iswolsky. Bloomington: Indiana University Press, 1984.

Balabanlilar, Lisa. "The Emperor Jahangir and the Pursuit of Pleasure." *Journal of the Royal Asiatic Society* 19 (2009): 173–186.

Beach, Milo Cleveland, and Ebba Koch. *King of the World: The Padshahnama, An Imperial Mughal Manuscript from the Royal Library, Windsor Castle*. Washington, DC: Sackler Gallery, 1997.

Begley, W. E., and Z. A. Desai. *Taj Mahal, The Illumined Tomb: An Anthology of Seventeenth-Century Mughal and European Documentary Sources*. Cambridge, MA: The Aga Khan Program for Islamic Architecture, 1989.

Behl, Aditya. "Pages from the Book of Religions: Encountering Difference in Mughal India." In *Forms of Knowledge in Early Modern Asia: Explorations in the Intellectual History of India and Tibet, 1500–1800*, edited by Sheldon Pollock, 210–239. Durham, NC: Duke University Press, 2011.

Berlekamp, Persis. *Wonder, Image, and Cosmos in Medieval Islam*. New Haven, CT: Yale University Press, 2011.

Bernier, François. *Travels in the Mogul Empire, A.D. 1656–1658*. 2nd ed. London: Oxford University Press, 1916.

Bihishti Haravi. *Nur al-mashriqain, safarnama-yi manzum az 'ahd-i Safavi*. Edited by Najib Ma'il Haravi. Mashhad: Astan-i Quds-i Razavi, 1998.

Bihishti Shirazi. *Ashub-i Hindustan*. Edited by Sayyada Khurshid Fatima Hussaini. New Delhi: Markaz-i Tahqiqat-i Farsi-yi Rayzani-yi Farhangi-yi Jumhuri-yi Islami-yi Iran, 2009.

Bokhari, Afshan. "The "Light" of the Timuria: Jahan Ara Begum's Patronage, Piety, and Poetry in 17th-century Mughal India." *Marg* 60 (2008): 53–61.

Brand, Michael, and Glenn Lowry, eds. *Fatehpur-Sikri: A Sourcebook*. Cambridge, MA: The Aga Khan Program for Islamic Architecture at Harvard University and the Massachusetts Institute of Technology, 1985.

Brookshaw, Dominic P. "Palaces, Pavilions and Pleasure-gardens: The Context and Setting of the Medieval *Majlis*." *Middle Eastern Literatures* 6 (2003): 199–223.

Browne, E. G. *A Literary History of Persia.* 4 vols. Cambridge, UK: Cambridge University Press, 1959.

Busch, Allison. "Poetry in Motion: Literary Circulation in Mughal India." In *Culture and Circulation: Literature in Motion in Early Modern India,* edited by Thomas de Bruijn and Allison Busch, 186–221. Leiden: Brill, 2014.

———. *Poetry of Kings: The Classical Hindi Literature of Mughal India.* New York: Oxford University Press, 2011.

Buzurg ibn Shahryar. *The Book of the Wonders of India, Mainland, Sea and Islands.* Edited and translated by G. S. P. Freeman-Grenville. London: East-West Publications, 1981.

Calmard, Jean. "Safavid Persia in Indo-Persian Sources and in Timurid-Mughal Perception." In *The Making of Indo-Persian Culture: Indian and French Studies,* edited by Muzaffar Alam, Françoise "Nalini" Delvoye, and Marc Gaborieau, 351–391. New Delhi: Manohar, 2000.

Casale, Giancarlo. *The Ottoman Age of Exploration.* Oxford: Oxford University Press, 2010.

Chandarbhan Brahman. *Chahar chaman.* Edited by M. Yunus Jaffrey. New Delhi: Markaz-i Tahqiqat-i Farsi-yi Rayzani-yi Farhangi-yi Jumhuri-yi Islami-yi Iran, 2007.

Chardin, Jean. *Travels in Persia, 1673–77.* New York: Dover, 1988.

Chida-Razvi, Mehreen. "Where is 'the greatest city in the East'? The Mughal City of Lahore in European Travel Accounts (1556–1648)." In *The City in the Muslim World: Depictions by Western Travel Writers,* edited by Mohammad Gharipour and Nilay Özlü, 79–100. London: Routledge, 2015.

Chojnacki, Christine. "Sanskrit Literary works by Jains in Mughal North India: The Historical Significance of a Reinvented Tradition." *Studies in People's History* 1 (2014): 49–62.

Cole, Juan R. I. "The Imagined Embrace: Gender, Identity, and Iranian Ethnicity in Jahangiri Painting." In *Safavid Iran and Her Neighbors,* ed. Michel Mazzaoui, 41–60. Salt Lake City: The University of Utah Press, 2003.

———. "Mirror of the World: Iranian 'Orientalism' and Early 19th-Century India." *Critique: Journal of Critical Studies of Iran and the Middle East* 8 (1996): 41–60.

Dale, Stephen F. *The Garden of the Eight Paradises: Babur and the Culture of Empire in Central Asia, Afghanistan and India (1483–1530).* Leiden: Brill, 2004.

———. *The Muslim Empires of the Ottomans, Safavids, and Mughals.* Cambridge, UK: Cambridge University Press, 2010.

————. "A Safavid Poet in the Heart of Darkness: The Indian Poems of Ashraf Mazandarani." *Iranian Studies* 36 (2003): 197–212.

Dalmia, Vasudha, and Munis D. Faruqui, eds. *Religious Interactions in Mughal India*. New Delhi: Oxford University Press, 2014.

Dara. *Divan-i Dara Shikoh*. Edited by M. Haidariyan. Mashhad: Navid, 1985.

Das, Asok Kumar. *Wonders of Nature: Ustad Mansur at the Mughal Court*. Mumbai: Marg, 2012.

Della Valle, Pietro. *The Travels of Pietro Della Valle in India: From the Old English Translation of 1664*. 2 vols. London: Hakluyt Society, 1892.

Devare, T. N. *A Short History of Persian Literature at the Bahmani, the Adilshahi and the Qutbshahi Courts—Deccan*. Poona: S. Devare, 1961.

D'Hubert, Thibaut. "Pirates, Poets, and Merchants: Bengali Language and Literature in Seventeenth-Century Mrauk-U." In *Culture and Circulation: Literature in Motion in Early Modern India*, edited by Thomas de Bruijn and Allison Busch, 47–74. Leiden: Brill, 2014.

Doniger, Wendy. *On Hinduism*. Oxford: Oxford University Press, 2014.

Dudney, Arthur. *Delhi: Pages from a Forgotten History*. New Delhi: Hay House India, 2015.

————. "Sabk-e Hendi and the Crisis of Authority in Eighteenth-Century Indo-Persian Poetics." *Journal of Persianate Studies* 9 (2016): 60–82.

Eaton, Richard M., and Phillip B. Wagoner. *Power, Memory, Architecture: Contested Sites on India's Deccan Plateau, 1300–1600*. New Delhi: Oxford University Press, 2014.

Elliott, Michael A., and Claudia Stokes, eds. *American Literary Studies: A Methodological Reader*. New York: New York University Press, 2003.

Elman, Benjamin A., ed. *Rethinking East Asian Languages, Vernaculars, and Literacies, 1000–1919*. Leiden: Brill, 2014.

Ernst, Carl. "A Princess of Piety." In *Women of Sufism, A Hidden Treasure: Writings and Stories of Mystic Poets, Scholars & Saints*, edited by Camille Adams Helminski, 128–131. Boston: Shambhala, 2003.

Faizi. *Divan-i Faizi*. Edited by A. D. Arshad. Tehran: Furughi, 1983.

Fakhruz-Zamani Qazvini, 'Abdun-Nabi. *Tazkira-yi Maikhana*. Edited by Ahmad Gulchin-Ma'ani. Tehran: Iqbal, 1961.

Fani. *Masnaviyat-i Fani Kashmiri*. Edited by S. A. H. Abidi. Srinagar: Jammu and Kashmir Academy of Arts, Culture and Languages, 1964.

al-Farabi. *Al-Farabi on the Perfect State: Abu Nasr al-Farabi's Mabadi' ara' ahl al-madina al-fadila, a Revised Text with Introduction, Translation and Commentary*. Translated and edited by Richard Walzer. Oxford: Clarendon Press, 1985.

Farishta. *Tarikh-i Farishta*. Edited by Muhammad Riza Nasiri. Tehran: Anjuman-i Asar va Mafakhir-i Farhangi, 2016.

Farooqi, Naimur Rahman. *Mughal-Ottoman Relations: A Study of Political and Diplomatic Relations between Mughal India and the Ottoman Empire, 1556–1748*. Delhi: Idarah-i Adabiyat-i Delli, 1989.

Faruqi, Shamsur Rahman. "The Strange Case of Persian and Urdu in the Nineteenth Century." *Annual of Urdu Studies* 13 (1998): 3–30.

Faruqui, Munis D. *The Princes of the Mughal Empire, 1504–1719*. Cambridge, UK: Cambridge University Press, 2012.

Fazli Beg. *A Chronicle of the Reign of Shah 'Abbas*. 2 vols. Edited by Kioumars Ghereghlou. Cambridge, UK: Gibb Memorial Trust, 2015.

Feldman, Walter. "Imitatio in Ottoman Poetry: Three Ghazals of the Mid-Seventeenth Century." *The Turkish Studies Association Bulletin* 21 (1997): 31–48.

Fetvaci, Emine. *Picturing History at the Ottoman Court*. Bloomington: Indiana University Press, 2013.

Findly, Ellison Banks. *Nur Jahan: Empress of Mughal India*. New Delhi: Oxford University Press, 1993.

Fleischer, Cornell H. *Bureaucrat and Intellectual in the Ottoman Empire: The Historian Mustafa Ali (1541–1600)*. Princeton: Princeton University Press, 1986.

Flores, Jorge. "Distant Wonders: The Strange and the Marvelous between Mughal India and Habsburg Iberia in the Early Seventeenth Century." *Comparative Studies in Society and History* 49 (2007): 533–581.

Foltz, Richard C. *Mughal India and Central Asia*. Karachi: Oxford University Press, 2001.

———. "Two Seventeenth-Century Central Asian Travellers to Mughal India." *Journal of the Royal Asiatic Society* 6 (1996): 367–377.

Foster, William, ed. *Early Travels in India, 1583–1619*. London: H. Milford, 1921.

Gandhi, Supriya. "The Prince and the *Muvahhid:* Dara Shikoh and Mughal Engagements with Vedanta." In *Monoliths and Multiplicities: Religious Interaction in India, 16th–20th Centuries,* edited by Vasudha Dalmia and Munis D. Faruqui, 65–101. New Delhi: Oxford University Press, 2014.

———. "Retelling the Rama Story in Persian Verse: Masihi Panipati's *Masnavi-i Ram va Sita*. In *There's No Tapping around Philology,* edited by Alireza Korangy and Daniel Sheffield, 309–324. Wiesbaden: Otto Harrassowitz, 2014.

Gazetteer of the Bombay Presidency. Vol. 4, *Ahmedabad*. Bombay: Government Central Press, 1879.

Ghalib. *Divan-i Ghalib Dihlavi.* Edited by Muhsin Kiyani. Tehran: Rauzana, 1997.

Ghani. *The Captured Gazelle: The Poems of Ghani Kashmiri.* Translated by Mufti Mudasir Farooqi and Nusrat Bazaz. New Delhi: Penguin Books, 2013.

Ghani, Abdul. *A History of Persian Language and Literature at the Mughal Court.* 2 vols. Allahabad: Indian Press, 1929.

Gharipour, Mohammad. *Persian Gardens and Pavilions: Reflections in History, Poetry and the Arts.* London: I. B. Tauris, 2013.

Ghazali. *Divan-i Ghazali Mashhadi (asar al-shabab).* Edited by Husain Qurbanipur Arani. Tehran: Intisharat-i 'Ilmi va Farhangi, 2008.

Glover, William. *Making Lahore Modern.* Minneapolis: University of Minnesota Press, 2008.

Gould, Rebecca. "How Gulbadan Remembered: The *Book of Humayun* as an Act of Representation." *Early Modern Women: An Interdisciplinary Journal* 6 (2011): 187–193.

Gulchin-Ma'ani, Ahmad, ed. *Karvan-i Hind.* 2 vols. Mashhad: Astan-i Quds-i Razavi, 1990.

———. *Shahrashub dar shi'r-i Farsi.* 2nd ed. Tehran: Rivayat, 2001.

Habib, Irfan. "Cartography in Mughal India." *The Indian Archives* 28 (1979): 90–95.

———. "Notes on the Economic and Social Aspects of Mughal Gardens." In *Mughal Gardens: Sources, Places, Representations, and Prospects,* edited by James L. Wescoat and Joachim Wolschke-Bulmahn, 127–138. Washington, DC: Dumbarton Oaks Research Library and Collection, 1996.

Hadi, Nabi. *Dictionary of Indo-Persian Literature.* New Delhi: Indira Gandhi National Centre for the Arts, 1995.

———. *Talib-i-Amuli (The Poet-Laureate of Jahangir): His Life and Times.* Aligarh: Muslim University, 1962.

Haidar Dughlat. *Mirza Haydar Dughlat's Tarikh-i Rashidi: A History of the Khans of Moghulistan.* Translated by Wheeler M. Thackston. Cambridge, MA: Harvard University, Department of Near Eastern Languages and Civilizations, 1996.

Hamadeh, Shirine. *The City's Pleasures: Istanbul in the Eighteenth Century.* Seattle: University of Washington Press, 2008.

Hanaway, William L., Jr. "Paradise on Earth: The Terrestrial Garden in Persian Literature." In *The Islamic Garden,* edited by R. Ettinghausen. Washington, DC: Dumbarton Oaks, 1976.

Haneda, Masahi. "Emigration of Iranian Elites to India during the 16th–18th Centuries." *Cahiers d'Asie Centrale* 3/4 (1997): 129–143.

Hasan, Hadi. *Mughal Poetry, Its Cultural and Historical Value.* Madras: Islamic Literature Society, 1952.

Hasrat, Bikrama Jit. *Dara Shikuh: Life and Works.* New Delhi: Munshiram Manoharlal, 1982.

Hodgson, Marshall. *Venture of Islam: The Gunpowder Empires and Modern Times.* 3 vols. Chicago: University of Chicago Press, 1974.

Husain, Ali Akbar. *Scent in the Islamic Garden: A Study of Literary Sources in Persian and Urdu.* 2nd ed. Karachi: Oxford University Press, 2012.

Husain, M. Hidayat. "The Mirza Namah (The Book of the Perfect Gentleman) of Mirza Kamran with an English Translation." *Journal of the Asiatic Society of Bengal* 9 (1913): 1–13.

'Inayat Khan. *The Shah Jahan Nama of 'Inayat Khan.* Translated by A. R. Fuller. Edited by W. E. Begley and Z. A. Desai. Delhi: Oxford University Press, 1990.

Inden, Ronald. "Kashmir as Paradise on Earth." In *The Valley of Kashmir: The Making and Unmaking of a Composite Culture?* edited by Aparna Rao, 523–561. New Delhi: Manohar, 2008.

———. "Paradise on Earth: The Deccan Sultanates." In *Garden and Landscape Practices in Precolonial India: Histories from the Deccan,* edited by Daud Ali and Emma Flatt, 74–97. New Delhi: Routledge, 2011.

Iqbal. *Ash'ar-i Farsi-yi Iqbal Lahauri.* Edited by Mahmud 'Ilmi. Tehran: Javidan, 1991.

Iskandar Beg Munshi. *History of Shah 'Abbas the Great.* 2 vols. Translated by Roger M. Savory. Boulder, CO: Westview, 1978–1986.

Islam, Riazul. *Calendar of Documents on Indo-Persian Relations, 1500–1750.* 2 vols. Tehran: Iranian Culture Foundation, 1979.

———. *Indo-Persian Relations: A Study of the Political and Diplomatic Relations between the Mughul Empire and Iran.* Tehran: Iranian Culture Foundation, 1970.

Jaffrey, Yunus. "Sati dar shi'r-i Sa'ib Tabrizi." In *Armaghan-i adabi: pizhuhishha-yi adabi dar adabiyat-i farsi-i Hind,* 284–289. Tehran: Mauqufat-i Duktur Mahmud Afshar, 1997.

Jahanara. "Risala-i Sahibiya." Edited with an Urdu translation by Muhammad Aslam. *Journal of the Research Society of Pakistan* 16 (1979): 78–110; 17 (1980): 69–107.

Jahangir. *The Jahangirnama.* Translated by Wheeler M. Thackston. New York: Oxford University Press, 1999.

Jayyusi, Salma Khadra. "Andalusi Poetry: The Golden Period." In *The Legacy of Muslim Spain,* edited by Salma Khadra Jayyusi, 317–366. Leiden: Brill, 1992.

———. "Nature Poetry in al-Andalus and the Rise of Ibn Khafaja." In *The Legacy of Muslim Spain*, edited by Salma Khadra Jayyusi, 367–397. Leiden: Brill, 1992.

Juneja, Monica. "On the Margins of Utopia—One More Look at Mughal Painting." *The Medieval History Journal* 4 (2001): 203–240.

Jutla, Rajinder S. "Fatehpur Sikri: A Utopian Approach to Urban Planning and Design." Unpublished manuscript, 1995. http://www.etsav.upc.es /personals/iphs2004/pdf/098_p.pdf.

Juya. *Divan-i Juya Tabrizi*. Edited by Parviz 'Abbasi Dakani. Tehran: Barg, 1999.

Kaicker, Abhishek. "Unquiet City: Making and Unmaking Politics in Mughal Delhi, 1707–39." PhD diss., Columbia University, 2014.

Kalhana. *Kings of Kashmira, being a translation of the Sanskrita work Rajataranggini of Kalhana Pandita by Jogesh Chunder Dutt*. Calcutta: I. C. Bose, 1879.

Kalim. *Divan-i Abu Talib Kalim Hamadani*. Edited by Muhammad Qahraman. Mashhad: Astan-i Quds-i Razavi, 1990.

Kanti Sagar, Muni. *Nagarvarnatmak Hindi padya sangrah*. Surat, 1948.

Keenan, Brigid. *Travels in Kashmir: A Popular History of Its People, Places, and Crafts*. Delhi: Permanent Black, 2006.

Khan, Dargah Quli. *Muraqqa'-e-Delhi: The Mughal Capital in Muhammad Shah's Time*, translated by Chander Shekhar and Shama Mitra Chenoy. Delhi: Deputy Publication, 1989.

———. *Muraqqa'-i Dihli*, edited with an Urdu translation by Nuru'l-Hasan Ansari. Delhi: Department of Urdu, University of Delhi, 1982.

Khan, Iqtidar Alam. "The Mughal Empire and the Iranian Diaspora of the Sixteenth Century." In *A Shared Heritage: The Growth of Civilization in India and Iran*, edited by Irfan Habib, 99–116. New Delhi: Tulika, 2002.

Khan, Pasha. "A Handbook for Storytellers: The *Tiraz al-akhbar* and the Qissa Genre." In *Tellings and Texts: Music, Literature and Performance in North India*, 185–207. Cambridge, UK: Open Book Publishers, 2015.

Kia, Mana. "Imagining Iran Before Nationalism: Geocultural Meanings of Land in Azar's *Atashkadeh*." In *Rethinking Iranian Nationalism and Modernity*, edited by Kamran Scot Aghaie and Afshin Marashi, 89–112. Austin: University of Texas Press, 2014.

———. "Limning the Land: Social Encounters and Historical Meaning in Early Nineteenth-Century Travelogues between Iran and India." In *On the Wonders of Land and Sea: Persianate Travel Writing*, ed. Roberta Micallef and Sunil Sharma, 44–67. Boston: Ilex, 2013.

Kinra, Rajeev. "Fresh Words for a Fresh World: *Taza-Gu'i* and the Poetics of Newness in Early Modern Indo-Persian Poetry." In *Sikh Formations: Religion, Culture, Theory* 3 (2007): 125–149.

———. "Handling Diversity with Absolute Civility: The Global Historical Legacy of Mughal *Sulh-i Kull.*" *The Medieval History Journal* 16 (2013): 1–45.

———. "Infantilizing Baba Dara: The Cultural Memory of Dara Shekuh and the Mughal Public Sphere." *Journal of Persianate Studies* 2 (2009): 165–193.

———. *Writing Self, Writing Empire: Chandar Bhan Brahman and the Cultural World of the Indo-Persian State Secretary.* Oakland: University of California Press, 2015.

Kirmani, Waris. *Dreams Forgotten: An Anthology of Indo-Persian Poetry.* Aligarh: Aligarh Muslim University, 1984.

Koch, Ebba. *The Complete Taj Mahal and the Riverfront Gardens of Agra.* London: Thames & Hudson, 2006.

———. "The Influence of the Jesuit Missions on Symbolic Representations of the Mughal Emperors." In *Mughal Art and Imperial Ideology: Collected Essays,* 1–11. New Delhi: Oxford University Press, 2001.

———. "Mughal Agra: A Riverfront Garden City." In *The City in the Islamic World,* edited by Salma K. Jayyusi, 555–588. Leiden: Brill, 2008.

———. "The Mughal Emperor as Solomon, Majnun, and Orpheus, or the Album as a Think Tank for Allegory." *Muqarnas* 27 (2010): 277–311.

———. "My Garden is Hindustan: The Mughal Emperor's Realization of a Political Metaphor." In *Middle East Garden Traditions: Unity and Diversity, Questions, Methods and Resources in a Multicultural Perspective,* 159–175. Washington, DC: Dumbarton Oaks Research Library and Collection 2007.

———. "The Taj Mahal: Architecture, Symbolism, and Urban Significance." *Muqarnas* 22 (2005): 128–149.

Lal, Ruby. *Domesticity and Power in the Early Mughal World.* Cambridge, UK: Cambridge University Press, 2005.

Landau, Amy S. "Man, Mode, and Myth: Muhammad Zaman ibn Haji Yusuf." In *Pearls on a String: Artists, Patrons, and Poets at the Great Islamic Courts.* Baltimore: Walters Museum of Art, 2016.

———. "Visibly Foreign, Visibly Female: The Eroticization of *zan-i farangi* in Seventeenth-century Persian Painting." In *Eros and Sexuality in Islamic Art,* edited by Francesca Leoni and Mika Natif, 99–129. Farnham: Ashgate, 2013.

Leach, Linda. *Mughal and Other Indian Paintings from the Chester Beatty Library.* 2 vols. London: Scorpion Cavendish, 1995.

Lefèvre, Corinne. "The Court of 'Abd-ur-Rahim Khan-i Khanan as a Bridge between Iranian and Indian Cultural Traditions." In *Culture and Circulation: Literature in Motion in Early Modern India*, edited by Thomas de Bruijn and Allison Busch, 75–106. Leiden: Brill, 2014.

Losensky, Paul. " 'The Equal of Heaven's Vault': The Design, Ceremony, and Poetry of the Hasanabad Bridge." In *Writers and Rulers: Perspectives on Their Relationship from Abbasid to Safavid Times*, edited by Beatrice Gruendler and Louise Marlow, 195–216. Wiesbaden: Reichert, 2004.

———. "The Palace of Praise and the Melons of Time: Descriptive Patterns in 'Abdi Širazi's *Garden of Eden*." *Eurasian Studies* 2 (2003): 1–29.

———. " 'Square like a Bubble': Architecture, Power, and Poetics in Two Inscriptions by Kalim Kashani." *Journal of Persianate Studies* 8 (2015): 42–70.

———. "Vintages of the *Saqi-nama*: Fermenting and Blending the Cup-bearer's Song in the Sixteenth Century." *Iranian Studies* 47 (2014): 131–157.

———. *Welcoming Fighani: Imitation and Poetic Individuality in the Safavid-Mughal Ghazal*. Costa Mesa, CA: Mazda, 1998.

Mahmud ibn Amir Vali. *The Bahr ul-Asrar, Travelogue of South Asia*. Edited by Riazul Islam. Karachi: Institute of Central & West Asian Studies, 1980.

Malik, Jamal. *Islam in South Asia: A Short History*. Leiden: Brill, 2008.

Mancini-Lander, Derek. "Dreaming the Elixir of Knowledge: How a Seventeenth-Century Poet from Herat Got His Name and Fame." In *Dreams and Visions in Islamic Societies*, edited by Özgen Felek and Alexander D. Knysh, 77–97. Albany: State University of New York Press, 2012.

Matthee, Rudi. *Persia in Crisis: Safavid Decline and the Fall of Isfahan*. London: I. B. Tauris, 2012.

Maurya, Anubhuti. "Of Tulips and Daffodils: Kashmir Jannat Nazir as a Political Landscape in the Mughal Empire." *Economic & Political Weekly* 52, no. 15 (2017): 37–44.

McGregor, Stuart. *Hindi Literature from Its Beginnings to the Nineteenth Century*. Wiesbaden: Harrassowitz, 1984.

Meisami, Julie S. "Allegorical Gardens in the Persian Poetic Tradition: Nezami, Rumi, Hafez." *International Journal of Middle Eastern Studies* 17 (1985): 229–260.

———. "Palaces and Paradises: Palace Description in Medieval Persian Poetry." In *Islamic Art and Literature*, edited by Oleg Grabar and Cynthia Robinson, 21–54. Princeton, NJ: Markus Wiener, 2001.

Miller, Sam. *A Strange Kind of Paradise: India through Foreign Eyes*. New Delhi: Penguin Books, 2014.

Mitchell, Colin. *The Practice of Politics in Safavid Iran: Power, Religion and Rhetoric.* London: Tauris, 2009.

Moin, A. Azfar. *The Millennial Sovereign: Sacred Kingship and Sainthood in Islam.* New York: Columbia University Press, 2012.

Morton, A. H. "The Transmission of Persian Texts Compared to the Case of Classical Latin." In *Literacy in the Persianate World: Writing and the Social Order,* edited by Brian Spooner and William H. Hanaway, 143–158. Philadelphia: University of Pennsylvania Museum of Archaeology and Anthropology, 2012.

Munir. *Karnama-yi Abu Barakat Munir Lahauri va Siraj-i munir-i Siraj al-Din 'Ali Khan Arzu.* Edited by S. M. A. Ikram. Islamabad: Markaz-i Tahqiqat-i Farsi-yi Iran va Pakistan, 1977.

———. *Surudaha va navishtaha-yi Munir Lahauri.* Edited by Farid Akram. Tehran: Bunyad-i Mauqufat-i Duktur Mahmud Afshar Yazdi, 2009.

Musta'id Khan. *Ma'asir-i 'Alamgiri.* Edited by Agha Ahmad 'Ali. Vol. 2. Calcutta: Asiatic Society of Bengal, 1871.

———. *Maasir-i-'Alamgiri.* Translated by Jadunath Sarkar. Calcutta: Royal Asiatic Society of Bengal, 1947.

Mutribi Samarqandi. *Khatirat-i Mutribi.* Edited by 'Abd al-Ghani Mirzayif. Karachi: Mu'assasa-yi Tahqiqat-i Asiya-yi Miyana va Gharbi, Danishgah, 1977.

Naik, Chhotubhai Ranchhodji. *'Abdu'r-Rahim Khan-i-Khanan and His Literary Circle.* Ahmedabad: Gujarat University, 1966.

Naim, C. M. "Mughal and English Patronage of Urdu Poetry: A Comparison." In *Urdu Texts and Contexts: The Selected Essays of C. M. Naim.* Delhi: Permanent Black, 2004.

Nau'i. *Burning and Melting, Being the Suz-u-Gudaz of Muhammad Riza Nau'i Khabushan.* Translated by Mirza Y. Dawud and Ananda K. Coomaraswamy. London, 1912.

———. *Divan-i Mulla Nau'i Khabushani.* Edited by Amir Husain Zakirzada. Tehran: Ma, 1995.

Necipoğlu, Gülru. "Framing the Gaze in Ottoman, Safavid, and Mughal Palaces." *Ars Orientalis* 10 (1993): 303–342.

———. "Visual Cosmopolitanism and Creative Translation: Artistic Conversations with Renaissance Italy in Mehmed II's Constantinople." *Muqarnas* 29 (2012): 1–81.

Nihavandi. *The Ma'asir-i-Rahimi.* 3 vols. Edited by Hidayat Husain. Calcutta: Asiatic Society of Bengal, 1925.

Nizamuddin Ahmad. *The Tabaqat-i-Akbari of Khwaja Nizamuddin Ahmad.* 3 vols. Translated by Brajendranath De. Delhi: Low Price Publications, 1992.

Ogura, Satoshi. "Transmission Lines of Historical Information on Kasmir: From *Rajataranginis* to the Persian Chronicles in the early Mugal Period." *Journal of Indological Studies* 22–23 (2010–2011): 23–59.

Orsini, Francesca. "The Multilingual Local in World Literature." *Comparative Literature* 67 (2015): 345–374.

Parodi, Laura E. "From *Tooy* to *Darbar*: Materials for a History of Mughal Audiences and Their Depictions." In *Garland of Gems: Indian Art between Mughal, Rajput, Europe and Far East*, edited by Joachim K. Bautze and Rosa M. Cimino, 51–76. Ravenna: Edizioni del Girasole, 2010.

Parvini, Neema. *Shakespeare's History Plays: Rethinking Historicism*. Edinburgh: Edinburgh University Press, 2012.

Pauwels, Heidi Rika Maria. *Cultural Exchange in Eighteenth-Century India: Poetry and Paintings from Kishangarh*. Berlin: EB-Verlag, 2015.

Pellò, Stefano. "Local Lexis? Provincializing Persian in Fifteenth-Century North India." In *After Timur Left: Culture and Circulation in Fifteenth-Century India*, edited by Francesca Orsini and Samira Sheikh, 166–185. New Delhi: Oxford University Press, 2014.

Pinder-Wilson, Ralph. "Three Illustrated Manuscripts of the Mughal Period." *Ars Orientalis* 2 (1957): 413–422.

Pollock, Sheldon I. *Literary Cultures in History: Reconstructions from South Asia*. Berkeley: University of California Press, 2003.

Qudsi. *Divan-i Hajji Muhammad Jan Qudsi Mashhadi*. Edited by Muhammad Qahraman. Mashhad: Danishgah-i Firdausi, 1996.

Rahim. *Rahim Granthavali*. Edited by V. Mishra and G. Rajnish. New Delhi: Vani Prakashan, 1994.

Rahman, M. L. *Persian Literature in India during the Time of Jahangir and Shah Jahan*. Baroda: Department of Persian and Urdu, M. S. University of Baroda, 1970.

Ramaswamy, Sumathi. "Conceit of the Globe in Mughal Visual Practice." *Comparative Studies in Society and History* 49 (2007): 751–782.

Rashidi, S. H., ed. *Tazkira-yi shu'ara-yi Kashmir*. 4 vols. Karachi: Iqbal Academy, 1967–1969.

Rashiduddin Fazlullah Hamadani. *Jami' al-tavarikh: Tarikh-i Hind va Sind va Kashmir*. Edited by Muhammad Raushan. Tehran: Miras-i Maktub, 2005.

Rathod, Vikramsinh, ed. *Rajasthani gajal sangrah*. Jodhpur: Rajasthan Shodh Sansthan, 1995.

Ray, Sukumar. *Humayun in Persia*. Calcutta: The Asiatic Society, 1948.

Razi. *Tazkira-yi haft iqlim*. Edited by Sayyid Muhammad Riza Tahiri "Hasrat." Tehran: Surush, 1999.

Rehman, Abdul, and Shama Anbrine. "Unity and Diversity of Mughal Garden Experiences." In *Mughal Gardens: Sources, Places, Representations, and Prospects,* edited by James L. Wescoat and Joachim Wolschke-Bulmahn. Washington, DC: Dumbarton Oaks Research Library and Collection, 1996.

Rice, Yael. "Between the Brush and the Pen: On the Intertwined Histories of Mughal Painting and Calligraphy." In *Envisioning Islamic Art and Architecture: Essays in Honor of Renata Holod,* edited by David J. Roxburgh, 148–174. Leiden: Brill, 2014.

Ritter, Valerie. *Kama's Flowers: Nature in Hindi Poetry and Criticism, 1885–1925.* Albany: State University of New York Press, 2011.

Roxburgh, David J. *Prefacing the Image: The Writing of Art History in Sixteenth-Century Iran.* Leiden: Brill, 2001.

Ruggles, D. Fairchild. *Islamic Gardens and Landscapes.* Philadelphia: University of Pennsylvania Press, 2008.

Rypka, Jan. *History of Iranian Literature.* Dordrecht: D. Reidel, 1968.

Sa'ib. *Divan-i Sa'ib Tabrizi.* 6 vols. Edited by Muhammad Qahraman. Tehran: Intisharat-i 'Ilmi va Farhangi, 1995.

Saidi. *Divan-i Saidi Tihrani.* Edited by Muhammad Qahraman. Tehran: Ittila'at, 1985.

Salik. *Divan-i Salik Qazvini.* Edited by 'Abdus-Samad Haqiqat and Ahmad Karimi. Tehran: Ma, 1994.

Salim. *Divan-i kamil-i Muhammad Quli Salim Tehrani.* Edited by Rahim Riza. Tehran: Ibn Sina, 1970.

Sarkar, Jadunath. "Adab-i 'Alamgiri." In *Studies in Aurangzib's Reign.* Calcutta: M. C. Sarkar & Sons, 1933.

Schimmel, Annemarie. *The Empire of the Great Mughals: History, Art and Culture.* Translated by Corinne Attwood. Edited by Burzine K. Waghmar. London: Reaktion Books, 2004.

———. *Islamic Literatures.* Wiesbaden: O. Harrassowitz, 1973.

———. "Turk and Hindu, a Poetical Image and its Application to Historical Fact." In *Islam and Cultural Change in the Middle Ages,* edited by Speros Vryonis, Jr., 107–126. Wiesbaden: Harrassowitz, 1975.

———. *A Two-Colored Brocade: The Imagery of Persian Poetry.* Chapel Hill: The University of North Carolina Press, 1992.

Seyller, John. *The Adventures of Hamza: Painting and Storytelling in Mughal India.* Washington, DC: Smithsonian Institution, 2002.

———. *Workshop and Patron in Mughal India: The Freer Ramayana and Other Illustrated Manuscripts of 'Abd al-Rahim.* Zurich: Artibus Asiae, 1999.

Shackle, Christopher. "Settings of Panegyric: The Secular Qasida in Mughal and British India." In *Qasida Poetry in Islamic Asia and Africa,* edited by Stefan Sperl and Christopher Shackle, 205–252. Leiden: Brill, 1996.

Shahnavaz Khan. *The Ma'asir al-umara.* 3 vols. Edited by Maulvi Mirza Ashraf 'Ali. Calcutta: Asiatic Society of Bengal, 1890.

Shamlu, Vali Quli. *Qisas al-khaqani.* 2 vols. Edited by Hasan Sadat Nasiri. Tehran: Vizarat-i Farhang va Irshad-i Islami, 1992–1995.

Sharafuddin 'Ali Yazdi. *Zafarnama.* Edited by Sa'id Mir Muhammad Sadiq and 'Abdu'l-Husain Navvabi. Tehran: Kitabkhana-yi Muzih va Markaz-i Asnad-i Majlis-i Shura-yi Islami, 2008.

Sharlet, Jocelyn. *Patronage and Poetry in the Islamic World: Social Mobility and Poetry in the Islamic World.* London: I. B. Tauris, 2011.

Sharma, Sandhya. *Literature, Culture and History in Mughal North India, 1550–1800.* New Delhi: Primus Books, 2011.

Sharma, Sunil. "Celebrating Writing and Books in Safavid and Mughal Court Poetry." In *Écrit et culture en Asie centrale et dans le monde turco-iranien, XIVe–XIXe siècles (Writing and Culture in Central Asia and the Turko-Iranian World, 14th–19th centuries),* edited by Francis Richard and Maria Szuppe, 231–250. Paris: Association pour l'Avancement des Etudes Iraniennes, 2009.

———. "The City of Beauties in the Indo-Persian Poetic Landscape." *Comparative Studies of South Asia, Africa and the Middle East* 24 (2004): 73–81.

———. "From 'Aesha to Nur Jahan: The Shaping of a Classical Persian Poetic Canon of Women." *Journal of Persianate Studies* 2, no. 2 (2009): 147–164.

———. " 'If There Is a Paradise on Earth, It is Here': Urban Ethnography in Indo-Persian Poetic and Historical Texts." In *Forms of Knowledge in Early Modern Asia: Explorations in the Intellectual History of India and Tibet, 1500–1800,* edited by Sheldon Pollock, 240–256. Durham, NC: Duke University Press, 2011.

———. "Kashmir and the Mughal Fad of Persian Pastoral Poetry." *Eurasiatica: Quaderni di studi su Balcani, Anatolia, Iran, Caucaso e Asia Centrale* 5 (2016): 183–202.

———. "The Nizamshahi Persianate Garden in Zuhuri's *Saqinama.*" In *Garden and Landscape Practices in Precolonial India: Histories from the Deccan,* edited by Daud Ali and Emma Flatt, 159–171. New Delhi: Routledge, 2011.

———. "Novelty, Tradition and Mughal Politics in Nau'i's *Suz u Gudaz.*" In *The Necklace of the Pleiades: Studies in Persian Literature Presented to*

Heshmat Moayyad on his 80th Birthday, edited by Franklin Lewis and Sunil Sharma, 251–265. West Lafayette, IN: Purdue University Press, 2007.

———. "The Production of Mughal *Shahnama*s: Imperial, Sub-Imperial, and Provincial Manuscripts." In *Ferdowsi's* Shahnama: *Millennial Perspectives,* edited by Olga M. Davidson and Marianna Shreve Simpson, 86–107. Boston: Ilex, 2013.

———. "Reading the Acts and Lives of Performers in Mughal Persian Texts." In *Tellings and Texts: Music, Literature and Performance in North India,* edited by Francesca Orsini and Katherine Butler Schofield, 283–302. Cambridge, UK: Open Book Publishers, 2015.

———. "Representation of Social Types in Mughal Art and Literature: Ethnography or Trope?" In *Indo-Muslim Cultures in Transition,* edited by Alka Patel and Karen Leonard, 17–36. Leiden: Brill, 2011).

Sheffield, Daniel. "The Language of Paradise in Safavid Iran: Speech and Cosmology in the Thought of Azar Kayvan and His Followers." In *There's No Tapping around Philology,* edited by Alireza Korangy and Daniel Sheffield, 161–183. Wiesbaden: Otto Harrassowitz, 2014.

Shibli Nu'mani. *Shi'r al-'ajam.* Vol. 3. Azamgarh: Dar al-Musannifin Shibli Academy, 1991.

Smith, Matthew. "Literary Connections: Bahar's *Sabkshenasi* and *Bazgasht-e Adabi.*" *Journal of Persianate Studies* 2 (2009): 194–209.

Storey, C. A. *Persian Literature: A Bio-Bibliographical Survey.* Vol. 1. London: The Royal Asiatic Society of Great Britain and Ireland, 1970.

Streusand, Douglas E. *Islamic Gunpowder Empires: Ottomans, Safavids, and Mughals.* Philadelphia: Westview Press, 2011.

Stronge, Susan. *Painting for the Mughal Emperor: The Art of the Book, 1560–1660.* London: V&A, 2002.

Subrahmanyam, Sanjay. "Iranians Abroad: Intra-Asian Elite Migration and Early Modern State Formation." *The Journal of Asian Studies* 51 (1992): 340–363.

———. "Monsters, Miracles and the World of *'Ajaib-o-gharaib:* Intersections between the Early Modern Iberian and Indo-Persian Worlds." In *Naturalia, mirabilia & monstrosa en los imperios Ibéricos (siglos XV–XIX),* edited by Eddy Stols, Werner Thomas, and Johan Verberckmoes, 274–306. Leuven: Leuven University Press, 2006.

Sufi, G. M. D. *Kashir, Being a History of Kashmir from the Earliest Times to Our Own.* 2 vols. Lahore: University of the Panjab, 1949.

Syed, Muhammad Aslam. "How Could Urdu Be the Envy of Persian (*rashk-i-Farsi*)! The Role of Persian in South Asian Culture and

Literature." In *Literacy in the Persianate World: Writing and the Social Order,* edited by Brian Spooner and William H. Hanaway, 279–310. Philadelphia: University of Pennsylvania Museum of Archaeology and Anthropology, 2012.

Talib. *Kulliyat-i ash'ar-i malik al-shu'ara Talib-i Amuli.* Edited by Tahiri Shihab. Tehran: Sana'i, 1967.

Taqi Auhadi. *Tazkira-yi 'Arafat al-'ashiqin va 'arasat al-'arifin.* 7 vols. Edited by Muhsin Naji Nasrabadi. Tehran: Asatir, 2009.

Thackston, Wheeler M. *Album Prefaces and Other Documents on the History of Calligraphers and Painters.* Leiden: Brill, 2001.

———. *A Century of Princes: Sources on Timurid History and Art.* Cambridge, MA: The Aga Khan Program for Islamic Architecture, 1989.

———. "Mughal Gardens in Persian Poetry." In *Mughal Gardens: Sources, Places, Representations, and Prospects,* edited by James L. Wescoat and Joachim Wolschke-Bulmahn. Washington, DC: Dumbarton Oaks Research Library and Collection, 1996.

———. "Persian Literature." In *The Magnificent Mughals,* edited by Zeenut Ziad, 84–111. Oxford: Oxford University Press, 2002.

———. *The Poetry of Abu-Talib Kalim, Persian Poet-Laureate of Shah Jahan, Mughal Emperor of India.* PhD diss., Harvard University, 1974.

Tikku, G. L. *Persian Poetry in Kashmir, 1339–1846.* Berkeley: University of California Press, 1971.

Truschke, Audrey. *Culture of Encounters: Sanskrit at the Mughal Court.* New York: Columbia University Press, 2016.

———. "Setting the Record Wrong: A Sanskrit Vision of Mughal Conquests." *South Asian History and Culture* 3 (2012): 373–396.

Tughra. *Arghavan-i shafaq: bar-guzida-yi divan-i Tughra-yi Mashhadi.* Edited by Muhammad Qahraman. Tehran: Amir Kabir, 2005.

———. *Rasa'il-i Tughra.* Kanpur: Matba'-i Mustafa'i, 1864.

'Urfi. *Kulliyat-i 'Urfi Shirazi,* ed. Javahiri Vajdi. Tehran: Kitabkhana-yi Sana'i, 1990.

Vahid, Tahir. "Gulzar-i 'Abbasi, ed. Bihruz Imani." *Ganjina-yi Baharistan: Adabiyat-i Farsi* 2 (2001): 643–674.

———. *Tarikh-i jahanara-yi 'Abbasi.* Edited by Sa'id Mir Muhammad Sadiq. Tehran: Pizhuhishgah-i 'Ulum-i Insani va Mutala'at-i Farhangi, 2004.

Valih, Daghistani. *Tazkira-yi riyaz al-shu'ara.* 5 vols. Edited by Muhsin Naji Nasrabadi. Tehran: Asatir, 2005.

Verma, Som Prakash. *Interpreting Mughal Painting: Essays on Art, Society, and Culture.* New Delhi: Oxford University Press, 2009.

Wade, Bonnie. *Imaging Sound: An Ethnomusicological Study of Music, Art, and Culture in Mughal India.* Chicago: University of Chicago Press, 1998.

Wescoat, James L. "Gardens, Urbanization, and Urbanism in Mughal Lahore: 1526–1657." In *Mughal Gardens: Sources, Places, Representations, and Prospects,* edited by James L. Wescoat and Joachim Wolschke-Bulmahn, 138–169. Washington, DC: Dumbarton Oaks Research Library and Collection, 1996.

Williams, Raymond. *The Country and the City.* Oxford: Oxford University Press, 1973.

Yildiz, Sara Nur. "Ottoman Historical Writing in Persian, 1400–1600." In *Persian Historiography,* edited by Charles Melville, 450–469. London: I. B. Tauris, 2012.

Zadeh, Travis. *Mapping Frontiers across Medieval Islam: Geography, Translation, and the 'Abbasid Empire.* London: I. B. Tauris, 2011.

Zafar Khan. *Masnaviyat-i Zafar Khan.* Edited by Muhammad Aslam Khan. Delhi: Indo-Persian Society, 1985.

———. *Zafar Khan Ahsan: Tahqiq dar ahval va asar va afkar va ash'ar.* Edited by Muhammad Aslam Khan. Delhi: Indo-Persian Society, 1976.

Zutshi, Chitralekha. *Kashmir's Contested Pasts: Narratives, Sacred Geographies, and the Historical Imagination.* New Delhi: Oxford University Press, 2014.

Acknowledgments

I am immensely grateful to Sharmila Sen and Heather Hughes at Harvard University Press for providing timely encouragement and assistance during the entire process that resulted in this book. The feedback of the two anonymous readers was thoughtful and welcome. I am indebted to my colleagues in various parts of the world—especially those in the fields of Persian and Mughal studies—students, and family, for many things ranging from discussions on the topics covered in the book to moral support.

Boston University's Center for the Humanities awarded a subvention to reproduce the images in this book. Scott Walker of the Map Collection at Harvard Library provided the map that appears in the beginning.

Illustration Credits

Figure 1   Ahsanallah b. Abu'l-Hasan, *Kitab-i Mathnawiyyat-i Zafar Khan,* unfinished autograph copy, ca. 1663. Royal Asiatic Society Manuscripts Collection, Cambridge University Library, Special Collections (RAS MS 310, Masnavi fol. 19b & 20a). Reproduced by kind permission of the Syndics of Cambridge University Library.

Figure 2   Abu'l-Hasan, *Tuzuk-i Jahangiri* or *Jahangirnama,* ca. 1615–1618. Institute of Oriental Manuscripts, Russian Academy of Sciences, St. Petersburg (IOM RAS: E-14, folio 21r).

Figure 3   "Emperor Jahangir hunting with hawks." Mughal Dynasty, late seventeenth century. The British Museum (1920,0917,0.1). © The Trustees of the British Museum. All rights reserved.

Figure 4   Outline by Tulsi the Elder, painting by Bandi, portraits by Madhav Khord. Folio from *Akbarnama,* ca. 1586–ca. 1589. South & South East Asia Collection, Victoria and Albert Museum (IS.2:91-1896). © Stephanie Fawcett for NEW PHO Invoicing / Victoria and Albert Museum, London.

Figure 5   "Shah Jahan examines jewels by the Dal Lake." Masterpieces of the Non-Western Book Collection, The Bodleian Library, University of Oxford (MS. Douce Or. a.1, fol. 23a).

Figure 6   Ahsanallah b. Abu'l-Hasan, *Kitab-i Mathnawiyyat-i Zafar Khan,* unfinished autograph copy, ca. 1663. Royal Asiatic Society Manuscripts Collection, Cambridge University Library, Special Collections (RAS MS 310, Masnavi fol. 11b & 12a). Reproduced by kind permission of the Syndics of Cambridge University Library.

Figure 7   Ahsanallah b. Abu'l-Hasan, *Kitab-i Mathnawiyyat-i Zafar Khan,*
             unfinished autograph copy, ca. 1663. Royal Asiatic Society
             Manuscripts Collection, Cambridge University Library, Special
             Collections (RAS MS 310, Masnavi fol. 25b & 26a). Reproduced by
             kind permission of the Syndics of Cambridge University Library.

Figure 8   "Carte nouvelle du Royaume de Kachemire," *Voyages de François
             Bernier,* 1723. Houghton Library, Harvard University (DS461.7.B5
             1723).

Figure 9   Mir Kalan Khan, "Village Life in Kashmir," ca. 1760. akg-images
             ltd / The British Library, London.

Figure 10   "Courtier Refusing Wine from Indian Courtesans," ca. 1650–1700.
             Arthur M. Sackler Museum, The Edwin Binney, 3rd Collection
             of Turkish Art, Harvard Art Museums, Imaging Department
             (2011.91). © President and Fellows of Harvard College.

Index

Page numbers in italics refer to illustrations.

Khandesh, 3, 96, 104

Khurasan, 37, 40, 47, 70, 110, 111, 137, 146, 208n45

Khurram, 45, 82, 106. *See also* Shah Jahan

Khusrau, Amir: Persian poetry of, 10, 37, 40–41, 61, 101, 193; poetry on India by, 17, 18, 64, 93–94, 105, 120, 186; reception of, 15, 19, 58, 61–62, 68–68, 93–94, 108, 219n25; tomb of, 119

Khvaja Jahan, 81

Khvaja Kalan, 69

Khvandamir, Ghiyasuddin, 100

Kinra, Rajeev, 11, 24

Koch, Ebba, 47, 77, 106, 113, 131

Kufri, 40

Lahijan, 125, 139

Lahore: as cultural center, 60, 109, 122, 154; in Hindi poetry, 124; Jahangir's tomb in, 88; Mughal men of letters from, 121, 177; in Persian literature, 95, 122–124, 138, 146, 161, 178, 182; Qadiri Sufi order in, 122, 160–161; topography of, 2, 82, 123, 146, 160, 178

Lakshmichandra, 118

Lefèvre, Corinne, 99

Lon Karan, Raja of Sambhar, 41

Losensky, Paul, 9, 12, 90, 94, 170

Mahabharata, 61, 186

Mahdavi movement, 33

Mahmud, Amir Vali, 185

Mahmud, Sultan, 64

Mahsati Haravi, 42

Majalis-i Jahangiri, 56

Makarim al-akhlaq, 100

Malik Mahmud Pyare, 42

Malik Qummi, 43

Manohar "Tausani," 41–42

Mansur, 80, 131

Manuchihri, 223n9

Marvels of the East, 63

Masih Panipati, 61

masnavi (poetic form), 6, 11, 61, 93, 95, 109, 111, 117, 127, 138, 143, 178, 182

Masnavi-yi 'ashiq u ma'shuq, 195

Mas'ud Sa'd Salman, 37, 123

Mathee, Rudi, 195

Mathuradas, 191

Mazhari Kashmiri, 30, 41, 42, 43

Meisami, Julie, 219n28

Mian Mir, 160, 161

Mihrunnisa. *See* Nur Jahan

Mir Hasan, 51

Mir Ilahi, 140, 156

Mir Jumla Shahristani, 109, 220n39

Mir Kalan Khan, 183

Mir Sayyid 'Ali, 20

Mir Taqi Mir, 51

mirza, 54, 60, 210n71

Mitchell, Colin, 22

Mubad Shah, 26

Mubarak, Shaikh, 33

Mughal India: as Arcadia, 4–5, 6, 24–25, 44, 73, 77, 83, 169, 184, 196, 198; architecture of, 47, 78, 91, 118, 124, 198; bibliophilia in, 57–59, 59–60; connections with the larger Persianate world, 3, 9, 13, 16, 19, 20, 22, 28, 29–30, 52, 60–61; contemporary view of, 198; cosmopolitanism in, 2, 7; émigrés in, 3–4, 8, 13, 16, 20, 23–24, 27, 138, 184, 204n8